Multimedia Projects in Education

Multimedia Projects in Education
Designing, Producing, and Assessing

Fourth Edition

Karen S. Ivers

Ann E. Barron

LIBRARIES UNLIMITED

AN IMPRINT OF ABC-CLIO, LLC
Santa Barbara, California • Denver, Colorado • Oxford, England

Library of Congress Cataloging-in-Publication Data

Ivers, Karen S.
   Multimedia projects in education : designing, producing, and assessing
/ Karen S. Ivers and Ann E. Barron. — 4th ed.
     p. cm.
 Includes bibliographical references and index.
  ISBN 978-1-59884-534-1 (pbk : alk. paper) — ISBN 978-1-59884-535-8
(ebook) 1. Media programs (Education) 2. Interactive multimedia. 3.
Instructional systems—Design. I. Barron, Ann E. II. Title.
LB1028.4.I95 2010
371.33'5—dc22   2010028475

ISBN: 978-1-59884-534-1
EISBN: 978-1-59884-535-8

14 13 12 11 10   1 2 3 4 5

This book is also available on the World Wide Web as an eBook.
Visit www.abc-clio.com for details.

Libraries Unlimited
An Imprint of ABC-CLIO, LLC

ABC-CLIO, LLC
130 Cremona Drive, P.O. Box 1911
Santa Barbara, California 93116-1911

This book is printed on acid-free paper ∞
Manufactured in the United States of America

Contents

    A Scenario 181
    Overview 181
    Sample Projects for Web-Based Development 182
    Summary 188
    Blackline Masters 188

10—Multimedia Projects: Presentation Tools 191
    A Scenario 191
    Overview 191
    Sample Projects for Presentation Tools 192
    Summary 197
    Blackline Masters 197

11—Multimedia Projects: Video 201
    A Scenario 201
    Overview 201
    Sample Projects for Video-Based Development 202
    Summary 208
    Blackline Masters 208
    References 208

    Glossary 213
    Index 219

Preface

There is nothing more rewarding for an educator to experience than the enthusiasm and joy created by students actively engaged in a learning activity. Students *willingly* seek knowledge, spend extra time on their projects, and take pride in their work. Both the teacher and the students enjoy coming to school!

Although there are no magic potions to guarantee positive student outcomes, teachers can use a variety of strategies to ensure that learning is an active, personally relevant, meaningful process. These strategies include cooperative learning, constructivism, identifying each individual student's needs and talents, and using a variety of alternative assessment techniques. *Multimedia Projects in Education: Designing, Producing, and Assessing* (4th ed.) takes advantage of the many benefits associated with the development of multimedia and video projects and provides educators with strategies and ideas for incorporating multimedia projects into the curriculum. It provides management and assessment techniques for integrating multimedia projects in the classroom, emphasizing the importance of identifying instructional goals and relative standards and addressing situations in which there may be a limited number of computers in the classroom, as well as one-to-one laptop environments.

Multimedia Projects in Education: Designing, Producing, and Assessing (4th ed.) begins by describing research in the areas of cooperative learning, multiple intelligences, and constructivism. It provides practical ideas as to how these theories can be applied to the development of multimedia projects and how developing multimedia projects can support 21st-century learning skills. Chapter 2 discusses the latest technology standards and introduces a model (DECIDE, DESIGN, DEVELOP, and EVALUATE) that is used to guide the reader through the rest of the book. Chapter 3 (DECIDE) discusses classroom management issues, grouping alternatives, computer-scheduling options, and other issues related to planning a project. Chapter 4 (DESIGN) introduces the reader to the design stages of multimedia development, including flowcharts, storyboards, and basic design issues. DEVELOP is divided into two chapters. Chapter 5 (Developing Media Elements) addresses and defines the various media components that are available for multimedia projects and includes background information about computer video production. Chapter 6 (DEVELOPE: Multimedia Development Tools) provides an overview of development tools. Chapter 7 (EVALUATE) discusses alternative assessment techniques and assessment strategies. It also includes information on rubric design and provides examples of multiple rubrics.

Following the chapters on DECIDE, DESIGN, DEVELOP, and EVALUATE, four activity chapters provide the reader with multimedia project ideas. The activities focus on various development tools in several content areas, and they address a variety of grade levels and standards.

Throughout the book, the emphasis is on student-learning outcomes and on managing the development of multimedia projects. Each chapter begins with a scenario illustrating the implementation of multimedia projects in an educational setting. The chapters contain detailed graphics, charts, and tables. In addition, blackline masters are included that can be copied for educational purposes. Teachers, media specialists, and administrators will find this book an invaluable resource for producing, designing, and assessing multimedia projects.

This book is designed from the educator's perspective and can be used to facilitate classroom instruction as well as inservice workshops on strategies for developing multimedia projects. It is appropriate for classroom teachers and for educational technology courses at both the undergraduate and graduate levels.

Impact of Multimedia on Student Learning

A SCENARIO

Mrs. Geftakys wanted to make learning inside the classroom just as meaningful as learning outside the classroom. Outside the classroom, students were engaged with their mobile devices, game systems, and social networking sites. Lectures, textbooks, and paper and pencil could no longer compete with the "real world." Businesses and educational leaders continued to emphasize the need for schools to focus on 21st-century learning skills and to use technology to help students analyze information, create, solve problems, communicate, collaborate, and innovate. Incorporating project-based multimedia projects into the curriculum was one way Mrs. Geftakys went beyond the classroom walls and engaged her students in 21st-century learning skills. In groups of four, students collected, analyzed, planned, and presented information related to a real-world issue. For example, the members of Troy's group researched and presented a multimedia report on their findings and recommendations for raising funds to extend the local library's hours. This was presented to the local city board and later approved.

Mrs. Geftakys' students realized that developing multimedia presentations was a multistage process that provided them with an opportunity to construct their own learning. Students were placed on teams and provided with the assignment's objectives, the various stages of the assignment, and how the assignment would be assessed. Each team devised a plan, assigning members to conduct research on the Internet, through interviews, and so on. After gathering, analyzing, and evaluating their research, the team would develop storyboards to organize and lay out their information. Once the storyboards were finished and approved by Mrs. Geftakys, the team would work together to develop the presentation on the computer. Each person would be assigned a role—graphics, text, navigation, or audio—as they worked through the project. The assignment allowed them to investigate a topic of interest, draw upon and examine multiple resources of information, share what they had learned through multimodalities, and actively engage in, learn from, and provide solutions to real-world issues.

OVERVIEW

Multimedia projects allow students to convey their understanding of a topic in a variety of ways, and they provide students with the opportunity to explain their work and ideas to others. Bennett (1996, 16) notes that students "know that they have learned something when they can explain their work and ideas to others or when they can successfully teach others difficult concepts or content." Multimedia provides students with a powerful communication medium and offers them new insights into organizing, synthesizing, and evaluating information. Multimedia has the potential to change the roles of teacher and learner and the interaction between them by allowing students to create their own interpretations of information.

In addition to content knowledge and skill development, developing multimedia projects offers students the opportunity to work collaboratively, engage in multiple modalities of learning and reflective thinking, and use a constructivist approach to learning. It supports 21st-century learning skills by helping students use their knowledge to analyze, create, solve problems, communicate, collaborate, and innovate (Cox 2009; Hersh 2009; International Society for Technology in Education [ISTE], Partnership for 21st Century Skills, and State Educational Technology Directors Association [SETDA] 2007; United Nations for Educational, Scientific and Cultural Organization 2008). This chapter defines multimedia and examines research addressing the benefits of developing multimedia projects. Topics include the following:

- Definition of multimedia

- Why use multimedia?

- Research on multimedia and student learning

  Howard Gardner's Theory of Multiple Intelligences

  Cooperative learning

  Constructivism

DEFINITION OF MULTIMEDIA

In general terms, *multimedia* is the use of several media to present information. Combinations may include text, graphics, animation, pictures, video, and sound. Educators have been using multimedia for years. For example, it is not uncommon for teachers to support a unit on Spain with digital video and audio from the Internet or DVDs, along with pictures, text, and artifacts. Today's technologies, however, allow educators and students to integrate, combine, and interact with media far beyond what was previously possible.

"Hyper" environments, such as hypertext and hypermedia, have added to the complexity and sophistication of multimedia's definition by providing electronic, nonlinear approaches to moving through a body of information. Hypertext facilitates interaction between readers and texts by organizing and linking information. This can create associations, definitions, examples, and other relationships between the text passages (Maccini, Gagnon, and Hughes 2002; Rouet, Levon, Dillion, and Spiro 1996; Vandendorpe 2009). Hypermedia adds video clips, graphics, or audio files to hypertext. Combining these elements results in greater comprehension, recall, and inference (Chambers et al. 2008; Jones 2003, 2009; Mayer and Moreno 2002; Panagiotakopoulos and Ioannidis 2002; Wilson 2008). These multimodal approaches to education effectively accommodate students with diverse learning and cognitive styles (Kay and Knaack 2009; Lachs 1998; Maccini, Gagnon, and Hughes 2002; Morse 2003; Rasmussen and Davidson-Shivers 1998; Spence 2009; Wieman, Perkins, and Adams 2008). In addition, hypermedia applications are better suited to transmitting knowledge that is not easily conveyed through print or verbal explanations (Ercetin 2003; Son 2003; Stelzer, Gladding, Mestre, and Brookes 2009; Urban-Woldron 2009).

Both hypertext and hypermedia can be considered subsets of multimedia. Combining the traditional elements of multimedia with hyper environments, Gayeski (1993, 4) defines *computer-based* multimedia as "a class of computer-driven interactive communications systems which create, store, transmit, and retrieve textual, graphical and auditory networks of information." In other words, computer-based multimedia involves the computer presentation of multiple media formats (e.g., text, pictures, sounds, and video) to convey information in a linear or nonlinear format. This book is based on this definition and focuses on multimedia projects created via authoring, presentation, video, and Web tools. It also touches on multimedia creations possible through word processing programs and other applications. Multimedia is driving today's technology; it is unusual for today's products not to be multimedia based! The purpose of this book is to help teachers and students design, produce, and assess multimedia projects using various multimedia development tools. Guidelines are provided for projects that take a couple of days or weeks to complete.

WHY USE MULTIMEDIA?

Multimedia projects encourage students to work in groups, express their knowledge in multiple ways, solve problems, revise their own work, and construct knowledge. Students have the opportunity to learn and apply real-world skills. They learn the value of teamwork; the impact and importance of different media, including design issues, media appropriateness and validity, and copyright laws; the challenges of communicating to different audiences; the importance of research, planning, and organization skills; the significance of presentation and speaking skills; and how to accept and provide constructive feedback. Creating multimedia projects helps to reinforce students' technology skills and to prepare them for the demands of future careers.

Engaging students in multimedia projects also makes effective use of technology in the classroom. To use technology effectively in the classroom, Yelland (1999, 44) notes that five goals must be met:

1. Integrating technology and curricula

2. Promoting active learning, inquiry, and problem-solving environments that engage the children in individual and collaborative work using higher-order thinking skills

3. Using technology to present and represent ideas

4. Developing new definitions of play and new conceptions of what constitutes a manipulative

5. Developing media literacy skills that involve critically analyzing the use of the technologies and the information derived from them

The act of creating multimedia projects addresses each of these criteria. Liu (2003) notes that the development of multimedia projects can address the 21 core cognitive skills as defined by Vockell and van Deusen (1989). These skills can be grouped into the following categories: focusing, information gathering, remembering, organizing, analyzing, generating, integrating, and evaluating.

The process of creating multimedia projects also addresses the new technology standards for students as described by ISTE. Focusing on 21st-century learning skills, students use technology to create and innovate; communicate and collaborate; research, assess, and apply information; think critically, problem solve, and make decisions; learn to become a digital citizen; and understand technology concepts (ISTE 2007).

Multimedia projects allow students to focus on course content; promote active and cooperative learning; engage students in higher-order thinking skills; present and represent ideas through a variety of media; manipulate various technology tools, onscreen objects, and information models; locate and determine the best tools and resources for gathering and producing information; and critically analyze, evaluate, and organize information.

RESEARCH ON MULTIMEDIA AND STUDENT LEARNING

Since the new century began, advancements in technology have made it possible for teachers and students to develop elaborate multimedia programs in the classroom. Using Macintosh and PC-based computers, as well as handheld and other mobile devices, students are able to express themselves through a variety of media—text, audio, video, graphics, animation, and sound—in linear and nonlinear formats. Research in the area of multimedia demonstrates that its use can be effective for teaching and learning (Mayer and Moreno 2002; Nikolova 2002; Sivin-Kachala and Bialo 2000; Vergara, Caudell, Goldsmith, Panaiotis, and Alverson 2009) with all levels of students, including second-language learners and those with special needs (Carnahan, Basham, and Musti-Rao 2009; Irish 2002; Morse 2003; O'Hara and Pritchard 2008; Poobrasert and Cercone 2009; Xin 1999). Multimedia learning environments can support higher-order thinking and problem-solving skills (Neo and Neo 2009; Su 2008), increase students' achievement (Chambers et al. 2008; Kingsley and Boone 2008; Tuzun, Yilmaz-Soylu, Karakus, Inal, and Kizilkaya 2009), and increase student motivation (Kasahara 2001; Marr 2000; Papastergiou 2009; Poobrasert and Cercone 2009; Tuzun, Yilmaz-Soylu, Karakus, Inal, and Kizilkaya 2009). In addition, creating multimedia projects reflects research on how the brain learns, helping students construct knowledge and making topics more meaningful and motivating to learn (Wolfe 2001). Bagui (1998, 4) suggests that "multimedia may make it easier for people to learn because of the parallels between multimedia and the 'natural' way people learn."

Viewing the learner as an active participant in the process of acquiring and using knowledge, educators are reexamining ways to activate appropriate learning strategies during the instructional process. Researchers and leading organizations note that technology must be used to empower students and to create a 21st-century learning environment in which students learn core subjects, 21st-century themes (global awareness; financial, economic, business, and entrepreneurial literacy; civic literacy; health literacy), and 21st-century skills (learning and innovation; information, media, and technology; life and career; Partnership for 21st Century Skills 2009).

The focus should not be on the technology itself but on how teachers are using technology with their students to promote such skills as critical thinking, problem solving, communication, collaboration, innovation, and global literacy in an increasingly digital world (ISTE, Partnership for 21st Century Skills, & SETDA 2007; United Nations for Educational, Scientific and Cultural Organization 2008). The design and development of multimedia projects support 21st-century learning by addressing students' multiple intelligences (i.e., how different students learn and communicate), encouraging cooperative learning and supporting constructive learning environments.

Howard Gardner's Theory of Multiple Intelligences

Several researchers have developed theories on various ways of knowing, suggesting that students possess several intelligences (Gardner 1983, 1999; Samples 1992; Sternberg 1994). Perhaps the most recognized theory of multiple intelligences is Howard Gardner's Theory of Multiple Intelligences (Gardner 1983, 1999). In his book, *Intelligence Reframed: Multiple Intelligences for the 21st Century*, Gardner reviews the seven intelligences he introduced in his first book, *Frames of the Mind: The Theory of Multiple Intelligences*, and adds another—the naturalist intelligence. Gardner defines *intelligence* as "a biopsychological potential to process information that can be activated in a cultural setting to solve problems or create products that are of value in a culture" (Gardner 1999, 33–34). He suggests that intelligences are neural conditions that will or will not be activated by opportunities, personal decisions, or values. He also states that everyone possesses these intelligences, noting that people acquire and represent knowledge in different ways. Gardner's proposed eight areas of intelligence include:

1. Linguistic Intelligence: the ability to use words effectively, whether orally or in writing.

2. Logical-Mathematical Intelligence: the capacity to use numbers effectively and to reason well.

3. Spatial Intelligence: the ability to perceive the visual-spatial world accurately and to perform transformations on those perceptions.

4. Bodily-Kinesthetic Intelligence: expertise in using one's body to express ideas and feelings and facility in using one's hands to produce or transform things.

5. Musical Intelligence: the ability to perceive, discriminate, transform, and express musical forms.

6. Interpersonal Intelligence: the ability to perceive and make distinctions in the moods, intentions, motivations, and feelings of other people.

7. Intrapersonal Intelligence: self-knowledge and the ability to act on the basis of that knowledge.

8. Naturalist Intelligence: expertise in recognizing and classifying living and nonliving forms within one's environment. Gardner (1999, 49) notes, "The young child who can readily discriminate among plants or birds or dinosaurs is drawing on the same skills (or intelligence) when she classifies sneakers, cars, sound systems, or marbles."

Gardner identified these intelligences based on a series of tests that included eight different criteria. Additional intelligences have been proposed—including spirituality, moral sensibility, sexuality, humor, intuition, and creativity—but it remains to be seen whether these proposed intelligences meet the required criteria (Armstrong 2009; Gardner 1999).

There are several important elements to remember about Gardner's Theory of Multiple Intelligences. In his book, *Multiple Intelligences in the Classroom*, Armstrong (2009) states that

- Each person possesses all eight intelligences.

- Most people can develop each intelligence to an adequate level of competency.

- Intelligences usually work together in complex ways.

- There are many ways to be intelligent within each category.

Many educators have successfully implemented Gardner's Theory of Multiple Intelligences into their classrooms (Delaney and Shafer 2007; Douglas, Burton, and Reese-Durham 2008; Kosky and Curtis 2008; Kunkel 2009). Applying Gardner's Theory of Multiple Intelligences can benefit all learners, including students with learning disabilities, gifted students, and students from diverse cultural backgrounds (Chen, Moran, and Gardner 2009; Perez and Beltran 2008).

Commercial multimedia applications and the development of multimedia projects encourage a multimodal approach to learning. Well-designed multimedia applications present content in several media formats and allow students to use their own individual learning styles. Although multimedia applications can effectively teach content, student-based multimedia projects allow students to gain skills beyond content-area knowledge. These skills include finding and interpreting information, articulating and communicating knowledge, and using the computer as a cognitive tool (Jonassen 2008; Neo and Neo 2009; Su 2008).

Applying the Theory of Multiple Intelligences to Multimedia Projects

One of the many benefits of developing multimedia projects is that it allows students to construct and communicate knowledge in various ways. Multimedia projects also encourage group work and social interaction, but they do not require a uniform experience for all students. According to Levin (1994), group work and social interaction are necessary for a multiple intelligences approach, but a uniform experience for all children is not.

When assigning multimedia design teams, students should be placed in groups that provide them with the opportunity to take advantage of their strengths, as well as nurture their weaknesses. For example, students who are identified as spatially intelligent might be responsible for the graphic content and layout of a multimedia project. Students who are identified as logical-mathematically intelligent might be responsible for designing the structure/flowchart of the project and the scripting or programming requirements. Table 1.1 correlates each intelligence with the observed student behaviors and recommended roles when developing a multimedia project.

It is important to note that all students have all intelligences, although one or more may be stronger than others. Placing students in design teams that capture the diversity of their intellectual profiles can provide them with the motivation, skills, and support necessary to learn. Armstrong (2009) comments that most students have strengths in several areas; hence, students may contribute to projects in multiple ways. For example, one student may lead the group in developing the text and music for the project, another student may lead the group in creating the graphics and flowcharts for the project, and so on.

Table 1.1. Roles of Multiple Intelligence in the Creation of Multimedia Projects

Intelligence	Observed Student Behaviors	Leadership Roles in Multimedia Projects
Linguistic	Loves to read books, write, and tell stories; good memory for names, dates, and trivia; communicates well	Gather and develop text for project; provide narration; keep journal of group progress
Logical-Mathematical	Excels in math; has strong problem-solving skills; enjoys playing strategy games and working on logic puzzles	Design flowchart; write scripting and programming code; develop navigation routes
Spatial	Needs a mental or physical picture to best understand things; draws figures that are advanced for age; doodles a lot	Create graphics, animation, and other visual media for project; design layout
Body-Kinesthetic	Excels in one or more sports; good fine-motor skills; tendency to move around, touch things, gesture	Keyboard information; manipulate objects with mouse; operate multimedia equipment
Musical	Remembers melodies; recognizes when music is off-key; has a good singing voice; plays an instrument; hums a lot	Identify works for content integration; create musical score for project; input audio/sound effects
Interpersonal	Enjoys socializing with peers; has leadership skills; has good sense of empathy and concern for others	Coordinate group efforts; help set group goals; help solve group disputes
Intrapersonal	Has strong sense of self; is confident; prefers working alone; has high self-esteem; displays independence	Conduct independent research to share with teammates; pilot test multimedia projects; lead multimedia presentations
Naturalist	Enjoys the outdoors, plants, and animals; easily recognizes and classifies things within his/her environment	Collect or videotape outside elements for incorporation into projects; organize project work

Intellectual profiles can change over time as intelligences develop in strength. Gray and Viens (1994, 24) note, "the differences among individual intellectual profiles are the result of personal and local factors as well as cultural influences." Working in diverse groups allows students to nurture their weaknesses and capitalize on their strengths. Students are able to make valuable contributions to group projects, as well as augment their intellectual profiles.

Cooperative Learning

Cooperative learning takes place when students work together to accomplish shared goals. Most cooperative conditions use small groups "so that students work together to maximize their own and each other's learning" (Johnson and Johnson 1999a, 5). Johnson and Johnson (2009, 1999b) suggest that a cooperative learning group has five defining characteristics:

1. Positive Interdependence. There is a group goal to maximize all members' learning beyond their individual abilities; members succeed only if the other members in their group succeed.

2. Individual Accountability. Group members hold themselves and each other accountable for high-quality work; students are held accountable for their share of the work.

3. Face-to-Face Promotive Interaction. Group members produce joint products, providing both academic and personal support; students promote each other's learning.

4. Social Skills. Group members are taught social skills and are expected to use them to coordinate their efforts; teamwork and task work are emphasized.

5. Group Processing. Groups analyze how well they are achieving their goals, working together, and learning.

The researchers note that a cooperative group is more than the sum of its parts and state that students often perform better academically than they would if they worked by themselves (Johnson and Johnson 1999b, 2009).

There are a variety of cooperative group techniques, including Student Teams Achievement Divisions, Teams Games Tournament, Team Assisted Individualization, Jigsaw, Group Investigation, and Learning Together (Slavin 1994, 1999, 2008; Vermette 1998), as described below.

Student Teams Achievement Divisions (STAD)—students learn something as a team, contribute to the team by improving their own past performance, and earn team rewards based on their improvements. Students are usually heterogeneously mixed by ability and take individual weekly quizzes. For example, student teams may study about the Westward Movement and take weekly quizzes on the content. Teams earn points based on each student's improvement from previous quizzes. If a student scores 5 out of 10 points on the first quiz and 8 out of 10 on the second quiz, he may earn 8 points for his team, plus 2 bonus points for improving. If a student scores 7 out of 10 points on the first quiz and 5 out of 10 on the second quiz, he may earn 5 points for his team, but no bonus points. If a student scores 10 points on both quizzes, she may earn a total of 12 points (10 points for the second quiz plus 2 bonus points for the perfect score) for her team.

Teams Games Tournament (TGT)—similar to STAD except that weekly tournaments replace weekly quizzes. Homogeneous, three-member teams are formed from the existing heterogeneous groups and compete against similar ability groups to earn points for their regular, heterogeneous group. As with STAD, high-performing teams earn group rewards. For example, existing heterogeneous groups may contain one each low-, average-, and high-ability student. During weekly tournaments (e.g., a game of Jeopardy), low-ability students form groups of three, average-ability students form groups of three, and high-ability students form groups of three. Low-ability groups compete against each other, average-ability groups compete against each other, and high-ability groups compete against each other. The winning homogeneous groups earn points for their heterogeneous teams.

Team-Assisted Individualization (TAI)—combines cooperative learning with individualized instruction. Students are placed into groups but work at their own pace and level. Team members check each other's work and help one another with problems. Teams earn points based on the individual performance of each member in the group. Team members encourage and support one another because they want their teams to succeed (Slavin 1994). For example, students at different spelling levels may be placed into heterogeneous groups. The group may consist of one low speller, two average spellers, and one advanced speller. Students are responsible for learning their assigned spelling words, but they have their team members to assist and encourage them. Groups earn points based on their team members' performance on weekly spelling tests. Members take responsibility for each other's learning, as well as their own.

Jigsaw—a cooperative group learning method that assigns each of its members a particular learning task. For example, learning about the Civil War may include famous men and women, battles, economic factors, and issues of slavery. Each member chooses a topic and is responsible for teaching his or her team members "all that there is to know" about that topic. Team members meet with members of other groups to form "expert groups" to discuss and research their topic. For example, the team members of the cooperative groups who chose famous women would meet together in a separate cooperative group focused on learning only about famous women of the Civil War. Following research and discussion, the students return to their own teams and take turns teaching their teammates about their topic. Afterward, students take individual quizzes and earn a team score.

Group Investigation—similar to the Jigsaw method, except students do not form expert groups. Students work in small groups toward an overall class project. Each group is assigned a different task or activity. Within each group, members decide what information to gather and how to organize and present their findings.

Learning Together—incorporates heterogeneous student groups that work on a single assignment and receive rewards based on their group product. For example, student groups may be assigned to draw and label the human skeletal system. Each student would receive the same final grade for the group product.

Cooperative learning groups differ from traditional learning groups in that most support positive interdependence, individual accountability, group processing, peer responsibility, and heterogeneous membership (Gillies and Boyle 2008; Johnson and Johnson 1999a, 2009). General findings conclude that:

- Cooperative groups are appropriate for any instructional task.

- Cooperative groups do just as well or better on achievement than competitive and individualistic learning conditions.

- Cooperative conditions appear to work best when students are heterogeneously grouped, although high-ability students do just as well or better in homogeneous groups.

- Group discussion promotes higher achievement.

- Cooperative learning is more likely to have an effect on student outcomes when cooperation is well defined.

- Stereotypes are likely to be reduced when using cooperative groups.

- Using cooperative groups promotes equality among perceived ability and leadership roles among males and females.

- Cooperative learning can reduce anxiety and create more interesting learning.

- Cooperative groups can be more cost-effective than individualistic learning conditions.

- Cooperative learning appears to be effective at all primary and secondary grade levels and with groups of two to five.

- Cooperative conditions can benefit all ability levels.

- Cooperative groups support achievement-oriented behavior and healthy social development.

- Cooperative grouping can increase student self-esteem and foster higher-order thinking skills.

Although researchers report many positive outcomes using cooperative learning (Calderon, Hertz-Lazarowitz, and Slavin 1998; Gillies 2008; Gillies and Boyle 2008; Johnson and Johnson 2009; Kumar 2009; Law 2008; Rothenberg, McDermott, and Martin 1998; Siciliano 2001; Slavin 1994, 1999; Tarim 2009), others note that there are pitfalls (Esmonde 2009; Johnson and Johnson 1999a; Slavin 1994; Vermette 1998). Pitfalls include the "free-rider effect" (members let the more capable members do all the work) and the "sucker effect" (more able members have the less able members do all the work). Individual accountability and grades based on the team's average individual scores can help avoid these pitfalls (Epstein 2007; Johnson and Johnson 1999a; Slavin 1994). Vermette (1998) suggests teacher monitoring, randomly calling on group members to summarize their group's progress or requiring each student to write a concluding summary or a description of his or her group's activity, including a retelling of each individual's role and contribution. Others recommend placing students in smaller groups so it is harder to hide or "free-ride," define individual expectations of group members, and assign roles that focus on the strengths of the students (Baloche 1998; Gillies and Boyle 2008; Marr 2000). In the case of chronic absenteeism, Baloche (1998) recommends:

- Group members phone or e-mail peers with what they have missed.

- Chronically absent students be placed in larger groups so that other group members are not as dependent on them.

- Group members have access to the other members' project information and material.

- Assessment is structured so group members are not penalized for work missed by the absent student.

- High expectations must be the norm for all students, with everyone viewed as a valuable member of the team.

Applying the Theory of Cooperative Learning to Multimedia Projects

Using cooperative groups in multimedia design and development has many benefits. These include peer teaching, increased use of metacognitive and elaboration strategies, the accommodation of individual differences, self-reflection, increased motivation and positive attitudes toward learning, and increased performance (Chen and McGrath 2003; Gillies and Boyle 2008; Marr 2000). The teacher's role is to guide and facilitate the cooperative groups' efforts. Table 1.2 provides examples of students' roles and responsibilities in different cooperative group settings. Cooperative group methods that require individual accountability and assign grades based on the average of the team's individual scores are recommended (see Chapter 7).

Table 1.2. Cooperative Group Settings and Responsibilities in Multimedia Projects

Cooperative Group Method	Multimedia Project Example and Evaluation	Student Roles and Responsibilities in Multimedia Projects
Student Teams Achievement Divisions (STAD)	Groups are provided with specific questions for research and content information on the Westward Movement. They display their knowledge through group multimedia projects. Announced weekly quizzes check individual content learning. A rubric can be used to evaluate final projects for a group grade.	Students learn about the Westward Movement as a team, helping each other understand the content. Groups may alternate project responsibilities to ensure everyone has a chance to explore the content in different ways.
Teams Games Tournament (TGT)	Similar to STAD, except weekly tournaments replace weekly quizzes, and students compete against similar ability groups to earn points for their heterogeneous group. Responsibilities remain the same.	
Team-Assisted Individualization (TAI)	Groups create projects on a select genre, such as mystery stories. Groups display information about several books. The project is evaluated based on each student's book report.	Each student is responsible for reading a select book (at the appropriate level) and reporting on it through multimedia. The team project introduces and links each report.
Jigsaw	Groups create projects on the Civil War. Students are evaluated on their group's final project and their individual knowledge of all the content areas researched for the Civil War.	Each member is assigned a particular content area of the Civil War, such as famous men and women, battles, economic factors, issues of slavery, and so on. Members meet with other groups' members assigned to the same content area. For example, members researching famous battles meet together and help each other become an "expert" on the topic. Members return to their groups and share what they have learned. Students design their portion of the group's multimedia project. (This approach may also be used to learn about different skills, such as creating animation, desktop videos, and so on.)
Group Investigation	Similar to the Jigsaw method except students do not form expert groups. Students work in small groups toward an overall class project. Each has a specific task or assignment.	
Learning Together	Groups decide on a multimedia project of interest (e.g., a project about volcanoes) and present their final project to the class. Each student receives the same final grade for the group product.	After deciding on the project, students determine each other's role and responsibilities based on their interests. Responsibilities and roles may change during the project. (Individual accountability may be weak.)

Cooperative group multimedia projects support small group interactions, positive socialization, peer teaching and learning, and the development of original projects that reflect the groups' collaboration (Ching and Kafai 2008; Marr 2000; Steelman, Grable, and Vasu 2004). In addition, cooperative groups can reduce the complexity and time commitment of creating multimedia projects by assigning students to specific design roles and responsibilities. Each student contributes to the project as a whole and has the opportunity to share his or her expertise with, as well as learn from, others. Techniques for establishing, monitoring, and assessing group projects are included in Chapters 3 and 7.

Constructivism

Cognitive psychologists believe in the process of learning through the construction of knowledge. They assert that "people learn by actively constructing knowledge, weighing new information against their previous understanding, thinking about and working through discrepancies (on their own and with others), and coming to a new understanding" (Association for Supervision and Curriculum Development 1992, 2). These ideas, combined with social learning, are not new. Kilpatrick (1918) expressed the need to base education on purposeful acts and social activity, which he designed into his project method of instruction. Dewey (1929) stated that "social tools" (reading, spelling, and writing) are best acquired in a social context. Piaget believed that people try to make sense of the world and actively create their own knowledge through direct experience with objects, people, and ideas (Woolfolk 1987). Vygotsky (1978, 88) argued that "human learning presupposes a specific social nature and a process by which children grow into the intellectual life of those around them."

Professional organizations, such as the National Council for Teachers of Mathematics (NTCM), the American Association for the Advancement of Science (AAAS), and the National Council for the Social Studies (NCSS) continue to emphasize the need to engage students in constructivist thinking—decision making, problem solving, and critical thinking. Researchers (Gagnon and Collay 2001; Marlowe and Page 1998; Shapiro 2003) define *constructivist teachers* as those who

- Encourage and accept student autonomy and initiative
- Use raw data and primary sources, along with manipulative, interactive, and physical materials
- Use cognitive terminology such as *classify*, *analyze*, *predict*, and *create*
- Allow student responses to drive lessons, shift instructional strategies, and alter content
- Inquire about students' understanding of concepts before sharing their own understandings of those concepts
- Encourage students to engage in conversations with the teacher and with one another
- Encourage student inquiry by asking thoughtful, open-ended questions and encouraging students to ask questions of each other
- Seek elaboration of students' initial responses
- Engage students in experiences that might create contradictions to their initial hypotheses and then encourage discussion
- Allow wait time after posing questions
- Provide time for students to construct relationships and create metaphors
- Nurture students' natural curiosity through frequent use of the learning cycle model (discovery, concept introduction, and concept application)

These teacher practices can help guide students in their understanding and intellectual and reflective growth. Developing multimedia projects provides an ideal forum for a constructivist approach.

Applying the Theory of Constructivism to Multimedia Projects

Research has demonstrated that developing multimedia projects can help students learn how to develop concepts and ideas, design plans, apply what they learn, refine questions, make predictions, collect and analyze research, communicate findings, and solve problems (Funk, 2003; Neo 2007; Schacter and Fagnano 1999). Researchers (Anderson 2008; Cooper and Brna 2001; Riddle 1995) report that students are more likely to show greater descriptive detail, unique perspectives, and diverse interests and skills when using multimedia software to create and add graphics, audio, and animation to their textual communications. Other researchers suggest that developing multimedia projects allows learning to occur in more meaningful contexts (Basden 2001; Katz 2002; Neo 2007; Rice and Wilson 1999). Designing multimedia projects can provide a concrete and meaningful context for developing higher-order thinking skills, engaging students in the learning process, and inviting them to use technology as a cognitive tool (Liu 2003; Liu and Hsiao 2002; Liu and Pedersen 1998; Neo and Neo 2009). While developing multimedia projects, students begin to see themselves as authors of knowledge, experts within their design teams, and active participants in the learning process (Katz 2002; Liu 2003; Liu and Pedersen 1998; Neo and Neo 2009; Schacter and Fagnano 1999).

According to Simons (1993), constructivist learning includes at least five components: active, cumulative, integrative, reflective, and goal-directed. Their definitions and relationship to the construction of multimedia projects are presented in Table 1.3. Gagnon and Collay (2001) describe similar elements but include a sixth—grouping—noting that "small groups are necessary for students to move from personal meaning to shared meaning in the social construction of knowledge" (p. 36). Design teams allow students to work in small groups.

Table 1.3. Constructivist Components and Their Relationships to Creating Multimedia Projects

Constructivist Learning Component	Definition	Relationship to Creating Multimedia Projects
Active	Students process information meaningfully.	Multimedia projects allow students to be active learners by defining the content and creating the media components.
Cumulative	Learning builds on prior knowledge.	Multimedia projects allow students to connect current knowledge to new ideas through a variety of formats.
Integrative	Learners elaborate on new knowledge.	Multimedia projects offer environments in which students can create increasingly complex programs, as well as present current and new knowledge in new ways.
Reflective	Students assess what they know and need to learn.	Multimedia projects incorporate multiple levels of assessment at various phases throughout the design and development process.
Goal-directed	Learners engage in purposeful learning activities.	When assigning multimedia projects, the teacher and students work together to define specific learning outcomes.

Herman, Aschbacher, and Winters (1992) also discuss the implications of aligning instruction and assessment with constructivist learning. Table 1.4 presents cognitive learning theories and their implications for instruction, assessment, and multimedia projects.

Table 1.4. Cognitive Learning Theories' Relationships to Multimedia Project Creation

Cognitive Learning Theory	Implications for Instruction/Assessment	Relationship to Creating Multimedia Projects
Learning is a process of creating personal meaning from new information and prior knowledge.	Encourage discussion, divergent thinking, multiple links and solutions, varied modes of expression, critical thinking skills; relate new information to personal experience; apply information to new situations.	Projects encourage knowledge construction and group efforts, stimulating discussion, and divergent thinking. Media elements provide various modes of expression.
Learning is not necessarily a linear progression of discrete skills.	Engage students in problem solving and critical thinking.	Developing flowcharts and storyboards requires problem-solving and critical-thinking skills to "chunk" and organize information into linear and nonlinear formats. Students see how data relate to each other.
There are a variety of learning styles, attention spans, developmental paces, and intelligences.	Provide choices in task, varied means of showing mastery and competence, time to think about and do assignments, opportunities for self-evaluation and peer review.	Design teams offer task options, allowing students to demonstrate their skills in many ways. The process of developing projects requires students to revise and rethink and provides students with hands-on, concrete learning experiences.
Students perform better when they know the goal, see models, and know how their performance compares to the standard.	Discuss goals and let students help define them (personal and class); provide and discuss examples of student work and allow them to have input into expectations; give students opportunities for self-evaluation and peer review.	Rubrics, goals, and expectations for projects can be decided as a whole class without sacrificing the teacher's basic objectives. Sample projects can help clarify project expectations. The process of developing projects encourages self-evaluation and peer review.
It is important to know when to use knowledge, how to adapt it, and how to manage one's own learning.	Provide real-world opportunities (or simulations) to apply or adapt new knowledge; provide opportunities for students to think about how they learn and why they like certain work.	Multimedia projects support real-world learning experiences, plus they have the potential to enhance students' communication and metacognitive skills.
Motivation, effort, and self-esteem affect learning and performance.	Motivate students with real-life tasks and connections to personal experiences; encourage students to see the relationship between effort and results.	Projects provide students with real-life tasks that they can connect to their personal interests and experiences. Projects serve as visual outcomes of students' efforts.
Learning has social components. Group work is valuable.	Provide group work; establish heterogeneous groups; enable students to take on a variety of roles; consider group products and group processes.	Multimedia projects encourage cooperative grouping techniques.

Multimedia projects can provide ideal learning environments for implementing a constructivist approach to learning. Creating multimedia projects encourages divergent thinking, multiple modes of expression, goal setting, critical-thinking skills, teamwork, opportunities to revise and rethink, and more. Students are active participants, constructing knowledge that is meaningful, applicable, and memorable. In addition, multimedia projects provide educators with multiple ways to assess students' progress. Assessment strategies are discussed in Chapter 7.

SUMMARY

Multimedia combines several media to present information. Computer-based multimedia uses computers to present multiple media formats that convey information in a linear or nonlinear format. Creating multimedia projects reinforces students' technology skills and invites them to work cooperatively and use a variety of media to express their understanding. It is a process approach to learning, encouraging students to think differently about how they organize and present information. Developing multimedia projects supports 21st-century learning skills. It supports a collaborative environment, self-reflection, authentic learning, and the use of technology as a cognitive tool. In addition, multimedia projects offer an effective alternative for assessing student learning and provide students with a real-world learning environment.

Research demonstrates that multimedia development tools provide students with opportunities to show greater descriptive detail, unique perspectives, and diverse interests and skills. It is possible that these tools may help students develop what may otherwise be paralyzed or "shut-down" intelligences. Opportunities to explore concepts and express understanding through multimedia may create positive turning points in the development of a student's intelligences. Students report a desire to learn, feel more confident, and consider themselves producers of knowledge rather than consumers when creating multimedia projects. By working cooperatively and constructing knowledge, students become empowered learners.

REFERENCES

Anderson, D. 2008. The low bridge to high benefits: Entry-level multimedia, literacies, and motivation. *Computers and Composition* 25(1): 40–60.

Armstrong, T. 2009. *Multiple intelligences in the classroom*. 3rd ed. Alexandria, VA: Association for Supervision and Curriculum Development.

Association for Supervision and Curriculum Development. 1992. Wanted: Deep understanding. "Constructivism" posits new conception of learning. *ASCD Update* 34(3): 1–5.

Bagui, S. 1998. Reasons for increased learning using multimedia. *Journal of Educational Multimedia and Hypermedia* 7(1): 3–18.

Baloche, L. A. 1998. *The cooperative classroom: Empowering learning*. Upper Saddle River, NJ: Prentice-Hall.

Basden, J. C. 2001. Authentic tasks as the basis for multimedia design curriculum. *T.H.E. Journal* 29(4): 16–21.

Bennett, D. T. 1996. Assessment through video. *Electronic Learning* 15(4): 16–17.

Calderon, M. R., Hertz-Lazarowitz, R., and Slavin, R. 1998. Effects of bilingual cooperative integrated reading and composition on students making the transition from Spanish to English reading. *Elementary School Journal* 99(2): 153–165.

Carnahan, C., Basham, J., and Musti-Rao, S. 2009. A low-technology strategy for increasing engagement of students with autism and significant learning needs. *Exceptionality* 17(2): 76–87.

Chambers, B., Slavin, R., Madden, N., Abrami, P., Tucker, B., et al. 2008. Technology infusion in success for all: Reading outcomes for first graders. *Elementary School Journal* 109(1): 2008–2015.

Chen, J., Moran, S., & Gardner, H. (Eds.). 2009. *Multiple intelligences around the world.* San Francisco: Jossey Bass.

Chen, P., and McGrath, D. 2003. Moments of joy: Student engagement and conceptual learning in the design of hypermedia documents. *Journal of Research on Technology in Education* 35(3): 402–422.

Ching, C., & Kafai, Y. 2008. Peer pedagogy: Student collaboration and reflection in a learning-through-design project. *Teachers College Record* 110(12): 2601–2632.

Cooper, B., and Brna, P. 2001. Fostering cartoon-style creativity with sensitive agent support in tomorrow's classroom. *Educational Technology & Society* 4(2): 32-40.

Cox, E. 2009. The collaborative mind: Tools for 21st-century learning. *MultiMedia & Internet@Schools* 16(5): 10–14.

Delaney, C., and Shafer, F. 2007. Teaching to multiple intelligence by following a "slime trail." *Middle School Journal* 39(1): 38–43.

Dewey, J. 1929. *The sources of a science of education.* New York: Horace Liveright.

Douglas, O., Burton, K., and Reese-Durham, N. 2008. The effects of the multiple intelligence teaching strategy on the academic achievement of eighth grade math students. *Journal of Instructional Psychology* 35(2): 182–187.

Epstein, E. 2007. Blending individual and group assessment: A model for measuring student performance using mathematics as an example. *Dissertation Abstracts International Section A: Humanities and Social Sciences*, 68(4): 1373.

Ercetin, G. 2003. Exploring ESL learners' use of hypermedia reading glosses. *CALICO Journal* 20(2): 261–283.

Esmonde, I. 2009. Ideas and identities: Supporting equity in cooperative mathematics learning. *Review of Educational Research* 79: 1008–1043.

Funk, C. 2003. James Otto and the pi man: A constructivist tale. *Phi Delta Kappan* 85(3): 212–214.

Gagnon, G. W., and Collay, M. 2001. *Designing for learning: Six elements in constructivist classrooms.* Thousand Oaks, CA: Corwin Press.

Gardner, H. 1983. *Frames of mind: The theory of multiple intelligences.* New York: Basic Books.

Gardner, H. 1999. *Intelligence reframed: Multiple intelligences for the 21st century.* New York: Basic Books.

Gayeski, D. M. 1993. *Multimedia for learning.* Englewood Cliffs, NJ: Educational Technology Publications.

Gillies, R. 2008. The effects of cooperative learning on junior high school students' behaviours, discourse and learning during a science-based learning activity. *School Psychology International* 29: 328–347.

Gillies, R., & Boyle, M. 2008. Teachers' discourse during cooperative learning and their perceptions of this pedagogical practice. *Teaching and Teacher Education: An International Journal of Research and Studies* 24(5): 1333–1348.

Gray, J. H., and Viens, J. T. 1994. The theory of multiple intelligences: Understanding cognitive diversity in school. *National Forum: Phi Kappa Phi Journal* 74(1): 22–25.

Herman, J. L., Aschbacher, P. R., and Winters, L. 1992. *A practical guide to alternative assessment.* Alexandria, VA: Association for Supervision and Curriculum Development.

Hersh, R. 2009. A well-rounded education for a flat world. *Educational Leadership* 67(1): 51–53.

International Society for Technology in Education. 2007. National educational technology standards students [online]. Available at: http://www.iste.org/Content/NavigationMenu/NETS/ForStudents/2007Standards/NETS_for_Students_2007.htm. Accessed on July 25, 2010.

International Society for Technology in Education, Partnership for 21st Century Skills, and State Educational Technology Directors Association. 2007. *Maximizing the impact: The pivotal role of technology in a 21st century education system* [online]. Available at: http://www.setda.org/c/document_library/get_file?folderId=191&name=P21Book_complete.pdf. Accessed on July 26, 2010.

Irish, C. 2002. Using peg- and keyword mnemonics and computer-assisted instruction to enhance basic multiplication performance in elementary students with learning and cognitive disabilities. *Journal of Special Education Technology* 17(4): 29–40.

Johnson, D. W., & Johnson, R. T. 1999a. *Learning together and alone: Cooperative, competitive, and individualistic learning* (5th ed.). Needham Heights, MA: Allyn & Bacon.

Johnson, D. W., & Johnson R. T. 1999b. Making cooperative learning work. *Theory into Practice* 38(2): 67–73.

Johnson, D., & Johnson, R. 2009. An educational psychology success story: Social interdependence theory and cooperative learning. *Educational Researcher*, 38, 365–379.

Jonassen, D. (Ed.). 2008. *Meaningful learning with technology.* Upper Saddle River, NJ: Pearson/Merrill Prentice Hall.

Jones, L. 2009. Supporting student differences in listening comprehension and vocabulary learning with multimedia annotations. *CALICO Journal* 26(2): 267–289.

Jones, L. C. 2003. Supporting listening comprehension and vocabulary acquisition with multimedia annotations: The students' voice. *CALICO Journal* 21(1): 41–65.

Kasahara, A. 2001. Students making media. *The Active Learner* 6(1): 18–23.

Katz, D. 2002. Multimedia projects. *English Teachers' Journal* 54: 72–79.

Kay, R., and Knaack, L. 2009. Analysing the effectiveness of learning objects for secondary school science classrooms. *Journal of Educational Multimedia and Hypermedia* 18(1): 113–135.

Kilpatrick, W. H. 1918. The project method: The use of the purposeful act in the educative process. *Teachers College Bulletin.* Columbia, SC: Columbia University.

Kingsley, K., & Boone, R. 2008. Effects of multimedia software on achievement of middle school students in an American history class. *Journal of Research on Technology in Education* 41(2): 203–221.

Kosky, C., & Curtis, R. 2008. An action research exploration integrating student choice and arts activities in a sixth grade social studies classroom. *Journal of Social Studies Research* 32(1): 22–27.

Kumar, R. 2009. Why is collaboration good for my child? Engaging families in understanding the benefits of cooperative learning. *YC Young Children* 64(3): 91–95.

Kunkel, C. 2009. Schooling built on the multiple intelligences. *School Administrator* 66(2): 24–25.

Lachs, V. 1998. Making the computer dance to your tune: Primary school pupils authoring hypermedia. *Journal of Computing in Childhood Education* 9: 57–77.

Law, Y. 2008. Effects of cooperative learning on second graders' learning from text. *Educational Psychology* 28(5): 567–582.

Levin, H. M. 1994. Commentary: Multiple intelligence theory and everyday practices. *Teachers College Record* 95(4): 570–575.

Liu, M. 2003. Enhancing learners' cognitive skills through multimedia design. *Interactive Learning Environments* 11(1): 23–39.

Liu, M., and Hsiao, Y. 2002. Middle school students as multimedia designers: A project-based learning approach. *Journal of Interactive Learning Research* 13(4): 311–337.

Liu, M., and Pedersen, S. 1998. The effect of being hypermedia designers on elementary school students' motivation and learning of design knowledge. *Journal of Interactive Learning Research* 9(2): 155–182.

Maccini, P., Gagnon, J. C., and Hughes, C. A. 2002. Technology-based practices for secondary students with learning disabilities. *Learning Disability Quarterly* 25(4): 247–261.

Marlowe, B. A., and Page, M. L. 1998. *Creating and sustaining the constructivist classroom*. Thousand Oaks, CA: Corwin Press.

Marr, P. M. 2000. Grouping students at the computer to enhance the study of British literature. *English Journal* 90: 120–125.

Mayer, R. E., and Moreno, R. 2002. Aids to computer-based multimedia learning. *Learning and Instruction* 12(1): 107–119.

Morse, T. 2003. Enhancing special education students' multiple literacies through multimedia activities. *Journal of Reading Education* 28(2): 39–40.

Neo, M. (2007). Learning with multimedia: Engaging students in constructivist learning. *International Journal of Instructional Media* 34(2): 149–158.

Neo, M., & Neo, T. 2009. Engaging students in multimedia-mediated constructivist learning—students' perceptions. *Journal of Educational Technology & Society* 12(2), 254–266.

Nikolova, O. R. 2002. Effects of students' participation in authoring of multimedia materials on student acquisition of vocabulary. *Language Learning and Technology* 6(1): 100–122.

O'Hara, S., & Pritchard, R. (2008). Hypermedia authoring as a vehicle for vocabulary development in middle school English as a second language classrooms. *The Clearing House* 82(2): 60–65.

Panagiotakopoulos, C. T., and Ioannidis, G. S. 2002. Assessing children's understanding of basic time concepts through multimedia software. *Computers & Education* 38(4): 331–349.

Papastergiou, M. 2009. Digital game-based learning in high school computer science education: Impact on educational effectiveness and student motivation. *Computers & Education* 52(1): 1–12.

Partnership for 21st Century Skills. 2009. *Framework for 21st century learning* [online]. Available at: http://www.p21.org/documents/P21_Framework.pdf. Accessed on July 25, 2010.

Perez, L., & Beltran, J. 2008. A Spanish intervention programme for students with special education needs: Effects on intellectual capacity and academic achievement. *European Journal of Special Needs Education* 23(2): 147–156.

Poobrasert, O., and Cercone, N. 2009. Evaluation of educational multimedia support system for students with deafness. *Journal of Educational Multimedia and Hypermedia* 18(1): 71–90.

Rasmussen, K. L., and Davidson-Shivers, G. V. 1998. Hypermedia and learning styles: Can performance be influenced? *Journal of Multimedia and Hypermedia* 7(4): 291–308.

Rice, M. L., and Wilson, E. K. 1999. How technology aids constructivism in the social studies classroom. *Social Studies* 90(1): 28–33.

Riddle, E. M. 1995. *Communication through multimedia in an elementary classroom* (Report no. 143; ERIC ED Document Reproduction Service No. 384 346). Charlottesville: Curry School of Education, University of Virginia.

Rothenberg, J. J., McDermott, P., and Martin. G. 1998. Changes in pedagogy: A qualitative result of teaching heterogeneous classes. *Teaching and Teacher Education* 14(6): 633–642.

Rouet, J., Levon, J. J., Dillion, A., and Spiro, R. J. 1996. An introduction to hypertext and cognition. In J. Rouet, J. J. Levon, A. Dillion, and R. J. Spiro (Eds.), *Hypertext and cognition* (pp. 3–8). Mahwah, NJ: Lawrence Erlbaum Associates.

Samples, B. 1992. Using learning modalities to celebrate intelligence. *Educational Leadership* 50(2): 62–66.

Schacter, J., and Fagnano, C. 1999. Does computer technology improve student learning and achievement? How, when, and under what conditions? *Journal of Educational Computing Research* 20(4): 329–343.

Shapiro, A. 2003. The latest dope on research (about constructivism): Part II: On instruction and leadership. *International Journal of Educational Reform* 12(1): 62–77.

Siciliano, J. I. 2001. How to incorporate cooperative learning principals in the classroom: It's more than just putting students in teams. *Journal of Management Education* 25(1): 8–20.

Simons, P. R. J. 1993. Constructive learning: The role of the learner. In T. Duffy, J. Lowyck, and D. Jonassen (Eds.), *Designing environments for constructive learning* (pp. 291–313). Heidelberg, Germany: Springer-Verlag.

Sivin-Kachala, J., & Bialo, E. R. 2000. *Report on the effectiveness of technology in schools* (7th ed.). Washington, DC: Software and Information Industry Association.

Slavin, R. E. 1994. *Cooperative learning: Theory, research, and practice* (2nd ed.). Needham Heights, MA: Allyn & Bacon.

Slavin, R. E. 1999. Comprehensive approaches to cooperative learning. *Theory into Practice* 38(2): 74–79.

Slavin, R. E. 2008. *Educational psychology theory and practice* (9th ed.). Boston: Allyn & Bacon.

Son, J. 2003. A hypertext approach to foreign language reading: Student attitudes and perceptions. *Australian Review of Applied Linguistics* 17: 91–110.

Spence, L. 2009. Developing multiple literacies in a website project. *Reading Teacher*, 62(7): 592–597.

Steelman, J., Grable, L., and Vasu, E. 2004. Expanding global awareness: The use of student-developed multimedia created in a cooperative learning environment. *International Journal of Social Education* 19(2): 41–50.

Stelzer, T., Gladding, G., Mestre, J., and Brookes, D. 2009. Comparing the efficacy of multimedia modules with traditional textbooks for learning introductory physics content. *American Journal of Physics* 77(2): 184–190.

Sternberg, R. J. 1994. Diversifying instruction and assessment. *Educational Forum* 59(1): 47–52.

Su, K. 2008. An informative study of integrating multimedia technology into problem-solving for promoting students' abilities in general chemistry. *International Journal of Instructional Media* 35(3): 339–353.

Tarim, K. 2009. The effects of cooperative learning on preschoolers' mathematics problem-solving ability. *Educational Studies in Mathematics* 72(3): 325–340.

Tuzun, H., Yilmaz-Soylu, M., Karakus, T., Inal, Y., and Kizilkaya, G. 2009. The effects of computer games on primary school students' achievement and motivation in geography learning. *Computers & Education* 52(1): 68–77.

United Nations for Educational, Scientific and Cultural Organization. 2008. *ICT competency standards for teachers: Policy framework.* [Online]. Available at: http://unesdoc.unesco.org/images/0015/001562/156210E.pdf (Accessed on July 25, 2010).

Urban-Woldron, H. 2009. Interactive simulations for the effective learning of physics. *Journal of Computers in Mathematics and Science Teaching* 28(2): 163–176.

Vandendorpe, C. 2009. From *papyrus to hypertext: Toward the universal digital library*. Chicago: University of Illinois Press.

Vergara, V., Caudell, T., Goldsmith, T., Panaiotis, and Alverson, D. 2009. Knowledge-driven design of virtual patient simulations. *Innovate: Journal of Online Education* 5(2). Available at: http://www.innovateonline.info/pdf/vol5_issue2/Knowledge-Driven_Design_of_Virtual_Patient_Simulations.pdf. Accessed on July 9, 2010.

Vermette, P. J. 1998. *Making cooperative learning work: Student teams in K–12 classrooms*. Upper Saddle River, NJ: Prentice-Hall.

Vockell, E. L., and van Deusen, R. M. 1989. *The computer and higher order thinking skills*. Watsonville, CA: Mitchell/McGraw-Hill Publishing Company.

Vygotsky, L. S. 1978. *Mind in society: The development of higher psychological processes*. Cambridge, MA: Harvard University Press.

Wieman, C., Perkins, K., and Adams, W. 2008. Oersted Medal Lecture 2007. Interactive simulations for teaching physics: What works, what doesn't, and why. *American Journal of Physics* 76(4/5): 393–399.

Wilson, A. 2008. Moving beyond the page in content area literacy: Comprehension instruction for multimodal texts in science. *Reading Teacher* 62(2): 153–156.

Wolfe, P. 2001. *Brain matters: Translating research into classroom practice*. Alexandria, VA: Association for Supervision and Curriculum Development.

Woolfolk, A. E. 1987. *Educational psychology* (3rd ed.). Englewood Cliffs, NJ: Prentice-Hall.

Xin, J. F. 1999. Computer-assisted cooperative learning in integrated classrooms for students with and without disabilities. *Information Technology in Childhood Education Annual 1999*: 61–78.

Yelland, N. 1999. Reconceptualizing schooling with technology for the 21st century: Images and reflections. *Information Technology in Childhood Education Annual 1999*: 39–59.

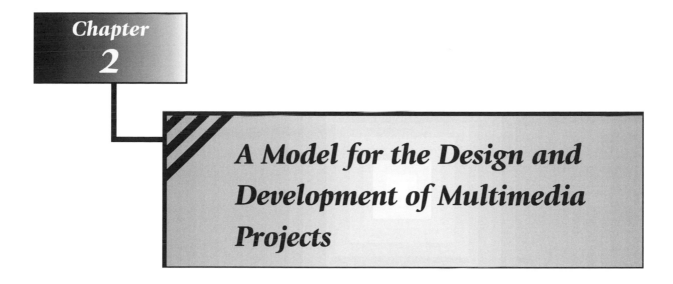

Chapter 2

A Model for the Design and Development of Multimedia Projects

A SCENARIO

As Marlena reviewed her students' multimedia projects, she couldn't believe it had been three years since the laptop initiative provided mobile computers for her school. In the beginning, she had been terrified—how could she possibly ensure that her sixth-grade students were prepared for the state achievement tests if they created multimedia projects instead of taking multiple-choice quizzes? She had discovered, however, that through careful planning, she could cover the topics in more depth, and the students appeared to understand the material better.

For example, the project they had recently completed involved a unit on the Civil War. After setting the instructional goals and aligning the objectives with state standards, she introduced the Gettysburg Address to her students and explained the meaning of the speech. Marlena then divided the students into groups of three and divided the lines of the Gettysburg Address so that each group was assigned several lines to study. After the lines of their part were memorized, each group used a computer to record themselves reciting their script.

Next, the students were asked to brainstorm and conduct research about images that would be appropriate to accompany their audio section. They were tasked with selecting and sequencing an appropriate number of germane pictures to match the length and meaning of their audio portion. Marlena provided guidance by outlining the flow of the speech and showing examples of how the screens should be formatted with titles and graphics. The students then downloaded copyright-free pictures from a Civil War website.

When the audio segments and images were ready, each group used iMovie to import the media elements and produce their own movie, combining the pictures with the recording of their portion of the speech. As the students worked with their projects, Marlena facilitated the activities by answering questions and providing guidance.

After all of the groups had completed their movie, Marlena combined the individual movies in iMovie to create a single production of the entire Gettysburg Address. In this lesson, positive social support was encouraged as students worked in groups, and students enhanced their knowledge by constructing a movie with images and audio from the Gettysburg Address. They (Marlena and her students) had agreed on a rubric for the projects before they started so that everyone knew exactly what was expected and how the projects would be evaluated.

As Marlena reflected on the project, she acknowledged that the classroom had been a little noisier than during a lecture, but the students stayed on task and were very enthusiastic. Over the three years that laptops had been available in the classroom, Marlena's comfort and the students' skills with technology had progressed tremendously, and now the laptops were used as a tool throughout the curriculum and throughout the school day.

OVERVIEW

Every teacher understands that good instruction involves careful planning. Whether or not a teacher creates detailed lesson plans, he or she understands the value of preparing the content, sequence, and instructional materials for each lesson. In addition, experienced teachers always have a backup plan (or two) in case the lesson does not progress as expected.

Careful planning is especially critical when integrating multimedia projects into the classroom. Planning saves time, reduces frustration, eliminates fragmented learning experiences, and results in increased student achievement. Following a systematic plan is recommended for teachers who are using technology for instruction, as well as for students who are creating multimedia projects. This chapter introduces a model for technology projects. It is based on three Ds and an E: DECIDE, DESIGN, DEVELOP, and EVALUATE. The topics of this chapter include the following:

- Overview of the DDD-E Model

- DECIDE phase: Planning activities for teachers and students

- DESIGN phase: Determining the project structure and implementation

- DEVELOP phase: Gathering and creating the media elements and facilitating the lesson

- EVALUATE phase: Reflecting on the project and the student achievement

THE DDD-E MODEL

Overview

Implementing multimedia projects in a classroom environment is a rewarding yet challenging undertaking. A multitude of issues will surface, such as the following: Which standards can be addressed? Should students work individually or in a group? Which media components are appropriate? Should the project result in a presentation, a digital movie, a webpage, or another venue? How many hours/days should the students work on the project? How should it be evaluated? The questions (and possible answers) are endless.

One way to address the numerous issues involved in designing and developing multimedia projects is to follow a process that outlines the analysis, design, development, and evaluation of the project. The model we propose consists of DECIDE, DESIGN, DEVELOP, and EVALUATE (DDD-E). This model is intended to serve as a general outline for projects, but it can be modified or expanded to meet individual project needs. It provides a framework for the phases of multimedia projects but does not negate a constructivist approach to individual project design or development.

Creating a multimedia project is similar to cooking a gourmet meal. First, you must DECIDE exactly which dishes you plan to serve (which will be influenced by who is coming to dinner and which groceries you have in the cupboard). If more than one person is cooking the meal, you also must decide who is going to be responsible for preparing each dish.

Next, the DESIGN of the meal includes locating the recipes and organizing the ingredients. Recipes, like flowcharts and storyboards, provide the structure for the dishes, detailing the required amounts of each ingredient and the sequence of cooking events.

Next, you DEVELOP the meal by gathering all of the components, mixing everything in the correct sequence, and combining the ingredients. As each individual dish is prepared, the overall meal must be considered. For example, appetizers are usually prepared first and served before the main course.

You EVALUATE throughout the process of making the meal (e.g., licking the spoon and making sure a dish is not burning). Dinner guests provide the final assessment by providing feedback after the meal has been served.

The DDD-E model consists of three main phases (DECIDE, DESIGN, DEVELOP), surrounded by EVALUATE (see Figure 2.1). This chapter provides a general outline of the model. Subsequent chapters (3 through 7) provide in-depth treatments of each phase, with recommendations for classroom implementation and modification.

Figure 2.1. The DDD-E model.

Each phase in the DDD-E model involves activities for both the teacher and the students. The DECIDE phase focuses on determining the goals and objectives; the DESIGN phase specifies the program structure; and the DEVELOP phase includes producing the media elements and completing the project. The EVALUATE phase occurs throughout the design and development processes. At each phase, the project should be reviewed, and, if necessary, revised. Table 2.1 outlines teacher activities and student activities for each phase in the DDD-E model. These activities will be introduced in this chapter. Detailed descriptions are provided in Chapters 3 through 7.

Table 2.1. Teacher and Student Activities in the DDD-E Model

Phase	Activities: Teacher	Activities: Student

DECIDE	PLANNING
	
	    Identify standards and set instructional goals
	    Decide on a project
	    Assess prerequisite skills
	    Determine assessment techniques
	
	ORGANIZING
	
	    Examine grouping alternatives
	    Create cooperative groups
	    Schedule computer time
	    Working in a one-to-one laptop classroom
	
	MANAGING
	
	    Brainstorming activities
	    Research activities
		Brainstorm content
		
		Conduct research

DESIGN	Present design guidelines and templates Conduct formative assessment	Outline content Create flowcharts Specify screen design and layout Write scripts or storyboards
DEVELOP	Manage media production Facilitate multimedia activities Conduct formative assessment	Create graphics Construct animations Produce audio Produce video Author program
EVALUATE	Provide student assessment Reflect on activity and revise for future	Debug program Evaluate peers Conduct self-evaluations

Decide

The first phase in a multimedia project is DECIDE. This phase sets the stage for the entire project. The DECIDE phase is influenced by many variables, including the content area, location and number of computers, available software, and students' experiences and expertise. The DECIDE phase includes the following activities for teachers and students.

Teachers

- Identify standards and set instructional goals
- Decide on a project
- Assess prerequisite skills
- Determine assessment techniques
- Examine grouping alternatives
- Create cooperative groups
- Schedule computer time

Students

- Brainstorm content
- Conduct research

Identify standards and set instructional goals (Teacher)

The first step in the DECIDE phase is to identify the standards and goals that will be addressed with the multimedia project. Standards and benchmarks for students exist at the national level for content areas. Many states and local districts also have standards and/or benchmarks to measure student achievement. Technology can be used as a tool in the classroom to address a multitude of standards and instructional goals—from science to reading.

Decide on a project (Teacher)

Before assigning a multimedia project, educators need to consider whether it is the most effective way to achieve the desired learning outcomes; alternative approaches might be more effective or efficient.

When assigning a multimedia project, consider the following:

1. It should be relevant to the student. Projects are more meaningful if the students can see how the areas of study affect them. In other words, a project about pollution can be introduced by focusing on how pollution has affected the beaches or air quality in the local area.

2. It should be relevant to the curriculum. Technology should be used as a tool, not as an end in itself. Therefore, each multimedia project should be closely related to instructional objectives.

3. There should be sufficient resources. Some topics do not lend themselves to multimedia simply because there are not enough resources. For example, it may not be appropriate to ask students to create a multimedia project about authors and assign Mark Twain to one group and Catherine Gregory to another. Likewise, it can be frustrating to implement a multimedia project without sufficient hardware and software. Before starting a multimedia unit, review the resources that the students will have available, such as books, clip media, the Internet, and computers. This will help teachers schedule computer time, arrange groups, and provide students with the necessary materials to complete their projects.

4. There should be sufficient time. Carefully evaluate the amount of time that can be devoted to project development. Short-term projects with well-defined scope could be completed in four hours or less. Long-term projects, involving research, synthesis of information, and complex production could take several weeks to complete.

Assess prerequisite skills (Teacher)

It is crucial that students have the necessary prerequisite skills for using the computer and multimedia tools. Teachers should ensure that students are familiar with basic computer skills (turning on and off the computer, saving and copying files, navigating through folders and directories, and handling the computer hardware) and the skills necessary for creating the assigned multimedia project.

In 2007, the International Society for Technology in Education (ISTE) updated the National Educational Technology Standards for Students (ISTE, 2007a). These standards provide technology foundations for students as well as profiles for technology-literacy. The technology standards are divided into six broad standards:

1. Creativity and Innovation

2. Communication and Collaboration

3. Research and Information Fluency

4. Critical Thinking, Problem Solving, and Decision Making

5. Digital Citizenship

6. Technology Operations and Concepts

ISTE also outlined technology profiles for four grade/age groups, including grades PK–2 (ages 4–8), grades 3–5 (ages 8–11), grades 6–8 (ages 11–14), and grades 9–12 (ages 14–18). "These profiles are based on ISTE's core belief that all students must have regular opportunities to use technology to develop skills that encourage personal productivity, creativity, critical thinking, and collaboration in the classroom and in daily life" (ISTE, 2007b, 1). The profiles are available at http://www.iste.org/Content/NavigationMenu/NETS/ForStudents/NETS_for_Students.htm.

Determine assessment techniques (Teacher)

When the project begins, it is important to inform the students about the goals and assessment methods. Students should be aware whether "paper" products, such as storyboards or content outlines, will be required, as well as which evaluation instruments and methods will be used.

Rubrics are common measurement tools for multimedia projects because they provide guidelines for assessment, while allowing room for creativity and subjectivity. In many cases, the teacher and students will work together to outline the requirements and establish the rubrics. Sample rubrics for multimedia projects are included in Chapter 7.

Examine grouping alternatives (Teacher)

Many of the multimedia projects will be completed by groups of two to six students. It is important to establish the size and membership of the groups early in the process because the group members will need to work together to brainstorm and research their approach.

There are many alternatives for assigning students to a group, including student learning styles, multiple intelligences, student interests, random assignment, and areas of expertise. Chapter 3 provides detailed information on alternatives in group size, group composition, and group structure.

Create cooperative groups (Teacher)

Teamwork and collaboration are important elements and outcomes of multimedia projects. Within each group, the members may take on the roles of a multimedia design and development team. The primary team members are listed in Table 2.2.

Table 2.2. Multimedia Team Members

Team Member	Roles in Multimedia Project
Project manager	• Organize the team members • Set the schedules • Track the progress
Instructional designers	• Determine the screen layout • Create the flowcharts • Specify the project design in the storyboards
Graphic artists	• Create the graphics • Create the animations
Production specialists	• Record and edit the audio • Record and edit the video
Program authors	• Produce the program • Debug and test the program

The team roles need not be independent of each other. In other words, one student may serve as both the program author and the graphic artist. Likewise, all students can take on all roles and work together for the final product. Chapter 3 provides more information about how to assign student roles.

Schedule computer time (Teacher)

It's not necessary to have a room full of equipment to implement multimedia activities; however, one of the first steps is to take an inventory of the hardware and software options that are available at your school or district. Once you know what is available, you can begin to schedule access to computers and other peripherals (see Chapter 3).

Working in a one-to-one laptop classroom (Teacher)

A promising trend is the increased access to laptop computers and other wireless devices in many schools. As technology becomes more ubiquitous, multimedia projects can be developed with less and less concern about equitable access for all students (see Chapter 3).

Brainstorm content (Students)

After establishing the design teams, allow students time to explore the project by brainstorming with their group members. There are two aspects of the project that students can explore—content and approach. For example, if a group is creating a program about Florida history, the students may begin by generating ideas about topics. The project might include explorers, soldiers, transportation, or hurricanes, among other things. (Note: Brainstorming is only effective if the students are somewhat familiar with the content.)

After they have exhausted the ideas for content, they can explore possible media and approaches. Given the Florida history project, they might suggest making a video about a reenactment of an historical battle, collecting pictures of the explorers, or generating maps showing settlement patterns. Be sure to allow plenty of time for the students to explore the content and approaches thoroughly. See Chapter 3 for effective techniques for managing student brainstorming activities.

Conduct research (Students)

Every project should include ample time for the students to research the content. For this step, students should have access to as many resources as possible, including the Internet, books, and journals. It may be necessary to help students get started and to provide a checklist of required components for the project. For example, if the project is focusing on a country, you may require students to include information about the imports, exports, history, geography, politics, culture, and so on. In addition to collecting the research, students should be encouraged to synthesize it and present it in a novel, concise manner. See Chapter 3 for information about managing research activities.

Design

The DECIDE phase outlines the goals and content of the project. In the DESIGN phase, the project often takes form through outlines, flowcharts, and storyboards. After teachers inventory available hardware and software, present design guidelines, demonstrate flowchart techniques, and provide storyboard templates, students organize the sequence and specify the exact text, graphics, audio, and interactions of the project. It is crucial to emphasize the importance of the DESIGN phase to students. If they do not dedicate sufficient time and energy to this phase, they may end up wasting valuable time during the DEVELOP (production) phase. The DESIGN phase should represent approximately 50 percent of the total time committed to the project.

Teachers

- Present design guidelines and templates
- Conduct formative assessment

Students

- Outline content
- Create flowcharts
- Specify screen design and layout
- Write scripts or storyboards

Present design guidelines and templates (Teacher)

Through the use of examples and non-examples, teachers can introduce students to design guidelines for text, menus, navigation, color, and other elements. Soon, the students will be critiquing each other and providing insight into effective presentations and projects.

Multimedia projects can be simplistic or complex, depending on the age of the students, the length of the project, and the instructional goals. Templates are useful tools to help students outline and structure their projects—the templates can be used as digital documents (the students fill them in on a computer), or they can be printed and filled in with paper and pencil. Information about guidelines and templates is provided in Chapter 4.

Conduct formative assessment (Teacher)

As students begin to design their projects, through the use of content outlines, flowcharts, storyboards, and so on, it is important to provide feedback on their progress. At this point, teachers can provide feedback to students about whether they are staying within the project scope, addressing the project goals, and working well with their team members. Chapter 7 focuses on assessment techniques.

Outline content (Students)

After the brainstorming and research steps of the DECIDE phase, the students should synthesize, organize, and outline the content for the project. This step helps set the stage for the flowcharts. Many factors influence the content outline, including the intended audience and the time allotted to the project. These and other factors will be covered in detail in Chapter 4.

Create flowcharts (Students)

The flowcharting process illustrates a program's sequence and structure. It is important that students visualize how the various parts of a project fit together. Students should be encouraged to experiment with different ways of presenting content. To help them determine the best options, ask questions such as, "Does one idea logically follow another throughout the program?" "Is there a central point from which all of the other ideas should be linked?" "Can you start with three or four choices and then subdivide the selections?" Be sure to demonstrate different projects with various structures to illustrate the alternatives. Additional information about flowcharts and project structure is provided in Chapter 4.

Specify screen design and layout (Students)

Storyboards for a project can detail all of the text, graphics, and interactions for each screen (page). Before students write the storyboards, work with them to determine the screen design (the layout or template for each screen). Each screen should contain specific functional areas (such as title, text, graphics, prompts, navigation options, and feedback) to make the program more consistent and easier to follow. Sample templates for projects are provided in Chapters 4, 8, 9, 10, and 11.

Write scripts or storyboards (Students)

After the screen templates and functional areas have been determined, the students can proceed with the scripts or storyboards. Storyboards should contain all the information that will be placed on the screens, as well as information that will help the programmer and production specialists develop the media components. At this point, the students (instructional designers) determine the best way to present the information, how much information goes on each screen, and the like. Sample storyboard templates are provided in Chapter 4.

Develop

After the storyboards are complete, the development process can begin. Depending on the complexity specified in the storyboards, the DEVELOP phase may involve producing audio elements, video segments, graphics, and/or text. Different members of the project team can develop these components simultaneously, or they can be developed in sequence by all of the members working together. The DEVELOP phase also includes the programming (often referred to as *authoring*) of the program.

As the class approaches the DEVELOP phase, teachers should ensure that they have the knowledge and skills necessary to work with the development tools (such as graphics programs or video editors). They should also emphasize the restrictions or constraints that may apply. For example, if the projects are being created for Web delivery, the file size will be an important factor. Activities in the DEVELOP phase include the following.

Teachers

- Manage media production
- Facilitate multimedia activities
- Conduct formative assessment

Students

- Create graphics
- Construct animations
- Produce audio
- Produce video
- Author program

Manage media production (Teacher)

The configuration and management of a multimedia activity will vary, based on the number of available computers (and other hardware), the grouping strategy, and other factors. Chapter 5 addresses various configurations for computer access and outlines the Jigsaw cooperative learning approach, wherein students assume various roles and interact with peer groups.

Facilitate multimedia activities (Teacher)

As the students engage in the multimedia activity, the teacher's role becomes that of a facilitator. This includes the following activities:

- Ensuring that all of the necessary equipment (batteries, software, etc.) is available
- Reviewing necessary prerequisite skills related to the technology or concepts related to the content
- Circulating the room, assisting students
- Monitoring the progress of each group or student
- Ensuring that students stay on task
- Troubleshooting hardware and software issues
- Conducting formative evaluation and providing ongoing feedback to students' progress
- Being aware of the time allotted for the activity in relation to the progress
- Having a backup plan (or two) in case the technology crashes
- Emphasizing the lesson's goals

Conduct formative assessment (Teacher)

Continuous feedback for students is important throughout the Develop phase. As students create their media elements, teachers should ensure that the elements are appropriate for the content, follow design guidelines, and are stored in the correct file formats. Chapter 7 focuses on assessment techniques.

Create graphics (Students)

Graphics—pictures, charts, diagrams, and drawings—can play a major role in conveying the content of a multimedia project. After the requirements are specified in the storyboards, students work to create the appropriate graphics. The procedures for creating graphics with software programs, scanners, and digital cameras are outlined in Chapter 5.

Construct animations (Students)

In some cases, the project may also include animations—graphics that move in rapid sequence to create the illusion of motion. Animations can convey many complex abstractions, such as water moving in a pipe, or they can be used to attract attention to a particular screen or project. Details on animation techniques are provided in Chapter 5.

Produce audio (Students)

All the sound elements of a program (narration, music, and sound effects) are referred to as *audio*. Students can record the audio elements of a project themselves, or they can incorporate sounds from the Internet or other sources. The procedures and alternatives for audio production are outlined in Chapter 5.

Produce video (Students)

Students are accustomed to viewing video (television, DVD, etc.). It is now more feasible than ever for students to use smartphones, camcorders and desktop computers to record video segments. The video clips can then be integrated into an application program or used to create a stand-alone video. Many factors must be considered when producing, editing, and implementing video segments; these factors are discussed in Chapter 5.

Author program (Students)

One of the last steps in the DEVELOP phase is to incorporate all the text, graphics, and other media components into a finished program. Many tools can be used to author a multimedia project, including application software (such as word processors, spreadsheets, or image programs) hypermedia programs, presentation programs (such as PowerPoint), Web-based editors (such as DreamWeaver or iWeb), and video editors (such as iMovie and MovieMaker). All of these options are inexpensive, relatively easy to use, and can include text, graphics, audio, and video. Chapter 6 outlines popular programming options for school-based projects. Chapters 8, 9, 10, and 11 focus on sample presentation, hypermedia, Web-based, and video projects.

Evaluate

The evaluation of multimedia projects is both formative and summative. Formative assessment is done throughout project development by both the teacher and the students. For example, the teacher should assess research and brainstorming during the DECIDE phase. She or he should also provide feedback for the students on their flowcharts and storyboards before they begin the development process. Summative evaluation takes place at the end of the project. The steps in the EVALUATE phase include the following.

Teachers

- Provide student assessment
- Reflect on activity and revise for future

Students

- Debug program
- Evaluate peers
- Conduct self-evaluations

Provide student assessment (Teacher)

Multimedia projects are a great way to provide alternate assessments for students. Rather than judging their knowledge based on a multiple-choice test, teachers can assess students' abilities to construct knowledge and communicate it through a variety of media. The exact method for determining a multimedia project's overall grade will vary. Most important is to provide a meaningful way to communicate the progress to students and their parents. See Chapter 7 for more information on student assessment and evaluation techniques.

Reflect on activity and revise for future (Teacher)

Reflection is an important aspect of all multimedia activities—for both students and teachers. Teachers who systematically reflect and modify their lessons will be better prepared to offer a similar, perhaps even more effective, lesson in the future.

Debug program (Students)

Throughout the project development, students should test and debug the project. This process includes testing the media elements on various computers, correcting grammar and punctuation errors, and testing the program for inoperative links. When students complete their projects, student groups should review each others' programs for possible bugs before the projects are submitted for final evaluation.

Evaluate peers (Students)

Group dynamics are an important part of most multimedia projects. Besides the teacher's assessment, students should be encouraged (or required) to evaluate their peers' projects. Instruments for peer evaluation are included in Chapter 7.

Conduct self-evaluations (Students)

It is also important for students to conduct self-evaluations and to report on their progress through checklists, journal entries or other assessment tools. For more information on self-evaluations, see Chapter 7.

DDD-E BENEFITS

There are many learning benefits for students who use technology as tools, information vehicles, and context to support knowledge construction, communication, and representation of ideas. Studies have also found that "producing multimedia is a more powerful way of learning than studying already produced materials" (Jonassen, Peck, and Wilson 1999, 102). Participating in the design and development of multimedia programs can improve students' creativity and attitudes and promote a deeper and more sophisticated understanding of the content. Table 2.3 outlines student activities and correlates them to some of the cognitive skills and activities that are involved in each phase of the DDD-E process.

Table 2.3. Cognitive Skills for Students

Phase	Student Activities	Cognitive Skills
DECIDE	• Brainstorm content • Conduct research	• Formulate questions • Design search strategies • Select and interpret information • Analyze and synthesize information
DESIGN	• Outline content • Create flowcharts • Specify screen design and layout • Write scripts or storyboards	• Organize and structure content • Allocate information to nodes/chunks • Chunk information into logical patterns • Sequence tasks into a timeline • Write meaningful scripts • Convey information through appropriate media • Demonstrate creativity
DEVELOP	• Create graphics • Construct animations • Produce audio • Produce video • Author program	• Translate storyboard information into media elements • Select appropriate media formats • Construct media elements
EVALUATE	• Debug program • Evaluate peers • Conduct self-evaluations	• Produce and verify program • Analyze program effectiveness • Engage in self-reflection

SUMMARY

Careful planning is critical when developing multimedia projects. Models such as DDD-E can help teachers and students structure the development of multimedia projects while encouraging student creativity. The DDD-E model provides a framework for students to work collaboratively in designing and developing their projects and allows opportunities for ongoing evaluation throughout each phase of the DDD-E process. Chapters 3 through 7 focus on each phase of the DDD-E model; Chapters 8 through 11 provide multimedia project ideas based on the DDD-E model.

REFERENCES

International Society for Technology in Education. 2007a. *NETS for Students2007*. Eugene, OR: ISTE. Available at http://www.iste.org/Content/NavigationMenu/NETS/ForStudents/2007Standards/ NETS_for_Students_2007.htm. Accessed on July 25, 2010.

International Society for Technology in Education. 2007b. *Profiles for technology (ICT) literate students*. Eugene, OR: ISTE. Available at http://www.iste.org/Content/NavigationMenu/NETS/ ForStudents/2007Standards/NETS-S_2007_Student_Profiles.pdf. on Accessed July 25, 2010.

Jonassen, D. H., Peck, K. L., and Wilson, B. G. 1999. *Learning with technology: A constructivist perspective*. Upper Saddle River, NJ: Merrill.

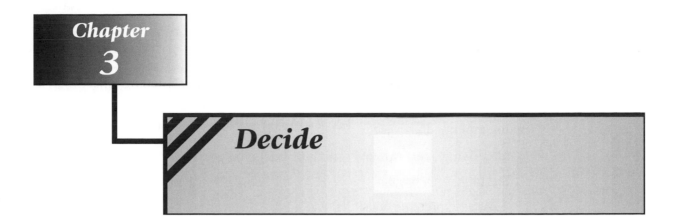

Chapter 3

Decide

A SCENARIO

Not everyone in Ms. Crawford's class had a computer at home. This made it that much more important for her to provide opportunities for her students to use and learn with technology in the classroom. Creating multimedia projects was a regular assignment in Ms. Crawford's classroom. She had four computers and established a computer schedule to ensure her student groups had access to a computer on a daily basis to work on their projects. Projects were based on content standards and provided students with the opportunities to collaborate and engage in authentic learning experiences. Her student teacher, Alma, questioned Ms. Crawford about her test scores, concerned that the students did not seem to be completing a lot of worksheets like the students in the other classrooms she had observed. Ms. Crawford smiled and assured Alma her students did quite well on standardized tests. Ms. Crawford explained that her students were very engaged in what they were doing, and what they were learning was meaningful to them. She also explained the planning and preparation that was involved in the assignments. "I'm not just placing groups of students at the computer," shared Ms. Crawford, "there is a significant amount of learning taking place." Alma commented that Ms. Crawford and the students made learning with technology look easy. "The key is enjoying what you do," noted Ms. Crawford, "If learning is not enjoyable or meaningful, kids check out. Using technology provides our students with real-world learning. The time I spend organizing these lessons are worth it. My students are worth it."

OVERVIEW

There are many things to consider before starting a multimedia project. For example, what content standard(s) will be addressed? Is a multimedia project appropriate? Are the necessary resources to support multimedia projects available? These questions and others are addressed in the first stage of the DDD-E process—the DECIDE stage. The DECIDE stage sets the foundation for the remaining stages of the DDD-E process; hence, the planning and organization of the DECIDE phase contribute to the overall success of the students' multimedia projects. The DECIDE stage includes determining the project's goals (deciding on relevant standards and benchmarks), establishing whether multimedia is appropriate, assessing students' prerequisite skills and background knowledge, deciding on assessment techniques, and planning grouping strategies and roles. Much of the teacher's time will be spent planning and organizing the projects. Students' time will be spent brainstorming and conducting research. Topics in this chapter include the following:

- Planning multimedia projects

  Identifying standards and setting instructional goals

  Deciding on a project

  Assessing prerequisite skills

  Determining assessment techniques

- Organizing multimedia projects

  Examining grouping alternatives

  Creating cooperative groups

  Scheduling computer time

  Working in a one-to-one laptop classroom

- Managing brainstorming and research activities

PLANNING MULTIMEDIA PROJECTS

DECIDE is the first phase of the DDD-E process, and it involves a significant amount of planning and organization. Planning includes setting instructional goals, deciding on a project, assessing and developing prerequisite skills, and deciding how the projects will be assessed.

Identifying Standards and Setting Instructional Goals

Educators are responsible for ensuring that students meet specific content standards across a variety of subject areas. District, state, and other tests are used to measure students' progress. Teachers are held accountable for their students' success and are expected to identify state or other standards that their lessons address, as well as learning objectives and outcomes. For many educators, this means strict adherence to textbooks and drill sheets for fear of not addressing a standard. However, standards can be met in a variety of ways through a multitude of instructional strategies, including the use of multimedia projects. In fact, as discussed in Chapter 1, students are more likely to retain what they have learned when constructing knowledge.

Multimedia projects can be used across all subject areas. When deciding to use a multimedia project to address a specific content standard or set of standards, consider the time needed to complete the project, how the standard(s) will be addressed through the project, and the students' ability levels. Consider whether such a project is the most effective way to achieve the desired learning outcomes. Textbooks, worksheets, independent research, field trips, or other hands-on activities may address an instructional goal more effectively. For example, students may more effectively classify objects (e.g., rocks, plants, leaves) in accordance with appropriate criteria by actually touching, handling, examining, testing, and manipulating the objects rather than researching and presenting a multimedia project about them. This is not to say that a multimedia presentation could not assist with students' learning; however, the students' time may be better spent with a hands-on science lesson than in the creation of a multimedia project.

When setting instructional goals for multimedia projects, it is critical that the goals reflect the identified content standard(s) and that there is a clear way to assess the students' learning. It is important that students learn something beyond technology skills and that the appearance of the final presentation does not overshadow the project's content. It is easy to become overly involved and influenced by multimedia special effects (such as sound, animation, video, transitions, and so on) and to forget about the purpose of the project. Assessing a multimedia project solely on its looks is comparable to rating a car based on its exterior instead of its engine or judging a cake's taste by its looks. Instructional goals and assessment criteria need to be introduced at the beginning of multimedia projects to ensure learning outcomes are addressed.

In addition to addressing specific content standards, instructional goals may be designed to:

- Accommodate multiple learning styles and interests

- Encourage cooperative learning and social skills

- Foster active learning by promoting interdisciplinary investigations

- Develop critical-thinking, reasoning, problem-solving, and metacognitive processes

- Enhance presentation and speaking skills

Instructional goals will vary depending on the ability level of the learner, available resources, and the learner's experience.

Deciding on a Project

After identifying the appropriate content standards and defining the instructional goals, the teacher can select and design a project to meet the desired goals. Assuming it is a multimedia project, the teacher will need to decide if the instructional goals can best be achieved through a program such as HyperStudio, Flash, DreamWeaver, a desktop video program (e.g., Apple's iMovie or Microsoft's MovieMaker), a presentation program (e.g., PowerPoint by Microsoft), or other applications. Teachers will want to choose multimedia production programs based on the ability level of their students. For example, younger or lower-ability students may benefit from Scholastic Keys (http://www.tomsnyder.com), a program that provides a kid-friendly interface for Microsoft Word, Excel, and PowerPoint. Ideas for projects are endless. Table 3.1 presents a variety of projects by subject area.

Table 3.1. Sample Project Ideas

Subject	Project Ideas
Language arts	Book reports; interactive and multiple ending stories; poetry collections; news reports; phonemic awareness activities for younger students; famous authors; parodies; mythology; reports on stories from multiple cultures or time periods; word origins; grammar, spelling, or vocabulary activities; rhyming games; story starters; prompted writing; creative writing
Mathematics	Problem-solving adventures; famous mathematicians; number recognition activities for younger students; number systems; geometry concepts; math puzzles and solutions; addition, subtraction, multiplication, or division concepts; history of mathematics; units of measure; currency exchange; stock market; inflation; finance; retailing; advertising; proofs
Science and health	Space exploration; pollution; animals; plant growth; weather; insects; nutrition; inventions and inventors; body systems; dissection; simple machines; chemical properties; ocean life; diseases; light and colors; science magic tricks; drugs, alcohol, or smoking; home remedies; exercise; senses; technology; volcanoes; plate tectonics; natural disasters; diet
Social studies	State or country reports; famous people in history; World Wars; Industrial Revolution; Civil War; Holocaust; Gold Rush; geography; Westward Movement; community events and history; family tree; explorers; hobbies and interests; government; careers; cultural holidays, foods, or celebrations; ancient civilizations; American Revolution; national symbols; current issues
Fine arts	Famous artists or musicians; film history; cinematography; music history; musical instruments; film or music genre; history of dance; music, movie, or play reviews; opera; music notation; song writing; animation; special effects; music and culture; famous paintings; art styles; famous entertainers

In addition to instructional goals, time is another consideration when deciding on a multimedia project. Students need to be given projects that can be completed within a prescribed time period. For example, if the multimedia project is part of a three-week unit on the California Gold Rush, teachers should limit the size and complexity of the project to what their students are capable of completing in a two- to three-week period.

Available resources affect the amount of time that may be needed to complete a multimedia project. Educators need to assess the number of computers and other resources (such as software, scanners, digital cameras, and so on) available for the project and what additional resources may be needed. This will help teachers schedule computer time, arrange groups, and ensure that the necessary resources are available. For example, teachers may need to plan additional time in the computer lab, borrow computers from other classrooms, have students bring in their own laptops, request Digital Video Disc Rewritables (DVD-RWs) media or flash (or keychain) drives for their students, or ensure that the necessary software is installed on all of the computers. Once a teacher has gathered all the necessary components, she or he is ready to introduce the project to the class.

Assessing Prerequisite Skills

Once the instructional goals and project have been defined, teachers must ensure that their students have the skills needed to complete the project successfully (see Chapter 2 for recommended technology profiles that have been outlined by ISTE). These include basic computer operations (e.g., properly turning on and off the computer, saving and printing files, opening and closing programs); the use of the assigned multimedia tools and peripherals; searching, evaluating, and citing Internet (and other) resources; understanding and following fair use and copyright laws; or other background knowledge teachers deem necessary for a particular project. Teachers can assess students' skills and background knowledge from past projects (if available), observations, skills tests and activities, and so on. Necessary skills may be taught as a whole class, in small groups, or by student experts (e.g., peer teaching). Review guides or index cards may be used to help students remember certain aspects of a program or device.

It is important that the use of technology does not obstruct the students' learning. Students should be made to feel comfortable with the technology prior to their use of the tool for content learning. Educators may use a jigsaw approach to teach certain elements of a complex program, ensuring each group has a member who is an "expert" in a particular part of the program. Additional or more advanced skills can be taught as the students design and prepare their projects.

Determining Assessment Techniques

In addition to identifying standards and setting instructional goals, deciding on a project, and assessing students' prerequisite skills, educators need to consider how they will monitor and assess students' work. This is actually a part of identifying standards and setting instructional goals, but its final form cannot be determined until the project has been identified and students have the necessary background knowledge and skills to proceed. The method of assessment will vary according to the type of the project, although a daily log or journal of the students' progress is something that may be applied across all projects. Chapter 7 discusses multiple strategies for assessing multimedia projects throughout each stage (Decide, Design, Develop, and Evaluate) to ensure instructional goals and standards are being met. Rubrics for formative and summative assessments are included, as are strategies for evaluating individual and group work. Educators may design their own assessment activities, borrow from others, use the examples in this book, or access websites such as RubiStar (http://rubistar.4teachers.org) for more ideas and resources for creating rubrics. Deciding on methods of assessment before students start their multimedia projects helps to ensure that students know what is expected of them, that they are on the right track, and that objectives are being met.

ORGANIZING MULTIMEDIA PROJECTS

In addition to planning, the DECIDE phase of the DDD-E process involves organizing the students' learning environment. This includes examining grouping alternatives, creating cooperative groups, and designing computer schedules.

Examining Grouping Alternatives

Depending on the project, students may work collaboratively or cooperatively. Students in collaborative groups work toward the same goal, but they are not necessarily accountable for each other's learning. Success may not depend on the efforts of all group members, allowing some students to loaf while others do all the work. Students in cooperative groups work toward a common goal and are accountable for each other's learning, providing both academic and personal support. Cooperative group members are taught social skills to help them coordinate their efforts, and teamwork is emphasized.

There are many types of cooperative group methods. These include Student Teams Achievement Divisions (STAD), Teams Games Tournament (TGT), Team-Assisted Individualization (TAI), Jigsaw, Group Investigation, and Learning Together. Groups may be heterogeneous or homogeneous. Most research supports heterogeneous groups (Johnson and Johnson 1999, 2009). Heterogeneous groups are usually formed with a mixture of ability, gender, or ethnicity; homogeneous groups consist of students with similar abilities or interests. Johnson, Johnson, and Holubec (1994, 26) state that "[h]eterogeneous groups tend to promote more elaborate thinking, more frequent giving and receiving of explanations, and greater perspective-taking during discussions about material, all of which increase students' understanding, reasoning, and long-term retention." Although heterogeneous groups are recommended, there are some instances when homogeneous groups are advantageous. For example, educators may find homogeneous groups best for specific class topics, students with specific needs, the creation of interest groups, or competition within groups (Fuchs, Fuchs, Hamlett, and Karns 1998; Johnson and Johnson 1999; Schullery and Schullery 2006).

Grouping Variables

Both grouping styles (heterogeneous and homogeneous) have advantages and disadvantages, depending on the grouping variable. Grouping variables include (but are not limited to) ability, learning style, intelligence, cognitive preference, gender, and background. Ability grouping is based on high, middle, and low achievement. Learning styles may include textual, visual, tactile, and auditory. Intelligences include linguistic, logical-mathematical, spatial, bodily-kinesthetic, musical, interpersonal, intrapersonal, and naturalist. Cognitive preference defines learners according to how they place themselves on a continuum between "global processing" and "analytical processing." Global individuals tend to be more sensitive to others, better communicators, and more socially oriented. Analytical individuals tend to be more introverted but are better at organizing and analyzing content. The next variable, gender, is self-explanatory. Background may include ethnicity, experiences, age, and likes and dislikes. Table 3.2 presents the advantages and disadvantages of these grouping variables.

In addition to heterogeneous and homogeneous grouping, groups may be established by interest or random assignment. For example, students whose favorite pet is a cat may work together to produce a multimedia project about cats, or students may be randomly assigned to groups by picking topics out of a hat. These grouping methods also have advantages and disadvantages. Interest groups may enhance communication among members and identify common interests and similarities among students. The disadvantage of interest groups is that they are self-selected, which may generate more off-task behavior, result in undesired homogeneous grouping (ability, ethnicity, or gender), and eliminate possibilities for students to expand their circles (Johnson, Johnson, and Holubec 1994).

Random assignment can provide variety and is perceived as one of the best ways to assign students to groups (Johnson and Johnson 1999). However, general random assignment may pair incompatible students. As an alternative, teachers may want to use stratified random assignment. This is the process of categorizing select groups (e.g., low-, average-, and high-ability students) and randomly selecting a member from each group to form a mixed team. For example, a teacher may randomly select a low-ability student, an average-ability student, and a high-ability student from predefined groups to serve as a three-member team rather than randomly select three students from one large group. Stratified random assignment may be used to ensure that certain students do not get placed together or that each group has students with one or two characteristics (e.g., reading level, math ability, or computer skills).

Stratified random assignment can be used to create groups of students with preferred intelligence. For example, by using stratified random assignment, the teacher can ensure that each group has one member with high linguistic intelligence, another member with high logical-mathematical intelligence, another member with high spatial intelligence, and another member with high interpersonal intelligence.

Table 3.2. Advantages and Disadvantages of Various Grouping Variables

Grouping Variable	Type	Advantages	Disadvantages
Ability	Heterogeneous	Best opportunity for peer support and tutoring	Free-rider effect
Ability	Homogeneous	Students tend to bond and communicate more effectively	Low-ability students are often at a significant learning disadvantage
Learning style, intelligence, or cognitive preference	Heterogeneous	Students are exposed to multiple perspectives and problem-solving methods, stimulating students' learning and cognitive development	May be hard to group if students display a preference for one dominant learning style, intelligence, or cognitive preference; communication skills may be more difficult to develop because of different interests
Learning style, intelligence, or cognitive preference	Homogeneous	Students tend to bond and communicate more effectively	Students' focus and exposure to different perspectives are limited
Gender or background	Heterogeneous	Reduces stereotypes, promotes equality among perceived ability and leadership roles	Teachers may need to ensure that social skills are in place to eliminate preconceived biases
Gender or background	Homogeneous	May benefit specific special interest groups or class topics	May cause unnecessary tension between groups; not representative of the real world

Groups can be teacher-selected or self-selected. Teacher-selected groups allow teachers to decide which students will work together, ensuring balance and the potential for positive relationships. At-risk students can be assigned to a group with supportive students in the class. Teachers can also ensure that students with non-achievement-oriented and disruptive behavior are not grouped together. Self-selected groups are the least recommended (Johnson and Johnson 1999). Typically, self-selected groups are homogeneous, spawning isolated groups of high achievers, males, minorities, socialites, females, and nonachievers. This leads to more off-task behavior and limited social experiences.

Group Numbers

In addition to grouping variables, the number of students placed in each group can make a difference in the group's success. Group numbers may depend on the students' abilities, number of computers in the classroom, time constraints, project requirements, cooperative group method, and other variables. Most studies on cooperative learning report group sizes ranging from two to six students. Johnson, Johnson, and Holubec (1994) provide the following points about group size:

1. As the size of the group increases, the range of abilities and viewpoints increases. Additional resources (members) may help the group succeed, and varying viewpoints will challenge the students to evaluate their own viewpoints and opinions more critically.

2. The larger the group, the more skillful the members must be at ensuring that everyone remains on task, has a chance to speak, reaches a consensus, understands the material being learned, and maintains good working relationships. Interactions increase as the group size increases, requiring additional interpersonal skills.

3. As group size increases, there is less face-to-face interaction among members and a reduced sense of intimacy. Lower individual responsibility may result, as well as a less cohesive group.

4. If a short period of time is available, smaller groups should be used. Smaller groups can take less time to get organized, and they may operate more quickly.

5. The smaller the group, the more difficult it is for students to avoid their share of the work. Small groups make students more accountable by increasing the visibility of their work.

6. The smaller the group, the easier it is to identify group difficulties, including leadership struggles, unresolved conflicts, and learning difficulties. Problems are more visible and more easily addressed in small groups.

Advantages and disadvantages of various group sizes for multimedia design teams are listed in Table 3.3.

Design teams generally consist of several people, depending on the size of the project and the number of available computers. With large groups, individuals or pairs of students can be assigned specific tasks. For example, following the group's research efforts, one person may be responsible for the graphics, one person may be responsible for the music and narration in the project, two more people may be responsible for completing the storyboards (based on a group-approved template), and two students may be responsible for entering information into the computer. Group members will have additional responsibilities as well; hence, it may not be possible for one member to complete his or her main responsibility until other members of the group complete their parts of the project. Students will need to ensure that everyone stays on task and assists other members.

Table 3.3. Advantages and Disadvantages of Various Group Sizes in Multimedia Design Teams

Group Size	Advantages	Disadvantages
One	• Work at own pace • Not dependent on others • May provide more hands-on computer time • Increases accountability	• Requires more classroom computer access time • Does not promote learning from different perspectives • Does not encourage cooperative problem solving • May take longer to complete a project • Individual may not be capable of handling all of the project's requirements
Two or three	• Learn from each other • Share project responsibilities • Supports real-world learning, learning from different perspectives, and cooperative problem solving • Classroom computer access time is cut in half because students can work together at the computer	• Need to ensure that everyone contributes and has a chance to speak
Four	• Learn from each other • Share project responsibilities • Supports real-world learning, learning from different perspectives, and cooperative problem solving • Increases classroom computer access time • More talent and resources are available to create the project • Projects may be completed in less time	• Need to ensure that everyone contributes and has a chance to speak • May be difficult to share computers • Requires greater interpersonal skills
Five or six	• Same as four	• Same as four • Easier for a member not to contribute • More chance of group disputes, leadership difficulties, and off-task behavior, which may delay project • Group dynamics may be more appropriate for older, more mature students

Creating Cooperative Groups

The success of cooperative groups depends on positive interdependence, a group goal, and individual and group accountability. Teamwork skills must be taught just as purposefully and precisely as academic skills. For most classroom multimedia projects, teamwork is essential.

Introducing Social Skills

Before placing students into cooperative groups, it is important to determine the goal of the multimedia project and what types of student interactions are desired. In most cases, students will need to be taught or reminded how to work cooperatively. Vermette (1998, 158) suggests the following working relationship skills:

- Acknowledging contributions

- Checking for agreement

- Disagreeing in an agreeable way

- Encouraging others

- Expressing support

- Inviting others to talk

- Keeping things calm and reducing tension

- Mediating

- Responding to ideas

- Sharing feelings

- Showing appreciation

The teacher may want to have groups model or practice these skills, as well as discuss the importance of listening, politeness, and other appropriate communication habits. Teachers may want to create social skill objectives. These may be defined by monitoring student groups and diagnosing the specific problems students are having working together or by asking students which social skill would improve their teamwork. Based on the teacher's observation and students' input, a social skill can be taught to help solve the problem.

Placing Students into Cooperative Groups

After social skills have been introduced, decide on the cooperative group method (e.g., STAD, TGT, TAI, Jigsaw, Group Investigation, or Learning Together) that will be most beneficial for the students and their assigned multimedia project. Depending on the project, desired interactions, and cooperative group method, assess students' strengths and weaknesses, their interests, who they like to work with, and so on. Consider group dynamics and create heterogeneous conditions. Along with the survey found at the end of this chapter (see the Self Survey blackline master), a teacher's own observation and background with his or her students can help facilitate student placement. Teachers may want to create their own surveys using online programs such as Zoomerang (http://www.zoomerang.com) or Survey Monkey (http://www.surveymonkey.com).

Students may be placed on design teams before or after introducing a multimedia project. Teachers may poll student interests before introducing the project or may wait to assess student interest until after the project has been introduced. For example, an informal survey might be created to assess students' interest in certain animals. On the basis of the survey results, the teacher can heterogeneously group students according to their interests before introducing a multimedia project about animals. Alternatively, the teacher could introduce a multimedia project about animals and let students group themselves according to their interests. Precautions must be taken, however, because of the disadvantages associated with self-selected groups. Hence, some students may choose groups based on the animal's popularity (not their true interest) and friends' choices. In addition, some animals may not draw enough students or they may attract too many students, creating bad feelings and a sense of unfairness if students are assigned to a different animal. Polling students' interests and assigning teams before introducing a project is recommended.

Assigning Roles

Another important aspect of cooperative group learning is role assignment. Assigning roles helps to ensure that all students participate and that no one person dominates a group. Roles may be based on group behaviors, computer tasks, or project assignments. For example, in a group of four students, one person may ensure that everyone gets a chance to speak (turn-taking monitor), one person may record the group's activities (record keeper), one person may ensure that the group's noise level is kept to a minimum (noise monitor), and one person may be responsible for keeping the group on task (task master). These group-behavior roles may be rotated on a daily basis. Computer tasks may include keyboarder (enters information into the computer), editor (oversees computer input), and record keeper (keeps track of the group's progress). Project assignment roles may include a graphic artist, instructional designer, production specialist, and program author.

Assignment roles may also become the basis for forming the groups. For example, a survey can be used to form the groups according to Gardner's Theory of Multiple Intelligences (see the Self Survey blackline master). Students are placed into teams based on their interests and observed strengths. Each design team might contain one student who ranked high in linguistics (I like to read books, write, and tell stories), one student who ranked high in logic-mathematics (I like math, strategy games, and working with puzzles), and two students who ranked high in spatial skills (I like to draw and I understand things better by looking at a picture). Student "linguistic experts" may take on the responsibilities of the subject matter experts, "spatial experts" may be considered the teams' graphic artists and storyboard designers, and "logical-mathematical experts" may be responsible for the project's flowchart and programming needs. Additional project roles may be assigned according to the students' self-rankings in the remaining areas of the survey: bodily-kinesthetic (I have a hard time sitting still), musical (I am a good singer and I know when music is off key), interpersonal (I get along well with others and I am a good listener), intrapersonal (I am dependable and self-confident), and naturalist (I enjoy the outdoors and can easily identify and classify the things around me).

Scheduling Computer Time

Until one-to-one laptop and wireless access are a standard in all schools, the most challenging aspect of designing and developing multimedia projects may be computer access. Various situations are possible. Computer labs are typically available for one 30- or 40-minute time slot a week. A computer assistant may or may not be available, and stations may range from 10 to 30 or more computers. Classrooms may have one or more computers, with or without a projection system. Some schools have mobile computer carts with laptops available for checkout, increasing the number of computers possible in a classroom. Mobile computer carts may not always be available if other teachers request them, however. There are several advantages and disadvantages for each situation when creating multimedia projects (see Table 3.4).

Table 3.4. Advantages and Disadvantages of Computer Situations

Computer Setting	Advantages	Disadvantages
Lab (10 to 15 computers)	• Working in groups, all students have access to the computers at the same time; teacher can facilitate whole-class instruction • Computer coordinator may be available to assist students • Students can take turns working individually on computers with computer coordinator while other students work on non-computer assignments with teacher • Less cost to secure and network computers	• Usually limited to 30 or 40 minutes a week • Fire drills, assemblies, and holidays, may cause lab time to be missed • Computer use is more likely to be an isolated activity than an integral part of the curriculum • Whole school uses the same computers and printers, causing more wear and tear on the systems, more variable problems, and additional software costs to meet everyone's needs • Instructional time is lost going to and from computer lab
Lab (20 or more computers)	• Same as other lab situation • Individual students have access to the computers at the same time; teacher can facilitate whole-class instruction • Additional computers may be available for multimedia purposes (e.g., making desktop videos)	• Same as other lab situation
One or two computers in the classroom	• Computer available every day for "teachable moments" • If a projector device or large monitor is available, can be used to facilitate whole-class/small group instruction • Some software is specifically designed for whole-class/small-group instruction (e.g., Tom Snyder Productions, Inc.) • Software funds can be used to purchase a variety of software that meets students' and teachers' individual needs vs. lab sets that may not be used by all teachers or students • Students may take better care of their "own" classroom computers	• Individual computer time is difficult to manage • Some group computer projects may take an undesirable length of time to complete due to limited access • More cost involved with purchasing computers and printers for every classroom, networking, and securing every room (alarm system)
Three or more computers in the classroom	• Same as other classroom situation • Student groups can have daily access • Computers are more likely to be used as an integral part of instruction and tool for learning	• Requires more classroom space than one or two computers • More cost involved with purchasing computers and printers for every classroom, networking, and securing every room (alarm system)
Mobile computer carts	• Can provide additional access for group projects • Can be removed from classroom and stored in secure location • Provides more flexibility (e.g., can be taken outdoors or on field trips)	• May not always be available • Time needed to move computer cart in and out of the classroom • Computers may be damaged in transit • May have batteries that need to be recharged

In most cases, a minimum of three computers in the classroom is necessary to ensure that every student gets some time at the computer during a single classroom period. This requires that students work in groups of three or four. While students are waiting for their group's turn at the computer, they work on a related, non-computer task. For example, students may be engaged in a silent reading activity, follow-up materials about the computer lesson, or another related activity. Teachers should resist teaching a directed lesson when students are actively engaged on classroom computers for several reasons:

1. Students on the computers are missing the lesson.

2. Students near the computers will more likely be watching their computer classmates rather than the teacher.

3. Some computer programs require sound (interrupting the teacher's directed lesson), and headphones are not always available.

4. The teacher cannot immediately assist students on the computers if he or she is involved in a directed lesson.

5. Students not on the computers may be more concerned about the clock and their turn at the computer than what the teacher has to say.

6. Scheduling may require students to take their computer turn during the middle of the directed lesson, as well as returning students to the directed lesson without having participated in the beginning of the lesson.

For many teachers, the thought of three or more computers in the classroom may seem unrealistic; however, computer access is improving. The National Center for Educational Statistics (2006) reports that about one in every four students has access to an instructional computer connected to the Internet. More schools are investing in one-to-one laptops programs. Wireless networks and lower costs have helped make one-to-one access a reality in many school districts. The trend is here, but how soon all teachers will have ample and updated technology in their classrooms is questionable. Change occurs slowly. In the meantime, teachers can place more computers in their classroom to facilitate multimedia projects by borrowing other classrooms' computers or arranging to borrow an additional computer from a computer lab. Parents and businesses may also lend support. Teachers may research organizations such as Share the Technology (http://www.sharetechnology.org) to locate equipment for donation or Computers for Learning (http://www.computers.fed.gov/School/user.asp) to learn how to receive excess federal computer equipment.

To help teachers address the various computer situations possible, computer schedules have been developed to assist teachers in managing multimedia projects in their classroom (see Figures 3.1 through 3.5).

Time	Computer Time	Project Assignments	Four-Computer Classroom Daily Computer Use (Version 1)
9:00 a.m. to 9:30 a.m.	A B C D	E F G H	24 to 32 students • 3 or 4 students per group • 30-minute rotation schedule • When students are not at computers, they work on related, non-computer project assignments. For example, Groups A, B, C, and D have computer time between 9:00 a.m. and 9:30 a.m. Groups E, F, G, and H work on related assignments.

Figure 3.1. Computer schedule for a four-computer classroom (version 1).

Time	Computer Time	Project Assignments		Four-Computer Classroom Daily Computer Use (Version 2)
		1	2	• 24 to 36 students
9:00 a.m. to 9:20 a.m.	A B C D	I J K L	E F G H	• 2 to 3 students per group • 20-minute rotation schedule • When students are not at computers, they work on related project assignments. For example, Groups A, B, C, and D have computer time between 9:00 a.m. and 9:20 a.m. Groups E, F, G, and H and groups I, J, K, and L work on related, non-computer assignments.
9:20 a.m. to 9:40 a.m.	E F G H	A B C D	I J K L	
9:40 a.m. to 10:00 a.m.	I J K L	E F G H	A B C D	

Figure 3.2. Computer schedule for a four-computer classroom (version 2).

Time	Computer Time	Project Assignments		Three-Computer Classroom Daily Computer Use
		1	2	• 27 to 36 students
9:00 a.m.	A	G	D	• 3 or 4 students per group
to	B	H	E	• 20-minute rotation schedule
9:20 a.m.	C	I	F	• When students are not at computers, they work on related project assignments. For example, Groups A, B, and C have computer time between 9:00 a.m. and 9:20 a.m. Groups D, E, F, G, H, and I work on related, non-computer assignments (projects 1 and 2).
9:20 a.m.	D	A	G	
to	E	B	H	
9:40 a.m.	F	C	I	
9:40 a.m.	G	D	A	
to	H	E	B	
10:00 a.m.	I	F	C	

Figure 3.3. Computer schedule for a three-computer classroom.

Time	Computer Time	Project Assignments			Two-Computer Classroom Daily Computer Use
		1	2	3	• 24 to 32 students
9:00 a.m.	A	C	E	G	• 3 or 4 students per group
to	B	D	F	H	• 15-minute rotation schedule
9:15 a.m.					• When students are not at computers, they work on related project assignments. For example, Groups A and B have computer time between 9:00 a.m. and 9:15 a.m. Groups C, D, E, F, G, and H work on related, non-computer assignments (projects 1, 2, and 3).
9:15 a.m.	C	E	G	A	
to	D	F	H	B	
9:30 a.m.					
9:30 a.m.	E	G	A	C	
to	F	H	B	D	
9:45 a.m.					
9:45 a.m.	G	A	C	E	
to	H	B	D	F	
10:00 a.m.					

Figure 3.4. Computer schedule for a two-computer classroom.

Time	Computer Time		Project Assignments				One-Computer Classroom MW/TTH Computer Use
	MW	TTH	MW	TTH	MW	TTH	
			1	2	3	4	
9:00 a.m. to 9:15 a.m.	A	E	B F G H	B F G H	C D E	A C D	
9:15 a.m. to 9:30 a.m.	B	F	F G H	B G H	A C D E	A C D E	
9:30 a.m. to 9:45 a.m.	C	G	A D E	A C D E	B F G H	B F H	
9:45 a.m. to 10:00 a.m.	D	H	A C E E	A C D E	B F G H	B F G	

One-Computer Classroom MW/TTH Computer Use:

- 3 or 4 students per group
- 24 to 32 students
- 15-minute rotation schedule
- Groups have computer time twice a week
- When students are not at computers, they work on related project assignments. For example, Group A has computer time from 9:00 a.m. to 9:15 a.m. on Mondays and Wednesdays. Groups B, F, G, and H and groups C, D, and E work on related, non-computer assignments (projects 1 and 3).
- On Friday, students are provided with additional time to complete their related, non-computer assignments. Groups may send one person to work with other groups to find clip art or research via the computer. For example, one person from each of groups A, B, C, and D may work together on the computer from 9:00 a.m. to 9:30 a.m., and one person from each of groups E, F, G, and H may work together on the computer from 9:30 a.m. to 10:00 a.m.

Figure 3.5. Computer schedule for a one-computer classroom.

Note that four computers in the classroom can provide students with 30 minutes of daily access to computers versus the 30 minutes of weekly access provided by computer labs. Two or three computers in the classroom can provide student groups with 75 to 110 minutes of computer time a week, respectively. One-computer classrooms provide limited group access, but they can be used to facilitate whole-class projects. For example, the class may decide to create a project about African American inventors to present to the community during Black History Month. Students may be placed in groups of three to research a specific inventor and to design a one-card or one-page presentation about their inventor. A template can be designed to assist students with their presentation. Student groups can take turns at the classroom computer (see Figure 3.5) inputting their data while others are finishing their research or working on a related small-group activity. A blackline master for scheduling computer time can be found at the end of this chapter. Teachers who are lucky enough to have one-to-one access in their classroom should not encounter problems scheduling computer time. Schedules may still be needed to share specific peripherals (still and video cameras, scanners, etc.) if these resources are limited or printers and Internet connections if the classroom is not wireless.

Working in a One-to-One Laptop Classroom

One-to-one laptop environments should not be equated to isolated learning environments. Students should still be encouraged to work in groups. As described earlier, each student can take on a different responsibility and work as a team. Each student can use his or her own computer to contribute to the team's progress. Tips for working in a one-to-one laptop classroom include the following:

- *Make sure the laptops are charged.* Establish a routine or procedure for ensuring laptop batteries are charged.

- *Have a backup plan.* Have outlets and cables available if laptops need to be recharged. Backup batteries are possible, too. Have a backup laptop or a "sharing" plan if a laptop is not working. Remember it is not always necessary for students to be working on their laptops at once. Some projects may require students to be conducting a different task on and off the computer.

- *Set rules and expectations and be consistent.* Let students know up front what you expect and the rules for using laptops in the classroom. Discuss consequences. You may want to have your students help to create these. Follow through and be consistent.

- *Make sure students are focused on you.* When students are working on their laptops and you need their attention, make sure you wait until all eyes are on you and not on their computer screens. One way to accomplish this is to ask students to place the lid of their laptop down. Another way is to use software (e.g., *SyncronEyes*) to control the students' laptops.

One-to-one laptop environments make it easier to integrate technology in the classroom if the teacher is ready to plan instruction to take advantage of the computer's resources and potential. Professional development opportunities can help teachers in one-to-one laptop environments increase student engagement and students' use of technology as a learning tool (Dawson, Cavanaugh, and Ritzhaupt 2008). Although one-to-one laptop programs are not a requirement to the creation of multimedia projects, they ensure that every student has the opportunity to engage in 21st century learning environments. One-to-one laptop programs support cooperative and collaborative learning, project learning, the teacher acting as coach or facilitator, independent research and inquiry, and highly focused academic class time (Dawson, Cavanaugh, and Ritzhaupt 2008). See the No Strings Attached website (http://etc.usf.edu/plans) to review exemplary models of technology integration in laptop classrooms. The lesson plans include video examples across numerous content areas for all grade levels.

MANAGING BRAINSTORMING AND RESEARCH ACTIVITIES

After the preliminary management issues of the DECIDE phase have been addressed, the teacher can provide students with time to brainstorm and research the topic of their project. This step should be prefaced with the purpose of the students' multimedia projects, and each group should be provided with guidelines and rubrics for their project (see Chapter 7). To solidify the groups, let teams develop their own name or "company" logo.

Brainstorming Activities

After student groups have established their project roles (e.g., graphic artist, instructional designer, production specialist, and program author), behavior roles (e.g., turn-taking monitor, noise monitor, record keeper, task master), and team name, provide students with time to brainstorm. Depending on the ability level and experience of the students, brainstorming may be conducted as a whole class or by individual groups. Teachers may wish to provide students with the BrainStorm or KWL Knowledge Chart blackline masters at the end of this chapter, or rely on brainstorming software such as Inspiration or Kidspiration (see http://www.inspiration.com). For high-ability and experienced groups, provide a rubric of questions or guidelines that covers the assigned instructional content. For example, if students are creating multimedia projects on Egypt, provide them with specific content questions and related pictures to research and include in their presentations. If students are creating a multimedia project about family history, provide them with guidelines as to the type of information that should be included. These guidelines can help focus the students' thoughts as they brainstorm ideas.

For younger and lower-ability students, make sure they have previous background knowledge in the assigned topics. Guide them through a KWL Knowledge Chart—What we Know, what we Want to find out, and what we Learned (see the KWL Knowledge Chart blackline master at the end of this chapter). Each student can participate in the chart activity at his or her desk as the teacher directs the whole class using a transparency of the chart on an overhead projector. Student groups can exchange their thoughts and share their ideas with the class. Following the introduction of the KWL Knowledge Chart, student groups can be assigned a particular outcome on the chart. For example, if the chart is about the solar system, student groups might be assigned to find out what the class wants to know about a particular planet. Group 1 might answer class questions about Jupiter, Group 2 might answer class questions about Mercury, and so on. The chart would be completed after the students presented their final multimedia projects.

Additional brainstorming techniques include recording students' sensory experiences. For example, many teachers pop popcorn in class to facilitate the student's creative writing skills. Students experience and discuss the sound, smell, taste, texture, and sight of popcorn before they write about it. A similar approach may be taken toward a particular multimedia project. For example, if the goal of the project is to develop and present a persuasive advertisement, such as why a group's hamburger is the best, educators may bring in different hamburgers for the students to sample, as well as let the students view videos of hamburger commercials, examine newspaper and magazine advertisements for hamburgers, inspect the packaging, and so on. As a class, the students can brainstorm and discuss how the hamburgers and their advertisements are the same or different and what issues (price, taste, nutrition, popularity, or convenience) may affect consumer choice. Following this whole-class experience, students can return to their groups and brainstorm strategies for their projects based on their new background knowledge. Final projects might include a persuasive presentation and samples of the group's hamburger creations.

Research Activities

After students have brainstormed about their topic, the teacher reviews the group's brainstorming chart and asks clarifying questions to ensure that the group is on track. After the group's work is approved, the students can begin researching the different areas of their topic. Students may want to assign each group member a specific task.

Research activities may take place on or off the computer. Computer schedules can be designed that allow students access to CD-ROMs, DVDs, and the Internet to further their research (see Figures 3.1 through 3.5). Students not assigned to computers can conduct research at the school library or in the classroom, using newspapers, textbooks, literature books, magazines, and other resources. High-ability students will need time to organize and synthesize gathered information and assign further research responsibilities. Younger and lower-ability students will need to work together to find the answers to their assigned questions from the KWL Knowledge Chart. Field trips, guest speakers, experiments, and other opportunities may be arranged to assist students with their research. Students can use a bibliography information sheet (see the Bibliography Information blackline master at the end of this chapter) to record and track their sources throughout the DDD-E process.

Students may also have the opportunity to conduct research outside the classroom. Groups may assign members to conduct research via the Internet, locate or create graphics, or develop narration or audio clips on their home computers or in the media center. Students can also create portions of their group's multimedia project at home, provided they have the appropriate software. Many Web tools and noncommercial programs (e.g., freeware) are free, allowing students to work on their projects at home. Never assume, though, that students have access to home computers, Internet access, or other research materials. It is inappropriate to assign homework if all of the students do not have the skills or resources to complete it. In situations where skills and access to technology are not an issue, teachers may incorporate the use of wikis, blogs, Google Apps, learning management systems (e.g., Blackboard, Moodle, etc.), and other online tools for group collaboration, journal entries, sharing of information, formative assessment, and so on.

Each group's record keeper should keep a journal (see the Journal Entry # blackline master at the end of this chapter) of his or her group's progress, including the time spent brainstorming. Journal entries can help students reflect on their work, social experiences, and how they are achieving their goals. Journals may be kept online as a wiki or other format, too. Teachers should review journal entries on a daily basis to help students keep focused and to address problems before they get out of hand. Groups can keep their journal entries in a binder and submit it with their final project. Groups may spend two to five class periods conducting the initial research for their projects.

SUMMARY

There are many variables to consider when assigning multimedia projects: standards and benchmarks, computer access, student experience, grouping variables, group size, student roles, time needed to complete the project, and so on. The DECIDE phase of the DDD-E process encourages teachers to address these variables before assigning multimedia projects.

After determining the project goals, appropriate background knowledge, guidelines, and rubrics are provided to assist student groups with the brainstorming and research activities. These activities provide the foundation for the next step of the DDD-E process: DESIGN. Journal entries continue throughout the DDD-E process, helping students to reflect on their progress and project goals.

There are multiple stages to creating multimedia projects, but the DECIDE phase is the most critical to their success. The stages that follow (discussed in Chapters 4–7) depend on the planning, organization, and research activities conducted in the DECIDE phase; each stage depends on its predecessor. The time needed to complete each stage will depend on the size and complexity of the projects, as well as the level and number of students in each group. Well-managed classrooms and organized projects will add to the success of students' multimedia endeavors and learning.

RESOURCES

Computers for Learning: http://www.computers.fed.gov/School/user.asp

Inspiration: http://www.inspiration.com/

Kidspiration: http://www.kidspiration.com/Kidspiration

No Strings Attached: http://etc.usf.edu/plans/

RubiStar: http://rubistar.4teachers.org

Scholastic Keys: http://www.tomsnyder.com/

Share the Technology: http://www.sharetechnology.org

Survey Monkey: http://www.surveymonkey.com/

SyncronEyes: http://smarttech.com/

Zoomerang: http://www.zoomerang.com/

BLACKLINE MASTERS

Several blackline masters are presented in this chapter to assist teachers with the DECIDE phase. These include:

- Self Survey: one method of organizing students into groups based on Howard Gardner's Theory of Multiple Intelligences

- Computer Schedule: a template for organizing classroom computer time

- BrainStorm: a webbing activity designed to help students link their ideas

- KWL Knowledge Chart: a chart to help students organize what they know and what they want to find out about a topic

- Bibliography Information: one way to record and identify sources used throughout the DDD-E process

- Journal Entry #_: a method of recording and tracking a group's progress.

Blackline masters may be copied for educational purposes. They may also be used to help educators create their own DECIDE activity and organization sheets, such as a modified survey, computer schedule, or bibliography information sheet.

REFERENCES

Dawson, K., Cavanaugh, C., and Ritzhaupt, A. 2008. Florida's EETT leveraging laptops initiative and its impact on teaching practices. *Journal of Research on Technology in Education* 41(2), 143–159.

Fuchs, L. S., Fuchs, D., Hamlett, C. L., and Karns, K. 1998. High achieving students' interactions and performance on complex mathematical tasks as a function of homogeneous and heterogeneous pairings. *American Educational Research Journal* 35(2): 227–267.

Johnson, D., and Johnson, R. 2009. An educational psychology success story: Social interdependence theory and cooperative learning. *Educational Researcher*, 38, 365–379.

Johnson, D. W., and Johnson, R. T. 1999. *Learning together and alone: Cooperative, competitive, and individualistic learning* (5th ed.). Needham Heights, MA: Allyn & Bacon.

Johnson, D. W., Johnson, R. T., and Holubec, E. J. 1994. *Cooperative learning in the classroom.* Alexandria, VA: Association for Supervision and Curriculum Development.

National Center for Educational Statistics. 2006. *Internet Access in U.S. Public Schools and Classrooms: 1994-2005* (NCES 2007-020). Washington, DC: NCES.

Schullery, N., and Schullery, S. 2006. Are heterogeneous or homogeneous groups more beneficial to students? *Journal of Management Education*, 30, 542–556.

Vermette, P. J. 1998. *Making cooperative learning work: Student teams in K–12 classrooms.* Upper Saddle River, NJ: Prentice-Hall.

Self Survey

Rank the following statements according to how well they describe you. Give the statement that describes you the best a "1," the second best a "2," and so on.

Name _____

☐   I like to read books, write, and tell stories.
(linguistics)

☐   I like math, strategy games, and working with puzzles.
(logic-mathematics)

☐   I like to draw and I understand things better by looking at a picture.
(spatial)

☐   I have a hard time sitting still.
(bodily-kinesthetic)

☐   I am a good singer and I know when music is off key.
(musical)

☐   I get along well with others and I am a good listener.
(interpersonal)

☐   I am dependable and self-confident.
(intrapersonal)

☐   I enjoy the outdoors and can easily identify and classify things around me.
(naturalist)

Computer Schedule

		Mon.	Tues.	Wed.	Thur.	Fri.	Sat.
Team Name:	Comp.						
	Time						
Team Members:							
	Role						
	Role						
	Role						
	Role						

		Mon.	Tues.	Wed.	Thur.	Fri.	Sat.
Team Name:	Comp.						
	Time						
Team Members:							
	Role						
	Role						
	Role						
	Role						

		Mon.	Tues.	Wed.	Thur.	Fri.	Sat.
Team Name:	Comp.						
	Time						
Team Members:							
	Role						
	Role						
	Role						
	Role						

BrainStorm

Create a web or "brainstorm" of your related ideas. Add additional thoughts as necessary.

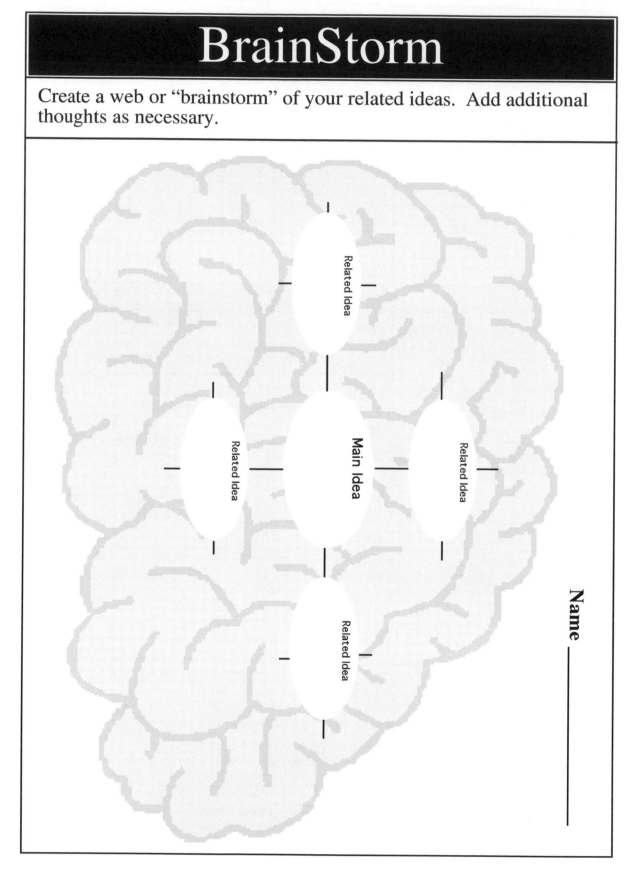

Main Idea

Related Idea

Related Idea

Related Idea

Related Idea

Name _____

KWL Knowledge Chart

What we know	What we want to find out	What we learned

From *Multimedia Projects in Education: Designing, Producing, and Assessing, Fourth Edition* by Karen S. Ivers and Ann E. Barron. Santa Barbara, CA: Libraries Unlimited. Copyright © 2010.

Bibliography Information

Team Name _____

Description	Media Type	Story-board#	Source

Journal Entry

Date _____   Team Name _____

Today's accomplishments: _____

_____

_____

_____

_____

Today's problems: _____

_____

_____

_____

Goals for tomorrow: _____

_____

_____

_____

Group dynamics: 1   2   3   Recorder's
                 poor   okay   great   initials:

Comments: _____

_____

_____

_____

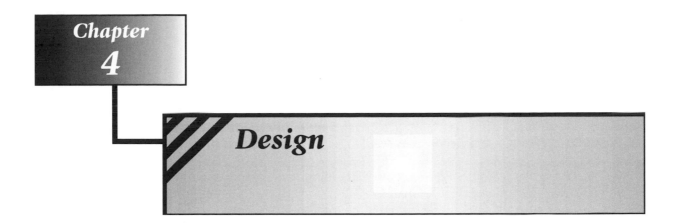

Chapter 4

Design

A SCENARIO

Ms. Stone was outlining the DESIGN phase requirements for an interactive science project. The students had already conducted their research and had the information they needed about their assigned habitat (physical description, geographic location, example animals, and resident plants). Their next activity would be to create flowcharts and storyboards for their projects.

To illustrate the importance of the flowcharts and storyboards, Ms. Stone demonstrated two projects from previous students. The first project seemed a bit disorganized. This group, Ms. Stone explained, had not created flowcharts or storyboards prior to development. Some of the pages had titles, some did not; some of the pages had a lot of text in a very small font, others had very little text and used a large font. There was also little consistency in the colors and graphics—it looked like the project was produced by several students who had used completely different approaches.

The second project she demonstrated was obviously well planned. The content was inviting, innovative, and extensive; yet the consistency of the presentation made the program easy to follow. "OK, I see your point," Sammy said. "But I'll bet the first group finished their project a lot faster!" "Actually," responded Ms. Stone, "It took them longer. Because they did not have a good plan; they had many disagreements and failed attempts in the DEVELOP phase of the project. For example, they spent a lot of time locating photographs that weren't relevant, and they revised the text over and over again because they had not written a script in advance."

Next Ms. Stone used Inspiration to demonstrate how the projects could be sequenced and flowcharts could be developed. For example, one group might decide on a linear format, in which they first show a title screen, then a screen with a map of the geographic location, followed by a screen with animals and a screen with plants. Another possible structure was the star format, in which the title screen could branch to either the geographic location, the animals, or the plants—all from the title screen.

She also showed them options for storyboarding (adding more details) for each screen. Some groups chose to expand the items within Inspiration to add the details; others decided to use Word or PowerPoint for the storyboards.

The students enjoyed using the technology tools to flowchart and storyboard their programs. As they progressed into the DEVELOP phase, they realized that the time and energy invested in the DESIGN phase could pay dividends later in the project.

OVERVIEW

The DESIGN phase is extremely important because it produces the blueprint for the entire project in the form of content outlines, screen templates, flowcharts, and storyboards. At the beginning of the DESIGN phase, teachers may want to show examples of well-designed projects as well as poorly designed projects. They should also set the parameters for the project, such as delineating the content, detailing the research requirements, and outlining the media components (number of slides, use of audio, etc.). Student teams should be provided with a list of other requirements or expectations. (See the Project Checklist blackline master at the end of this chapter.)

To assist teachers with aspects of the DESIGN phase, this chapter provides techniques for introducing topics that are important to design; it also presents design guidelines and recommendations for structuring and formatting multimedia projects. Keep in mind that the scope and complexity of projects will vary, as will the components of the design. The chapter concludes with several blackline masters that are correlated to the activities in the DESIGN phase. Topics that the teacher should present to the students include:

- Outlining the content
- Creating flowcharts

    Linear structures

    Tree structures

    Cluster structures

    Star structures

    Flowchart symbols

- Specifying screen design
- Creating storyboards

    General planning sheet

    Detailed storyboards and scripts

- Reviewing design guidelines

    Text

    Menus

    Icons and navigation

    Color

OUTLINING THE CONTENT

In the DECIDE phase, the broad instructional goals are stated for the project, and a brainstorming session may help to determine the possible topics. In addition, research can be conducted to further delineate the topics that will be included in the project.

As the students enter the DESIGN phase, the content can be solidified with outlines, flowcharts, and storyboards. Several factors will influence the content, including the timeline, age of students, subject area, and the venue for the project.

When a project is assigned, it is often wise for the teacher to specify the project requirements in terms of content and components. For example, teachers may assign a topic, such as a famous author, and require that the students provide background information on the author's childhood, a synopsis of his or her publications, and the author's impact on society. An Intention Outline or similar template can be used to help students specify the goals and outcomes of the project, its target audience, and an outline of the content (see blackline masters at the end of this chapter).

When the intention outlines are complete, the teacher should review them to ensure that the students' goals are clearly stated and aligned with the assignment's instructional objectives, that the content outline contains the depth required for the project, and that the topics are organized logically.

The teacher should also determine the primary venue for the project and how the audience might influence the content. Venues might include presentations for classroom peers, school assemblies, community groups, or external audiences via the Internet. If a project is designed for third graders, the content, presentation, and elements will be noticeably different from the content, presentation, and elements of a project designed for adults.

CREATING FLOWCHARTS

After the Intention Outline is complete, students should be encouraged to think through the flow of the project. A flowchart can be used to visually depict the sequence and structure of a program. This is especially pertinent if the project involves interactivity and branching. To introduce the logic of flowcharts, teachers can use exercises such as "The Bunny Hop" or "Medusa's Market" (see blackline masters at the end of this chapter). Such exercises encourage students to think through decision points and represent their paths in a logical manner.

There are several common flowchart structures, including linear, tree, star, and cluster. Teachers should demonstrate various projects that use different structures and point out the advantages and disadvantages of each. The Project Structures blackline master at the end of this chapter can be used to help students differentiate among the various options for project flow and choose the appropriate structure for their projects. Students should be encouraged to experiment with different ways of presenting content. Content mapping programs, such as Inspiration and Kidspiration, are excellent tools for developing flowcharts.

Linear Structures

Linear structures are appropriate when there is a specific sequence or a step-by-step procedure (see Figure 4.1). For example, a student may create a linear project that details the process required to dissect a frog. Projects designed as presentations (such as those created with PowerPoint) and videos are usually linear in design.

Figure 4.1. Linear structure.

Movement options in a linear structure may provide options for branching forward or backward. Most linear programs also include a method for starting over at the beginning.

Tree Structures

A tree structure is appropriate when the main idea branches into a few other topics, which in turn are subdivided further. Tree structures are common in both Web and hypermedia projects. For example, Figure 4.2 illustrates a tree-shaped project in which the user can select any of three states from a Main Menu. When he or she clicks on a state, a submenu appears with state politics and state history.

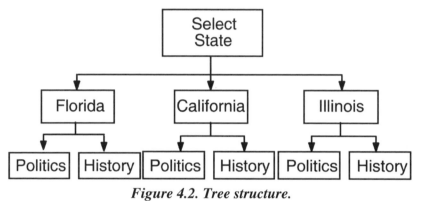

Figure 4.2. Tree structure.

Movement options in a tree structure usually allow users to branch forward and backward, return to the previous menu, or return to the Main Menu.

Cluster Structures

The cluster approach combines tree and linear structures. For example, Figure 4.3 illustrates a Main Menu where the user can select an option, then proceed to a linear presentation about adding or multiplying fractions.

Movement options in a cluster structure allow users to branch forward and backward within the linear segments or return to the Main Menu. In most cases, the linear segments should not contain more than five or six screens.

Star Structures

Star structures are used when one idea or screen branches to several other, single ideas. Many webpages and hypermedia programs are designed with a star format. For example, a webpage may provide information

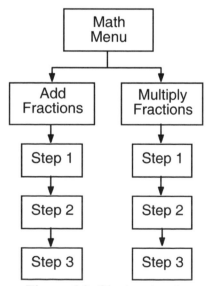

Figure 4.3. Cluster structure.

about a school (see Figure 4.4). From the main page, hyperlinks allow access to other pages with the sports schedule, school address, student activities, and so on. Each of the linked pages branches directly back to the introduction/menu page.

A star structure allows the user to branch out in any direction from the Main Menu. In most cases, the only option thereafter is to branch back to the Main Menu to make another selection.

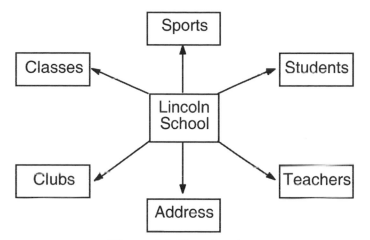

Figure 4.4. Star structure.

Flowchart Symbols

Students should be encouraged to flowchart their lessons after the content outline is complete. Several standard symbols are used in flowcharts. For example, a diamond generally represents a decision point, and a small circle serves as a connector from one part of the flowchart to another. These symbols can be created by hand, with rulers, with drawing templates, or with computer programs (such as Inspiration). Figure 4.5 illustrates common flowchart symbols.

Figure 4.5. Common flowchart symbols.

When creating flowcharts, ask the students to label each element. With proper labeling, they will be able to easily match the flowchart components with the details of the program. Figure 4.6 is a flowchart of a program about Florida that was created with Inspiration. Each symbol in the figure has a short title, and connectors are used to return to the menu.

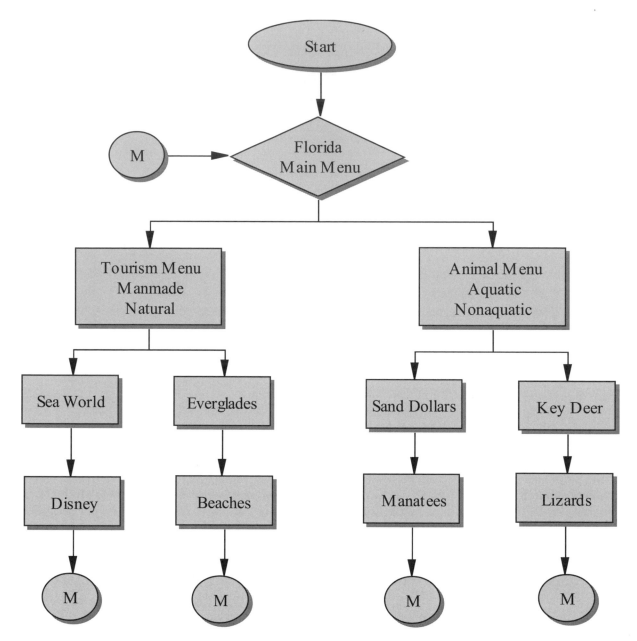

Figure 4.6. Flowchart for project about Florida (created in Inspiration).

Young students can also create flowcharts using the symbol libraries in Kidspiration. For example, the flowchart in Figure 4.7 was created for a third-grade presentation about farm animals.

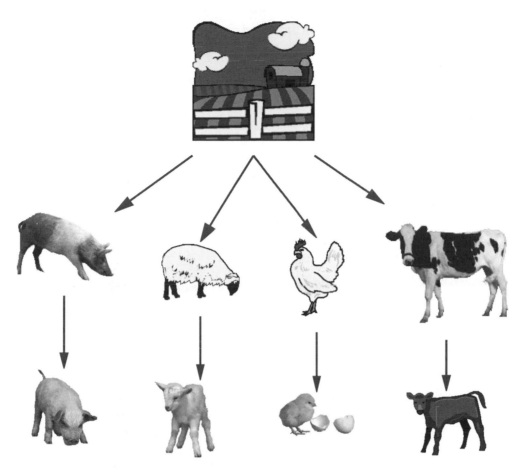

Figure 4.7. Flowchart for project about farm animals (created in Kidspiration).

SPECIFYING SCREEN DESIGN

After the general flow of the project is diagrammed, the students should determine the "look and feel" of the screens that will be used in the project. This may include defining the color scheme and the location and size of graphics, icons, and other items.

Depending on the intended venue and the method of delivery, the navigation within a project may vary considerably. For example, if the project will be projected for a class presentation, the students will not have to include extensive navigation options, because they will be controlling the navigation. However, if the project is designed for individual use or as an external website, there must be sufficient prompts to help users navigate through the project.

For consistency, each screen should contain defined functional areas. The functional areas will vary based on the purpose of each screen (menu versus presentation) and on the programming tool used (PowerPoint versus HTML). The primary functional areas for a presentation or instructional screen may include:

- *Title.* The title of each screen is usually located at the top or on the left side.

- *Informational/instructional text.* The text should be located in a consistent area of the screen.

- *Graphics.* The graphics can be placed on the side of the text, above it, or below it (see Figure 4.8).

- *Directions or student prompt.* If user input is required, a prompt area should be included.

- *Icons or navigation options.* The navigational options (icons or buttons) are usually located along one of the edges of the screen.

Figure 4.8. Presentation or instructional screen template.

Note that in Figure 4.8, the text is on the left, the graphic is on the right, and the navigation options are on the bottom. This is only one example of the numerous possibilities for instructional templates. For example, the text could be above the graphic; or it might be a text-only screen.

Menu screens and question screens will have slightly different functional areas. For example, Figure 4.9 contains the following areas:

- *Title.* The title of each screen is usually located at the top or on the left side.

- *Directions and Question.* The question should be located in a consistent area of the screen.

- *Answer Choices.* The answers choices might consist of textual options or graphical areas.

- *Graphics.* Graphics may be used as part of the question or as answer options.

- *Feedback.* Feedback may appear in a pop-up dialog box or in a consistent location on the screen.

- *Icons or navigation options.* The navigational options (icons or buttons) are usually located along one of the edges of the screen.

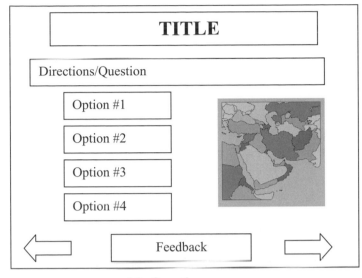

4.9. Question screen.

The menu template in Figure 4.9 is based on four text options (it is best to provide between three and six menu options). The menu selections can be text or graphics, and they might be arranged horizontally, vertically, or in another pattern. Prompts and Exit options may also be included.

CREATING STORYBOARDS

After the content has been outlined and the screen designs have been determined, the storyboards can be created. Storyboards contain all the information that will be placed on the screens as well as information that will help the programmer and production specialists develop the media components. Storyboards can be thought of as "blueprints" for the program or project. They provide the visual representation of the screen, as well as scripts for the audio, details for the video, and branching information.

General Planning Sheet

Before beginning the storyboards, it may be helpful to have the students fill out a general planning sheet. This sheet provides an opportunity for the students to allocate, or chunk, the information into separate screens without specifying all the details. Figure 4.10 illustrates the manner in which a title screen and instructional screen can be completed. (A Planning Sheet blackline master is provided at the end of this chapter as a tool for students.)

An alternative to using a planning sheet is to have the students outline their screens on 3- × 5-inch or 5- × 8-inch index cards. Each card can be used to represent one computer screen or page. The students can divide each card into functional areas and place the content (text and graphics) on the screen in the appropriate places. The backs of the cards can be used to provide information for navigation and media elements. An advantage of using this method is that the students can arrange (and rearrange) the cards on a desk in the sequence appropriate for the program, before finalizing the storyboards.

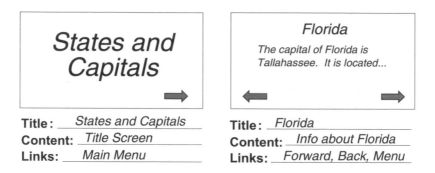

Figure 4.10. General planning sheet.

Detailed Storyboards and Scripts

After the general plan is outlined, encourage the students to write detailed storyboards and scripts for the project, especially if it is complex. Storyboards are more detailed than planning sheets because they contain all the descriptive information required to produce the text, graphics, animations, audio, and video for the project. In addition, the links for each button or interaction are specified. Several storyboard templates are provided at the end of this chapter.

The storyboards should provide all the information that will appear on the final screens. At this point, the students will determine the best way to present the information, how much information goes on each screen, and which media elements are appropriate. Each storyboard should contain a display area, branching information for the programmer (if appropriate), details about the font size and color, and a list of media elements.

Blackline masters are provided at the end of this chapter for creating storyboards for hypermedia, presentation, Web-based, and video projects. These storyboards can be copied and distributed to the students. Advanced students may want to create their own storyboards in a word processor, database, or other application. Storyboard tools and templates are also available on the Web (see the Resources section at the end of this chapter).

Storyboards for Hypermedia Programs

Hypermedia programs, such as HyperStudio, usually contain at least three screen types: instructional screens, menu screens, and question screens. Because of their branching ability, questions and other types of interactions are common in hypermedia programs. The feedback for correct and incorrect responses may be provided by branching to a different screen, or a pop-up dialog box might provide the feedback. Note that the Hypermedia Storyboard template provides a large, blank area for the students to diagram exactly how each screen will be formatted, as well as areas to specify the navigation, text, audio, and video components. See Chapter 8 for hypermedia project ideas.

Presentation Programs

Presentation programs, such as PowerPoint, are not designed to provide as much interactivity as hypermedia programs (although buttons can be inserted to provide basic branching capabilities). Presentation programs generally include design templates and backgrounds that have been professionally developed. Figure 4.11 illustrates some of the basic layouts that are provided with

PowerPoint. Note that these layouts and templates are generally designed for projecting to a large audience. In most cases, the font is large and the text is presented in bulleted lists. See Chapter 10 for project ideas using presentation programs.

Figure 4.11. PowerPoint layouts.

Web-Based Programs

A wide variety of screen templates are appropriate for webpages. Because large graphics take longer to transfer over the Internet, it is usually advisable to use text, with small images, graphic banners or bullets. Navigational links on a webpage should be well defined so users will know where the links will lead.

Although feedback in the form of pop-up windows is possible on webpages, the programming is more complex. In most cases, school-based webpages will consist of text, graphics, and hyperlinks to other pages or media files. Templates and examples of Web-based pages and projects are provided in Chapter 9.

Video Projects

Digital video files can be integrated into hypermedia, presentation, or Web-based programs, or they can be "stand-alone" projects, consisting entirely of video. In either case, the video window may be set within a graphical backdrop that contains control options. For example, Figure 4.12 represents a digital video program that is displayed on a television-like screen. Video storyboards are used to specify the different screen shots (such as close-up, wide shot, over the shoulder, etc.), the audio components, and the actors that will be used in production. Sample video projects are provided in Chapter 11.

Figure 4.12. Video window.

Storyboarding is not an easy task for many students. One way to encourage good techniques is to review and "sign-off" on the storyboards before the students begin producing the projects (see the Storyboard Review blackline master at the end of this chapter). If the students have thoroughly outlined their content and approach via storyboards, their time spent on the computer or with the video camera will be much more efficient. Keep in mind, however, that the level of detail required in storyboards may vary based on the age of the students, the complexity of the project, the time allotted to the project, and other factors.

REVIEWING DESIGN GUIDELINES

As students add details to their storyboards, they will have to make numerous decisions. The following design guidelines can help students specify information related to text, menus, icons and buttons. Guidelines for media elements, such as graphics, animations, audio, and video are provided in Chapter 5. Information about development programs, such as HyperStudio, PowerPoint, HTML, Inspiration, and more, are included in Chapter 6.

Guidelines for Text

- Left-justify the text (not centered).

- Use mixed case (not all caps).

- Avoid long lines of text.

- Double space text if possible.

- Keep sentences short and sweet.

- Use active tense.

- Chunk information into short paragraphs.

- Do not blink text unnecessarily.

- Use at least 12-point font size for hypermedia and webpages.

- Use at least 24-point font size for presentation projects.

- Use generic fonts that are available on all computers.

- Do not place text on a background that has a pattern or graphic.

Guidelines for Menus

- Provide between three and six options on a menu.

- Include an exit option on all menus.

- Clearly state the directions for selecting menu options.

- Include titles on all menus.

- Place menu options in logical sequence.

Guidelines for Icons and Navigational Buttons

- Place icons in consistent locations throughout the program.

- Use common icons (such as arrows) for navigation.

- If an icon is inactive, remove it or make it dim.

- Make icons big enough for users to click on them easily.

- Provide instructions to help users navigate.

- Make permanent buttons small and unobtrusive.

- Place permanent buttons along the edge of the screen.

- Include options for users to back up and exit.

Guidelines for Color

- Use fewer than seven colors per screen.

- Use consistent background colors.

- Use consistent text colors.

- On dark backgrounds, use light text.

- On light backgrounds, use dark text.

- Highlight key words in a contrasting color.

- Do not use red backgrounds.

SUMMARY

The DESIGN phase is crucial to developing a successful multimedia project. Teachers should emphasize the importance of outlining the content of the project and present design guidelines through the use of examples and non-examples. In addition, teachers can demonstrate the use of storyboards and scripts to help students plan and structure their projects prior to the production of graphics, video, and other media. The blackline masters at the end of this chapter, as well as Internet resources, can assist teachers and students in the design aspects of multimedia projects.

RESOURCES

Flowchart (Studio 1151): http://www.mcli.dist.maricopa.edu/authoring/studio/guidebook/flow.html

Inspiration: http://www.inspiration.com/

Kidspiration: http://www.kidspiration.com/Kidspiration

Multimedia in the Classroom: http://fcit.usf.edu/multimedia/

Storyboard Pro (Atomic Learning): http://www.atomiclearning.com/storyboardpro

Success Is in the Planning: http://www.create.cett.msstate.edu/create/howto/storyboard_Handout.pdf

BLACKLINE MASTERS

A variety of blackline masters are presented in this chapter to help teachers and students design a multimedia project. Practice activities are included to help students with flowcharting. The following blackline masters conclude this chapter:

- Project Checklist: a general checklist of expectations for multimedia projects

- Intention Outline: an outline of intent that specifies the goals and content of a project

- Project Structures: illustrations of different flowcharts

- The Bunny Hop: a flowchart sequencing activity

- Medusa's Market: a flowchart sequencing activity

- Planning Sheet: a tool to assist students in planning their storyboards

- Hypermedia Storyboard: a sample hypermedia storyboard template

- Presentation Storyboard: a sample presentation storyboard template

- Web Storyboard: a sample storyboard template for Web projects

- Video Storyboard: a sample storyboard for digital video projects

- Storyboard Review: a preliminary evaluation sheet to help students produce and revise their storyboards.

Project Checklist

Team Name _____

Before developing your project at the computer, complete the following:

☐ Intention Outline   ☐ Flowchart

☐ Planning Sheet   ☐ Storyboards

Make sure your project has:

☐ a minimum of _____ pages (or cards).

☐ a maximum of _____ pages (or cards).

☐ a Title page (or card).

☐ credits (designers and bibliography information).

☐ a Main Menu.

☐ appropriate navigation options.

☐ text that is easy to read and is accurate.

☐ complete sentences with correct punctuation, grammar, and spelling.

☐ the assigned media requirements.

_____ Clip Art   _____ Animation   _____ Video

_____ Scanned Image   _____ Digitized Camera Photo

_____ Original Audio   _____ Clip Sound (digitized)

_____ MIDI File   _____ Original Graphic

☐ Other: _____

_____

Intention Outline

Project Title: _____

General Goal: _____

Specific Outcomes: _____

_____

Audience

Who will use this project (e.g., students, teachers, parents)?

Content Outline

I. _____

    A. _____

    B. _____

    C. _____

II. _____

    A. _____

    B. _____

    C. _____

III. _____

    A. _____

    B. _____

    C. _____

From *Multimedia Projects in Education: Designing, Producing, and Assessing, Fourth Edition* by Karen S. Ivers and Ann E. Barron. Santa Barbara, CA: Libraries Unlimited. Copyright © 2010.

Project Structures

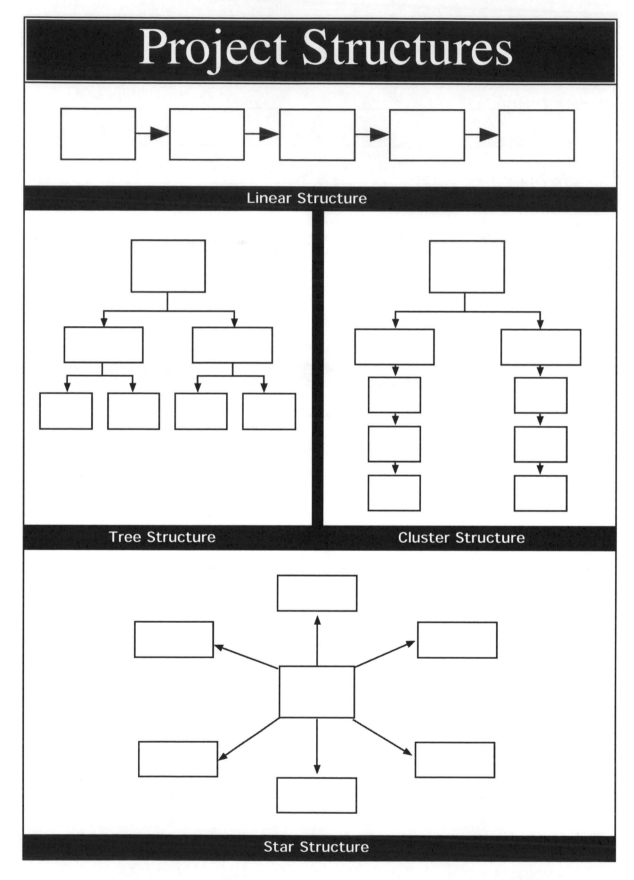

Linear Structure

Tree Structure

Cluster Structure

Star Structure

The Bunny Hop

Benjamin Bunny is helping his friend hide eggs. Help Benjamin figure out what to do by placing a letter in the correct section of the flowchart. Remember that diamond shapes are for asking questions and box shapes are for decisions. Two are already done for you.

_____ A. Wait ten minutes.

_____ B. Hide egg.

_____ C. Is anyone peeking?

_____ D. Continue to hop down the bunny trail.

_____ E. Place colored eggs into basket.

_____ F. Are there eggs in the basket?

_____ G. Hop down the bunny trail.

_____ H. Look for a place to hide egg.

_____ I. Go home.

Extension ideas: Create a flowchart for getting ready for school in the morning, cooking your favorite meal, or packing for a vacation.

Answer: E, G, H, C (yes is A), B, F (yes is D), I

From *Multimedia Projects in Education: Designing, Producing, and Assessing, Fourth Edition* by Karen S. Ivers and Ann E. Barron. Santa Barbara, CA: Libraries Unlimited. Copyright © 2010.

Medusa's Market

Medusa needs to go to the grocery store. Help her get into her car and drive to the grocery store's parking lot by placing a letter in the correct section of the flowchart. Remember that diamond shapes are for asking questions and box shapes are for decisions. Three are already done for you.

_____ A. Insert ignition key.

_____ B. Shut door.

_____ C. Is the light green?

_____ D. Put on safety belt.

_____ E. Open door.

_____ F. Wait.

_____ G. Is there a parking space?

_____ H. Get into car.

_____ I. Pull into parking space.

_____ J. Drive to stop light.

_____ K. Drive into parking lot.

_____ L. Look for parking space.

_____ M. Turn off ignition.

_____ N. Exit parking lot.

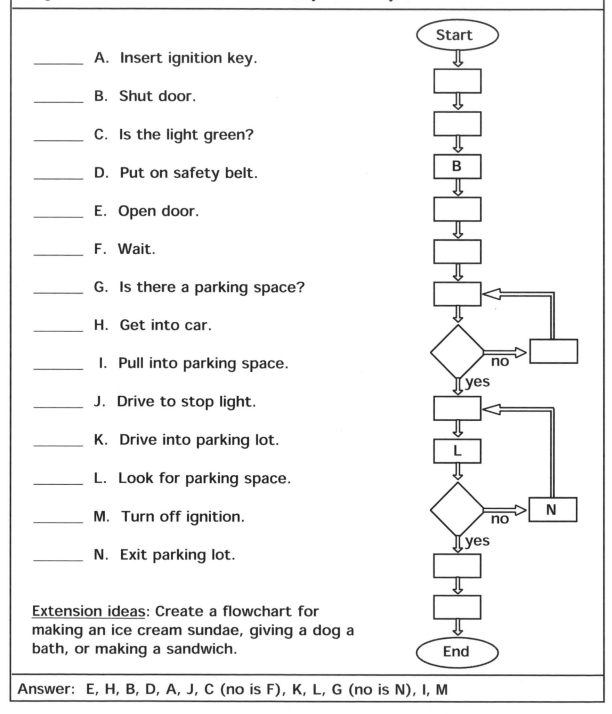

Extension ideas: Create a flowchart for making an ice cream sundae, giving a dog a bath, or making a sandwich.

Answer: E, H, B, D, A, J, C (no is F), K, L, G (no is N), I, M

From _Multimedia Projects in Education: Designing, Producing, and Assessing, Fourth Edition_ by Karen S. Ivers and Ann E. Barron. Santa Barbara, CA: Libraries Unlimited. Copyright © 2010.

Planning Sheet

Name of group: _____

Use this sheet to plan the general content of your pages.

[ ]

Title: _____
Content: _____
Links: _____

[ ]

Title: _____
Content: _____
Links: _____

[ ]

Title: _____
Content: _____
Links: _____

[ ]

Title: _____
Content: _____
Links: _____

[ ]

Title: _____
Content: _____
Links: _____

[ ]

Title: _____
Content: _____
Links: _____

From *Multimedia Projects in Education: Designing, Producing, and Assessing, Fourth Edition*
by Karen S. Ivers and Ann E. Barron. Santa Barbara, CA: Libraries Unlimited. Copyright © 2010.

Hypermedia Storyboard

Name of group: _____ Storyboard Number: _____

Use this sheet to specify the details of the project.

Navigation

Button: _____ Link to: _____ Action: _____
Button: _____ Link to: _____ Action: _____
Button: _____ Link to: _____ Action: _____

Text

Color: _____ Size: _____ Font: _____

Audio

Source: _____
File: _____
Description: _____
_____
_____

Video

Source: _____
File: _____
Description: _____
_____
_____

Presentation Storyboard

Name of group: _____ Storyboard Number: _____

Use this sheet to specify the details of the project.

Template

Name: _____ Color: _____ Layout: _____

Text

Color: _____ Size: _____ Font: _____

Transition: _____ Build: _____

Audio

Source: _____
File: _____
Description: _____
_____
_____

Video

Source: _____
File: _____
Description: _____
_____
_____

From *Multimedia Projects in Education: Designing, Producing, and Assessing, Fourth Edition* by Karen S. Ivers and Ann E. Barron. Santa Barbara, CA: Libraries Unlimited. Copyright © 2010.

Web Storyboard

Name of group: _____ Storyboard Number: _____

Use this sheet to specify the details of the project.

Navigation

Hyperlink: _____ Link to: _____

Hyperlink: _____ Link to: _____

Hyperlink: _____ Link to: _____

Text and Background

Text Color: _____ Size: _____ Font: _____

Background Color: _____ Background Graphic: _____

Audio

Source: _____

File: _____

Description: _____

_____

Graphic

Source: _____

File: _____

Description: _____

_____

Video Storyboard

Name of group: _____ Storyboard Number: _____

Use this sheet to specify the details of the project.

Video Details

Description of Scene: _____

_____

Actors: _____

Lighting: _____ Camera Shot: _____

Scenery: _____

Props: _____

Transition Effect: _____

Audio

Source: _____

File: _____

Description: _____

_____

Special Graphics

Source: _____

File: _____

Description: _____

_____

Storyboard Review

Students included:	Yes	No	N/A
a title screen	——	——	——
a credit screen	——	——	——
directions/information for the user	——	——	——
a main menu	——	——	——
forward and back links	——	——	——
factual and interesting information	——	——	——
consistent and clear layout designs	——	——	——
required media elements	——	——	——
font information for text boxes	——	——	——
font information for titles	——	——	——
background information	——	——	——
_____	——	——	——
_____	——	——	——
_____	——	——	——

Comments:

_____

_____

_____

_____

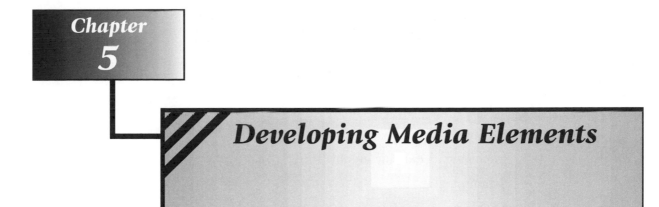

Chapter 5

Developing Media Elements

A SCENARIO

Molly, Brooke, and Luis decided to create an oral history about the town square in their village for the multimedia research project in social studies. They knew that the cannon in the square had been there a long time, but they did not know the details of the history.

Their first step was to conduct Web searches and look in the town's library for relevant information and photographs related to the village's history. Next, they wrote questions that they could ask and set up interviews with the mayor and a few elderly veterans.

Luis suggested that they use his iPod to record the interviews. It worked great—they attached a microphone to the iPod, conducted the interviews, saved the files, and transferred the audio to a computer through a cable. After the files were on the computer, they were easy to modify with the audio editor. Brooke cropped parts of the audio they didn't need and adjusted the volume levels to make everything consistent. Then Molly added some background music that she had created in GarageBand.

They decided that a good way to share the oral histories would be to create a series of podcasts (audio and/or video files that could be listened to via the Internet or downloaded into a mobile device or computer). Brooke saved each audio file in the MP3 format and uploaded them to the school's webmaster so he could link them to the school's website.

To reach an even broader audience, Molly, Brooke, and Luis imported the audio into iMovie and sequenced the historical images they had scanned to create a movie file. After their teacher reviewed the content, the digital movie was uploaded into YouTube. Now everyone could find out more about the history of that old cannon in the square.

OVERVIEW

The third phase of the DDD-E model is DEVELOP, which includes producing the media components, such as text, graphics, animations, audio, and video. It also covers the programming (or authoring) of the program. This chapter focuses on designing and producing the media; Chapter 6 outlines the tools available for authoring and delivery.

Media elements (graphics, animation, audio, and video) are key components of multimedia projects. They can help bring a presentation to life by providing realism, color, motion, and sound. Used effectively, media elements add many instructional benefits, enhance visual literacy, and address multiple intelligences and learning styles. This chapter outlines the procedures for creating and editing graphics, animations, audio, and video elements. Guidelines for implementing media elements and an appendix of media resources are also provided. Topics include:

- Graphics

  Creating a graphic

  Importing an existing graphic file

  Scanning graphics

  Capturing digital images with a camera

  Guidelines for graphics

- Animations

  Frame animations

  Path animations

  Guidelines for animations

- Audio

  Digital audio

  Recording audio with computers

  Synthesized speech

  Music

  Digital audio file formats

  Using existing audio files

  Podcasting audio

  Guidelines for audio

- Digital video

  Digitizing and editing video

  Digital video file formats

  Guidelines for video

GRAPHICS

The term *graphics* refers to images or any information that is presented via pictures, drawings, or paintings. There are many ways to obtain graphics for a computer project: they can be created from scratch with a computer program, they can be imported from an existing file, they can be scanned from a hard copy, or they can be digitized with a camera. Each method has advantages and disadvantages.

Creating a Graphic

Many image programs are available, including Adobe Photoshop, CorelDraw, Microsoft Paint, and GIMP. These programs vary in price, sophistication, and many other attributes, but they can all be used to create and manipulate computer graphics and then save them in various file formats. Computer graphics (and image programs) can be roughly divided into two types: paint (bitmapped) or draw (vector).

Paint (Bitmapped) Graphics

To visualize bitmaps, think of a piece of graph paper. Each of the individual small squares represents a *pixel* (which means *pic*ture *el*ement). When you are "painting" a bitmapped image, all you are doing is filling in each individual pixel or group of pixels with a solid color. The small pixels can be arranged to form a graphic, similar to a Lite-Brite toy. In this type of program, the pixels retain their independence. In other words, even if the pixels are positioned to form the appearance of a square, when you zoom in, you can see that the square is made up of tiny, individual pixels (see Figure 5.1).

Figure 5.1. A bitmapped graphic is made up of individual pixels.

If the pixels are small, the picture will look sharper. The number of pixels you have for your image is called the image resolution. The resolution of a computer screen or graphic is expressed as the number of pixels wide by the number of pixels tall. For example, a resolution of 1024×768 means it is 1024 pixels wide by 768 pixels tall.

There are numerous software programs that can be used to create and manipulate bitmapped graphics; they are often referred to as *paint programs*. Popular examples include Adobe Photoshop, Microsoft Paint, and Picasa. With these programs, you can easily add effects such as distortions, textures, or gradients. All of the images created with these tools will be bitmapped and will consist of individual pixels. If students want to move a graphic (such as a square) after it has been created, they must use a selection tool (such as the lasso) to select all of the pixels that are to be moved.

Draw (Vector) Graphics

A vector (object-oriented) graphic might look similar to a bitmapped image when it appears on the computer screen, but it is stored in a very different manner. Object-oriented drawings consist of geometric shapes instead of individual pixels, and they work more like a collage (made up of shapes). When you draw an object (for example, a square), the computer knows it as a square and will always treat it as a square. If you were to zoom into the graphic, you would not see individual pixels (see Figure 5.2).

Figure 5.2. Vector graphics do not contain individual pixels.

Object-oriented images are ideal for geometric drawings such as blueprints, charts, or line drawings. Because the images consist of geometric figures, they can be layered on top of each other and still retain their identity. When an object is "selected," tiny handlebars appear to allow you to change the size of the image. It is possible to select an object and bring it on top, push it back, or move it around, without affecting anything else on the screen. Any object can be selected at any time, and you can change its attributes, such as line thickness, line color, line style, and so forth. If the object is a closed figure, you can also determine the color and pattern that fill the enclosed region.

Popular software programs for vector graphics include CorelDraw and Adobe Illustrator. Software applications, such as PowerPoint and Word, also contain drawing features that can be used to create vector graphics.

One of the main differences between bitmaps and vector drawings is that bitmaps are resolution dependent whereas vector drawings are resolution independent. That means that if you create a bitmapped image at a certain size, it should be viewed at that size. Enlarging it would make it look awful—all of the pixels would be stretched, and the image would look very pixilated (blocky). Vector drawings however, can be enlarged to any size, even stretched to different aspect ratios, and they will always look smooth, because they will adjust to the resolution of the screen or printer. For example, the first image in Figure 5.3 was created as a bitmap and then stretched; the second figure was created as a vector graphic and then stretched. Note that the lines on the second image are smooth.

Figure 5.3. Stretching bitmaps and vector images.

Importing an Existing Graphic File

In some cases, students may not have the time or software programs required to create their own graphics, and they may find it more expedient to use existing images. Many programs provide a collection of clipart that can be easily imported. For example, HyperStudio and PowerPoint both have options to *"Insert Clip Art."* In addition, there are numerous clipart sites available on the Internet (see Graphics and Animation Resources at the end of this chapter). You can also go to Google and click on "Images" to search the Web for images.

Some clipart is *public domain* (meaning it is free for anyone to use), and some may be *royalty free* (meaning that someone owns the copyright but allows you to use it with certain restrictions). Many people incorrectly believe that everything posted on the Internet is public domain; the truth is the exact opposite. All images and documents are protected by copyright laws, whether they are on the Internet or not. If you or your students see a graphic on a webpage that you would like to use, you must read the copyright notice, and, if necessary, request permission from the artist who created it—especially if it will be used beyond the classroom.

The key to importing existing graphics files into a program is to make sure that the files are in a compatible format. For example, PowerPoint will open and display graphics files that have the extension BMP, PICT, TIFF, GIF, JPG, and others, whereas graphics files on websites are almost always stored in GIF, JPEG, and PNG format. See Table 5.1 for a list of common graphics formats.

Table 5.1. Common Graphic Formats

Extension	Description	Platform	Application
BMP	Microsoft Bitmap	Windows	Windows applications
WMF	Windows Metafile	Windows	Windows applications
PICT	Macintosh Picture Format	Macintosh	Macintosh applications
TIFF	Tagged Image File Format	Windows, Macintosh	Common format for exchanging files between platforms
EPS	Encapsulated PostScript	Windows, Macintosh	Common for printed documents
GIF	Graphics Interchange Format	Windows, Macintosh	Common on the Web
JPEG (JPG)	Joint Photographic Experts Group	Windows, Macintosh	Common on the Web
PNG	Portable Network Graphic	Windows, Macintosh	Common on the Web

If you have a graphic that is not in the appropriate format, you can use an image program or a graphic converter to change the format. For example, if you had a PICT graphic and you wanted to place it on a webpage, you could open it in Adobe PhotoShop and save it as a GIF file. There are several shareware programs, such as Graphic Converter (available at http://www.lemkesoft.de/en/graphcon.htm), that can be used to convert image formats. It is important to note that the file extension (such as image.gif) only indicates the type of file format; it is not the file format itself. Merely changing the extension on a file does not change the file's contents anymore than changing the label on a can of peas will turn it into applesauce. To change a file from one format to another, you must use an image editor or a conversion program.

Scanning Graphics

There are many times when students may want to use an image in a multimedia program that currently exists only as a hard copy, such as a photograph or a drawing in a book. *Scanners* are computer peripherals used to convert print materials (hard copies) and other objects into images on a computer. Capturing images with a scanner makes it possible to incorporate a wide variety of photographs and other images into multimedia projects.

The typical scanning process is similar to copying a piece of paper on a photocopy machine. The paper copy is placed on a scanner, a light passes under it, and a bitmapped image is created. The difference is that instead of producing a copy on paper, the image is transferred to the computer screen.

Scanners come with software that offers several settings. These settings can have an impact on the quality of the scanned image and the size of the file. When students scan graphics, caution them to scan only the portion of the picture that they need. Also, they should select a resolution of about 72 dots per inch (dpi) or pixels per inch (ppi). Scanning at a higher resolution for display on a computer screen will result in a very large file, with little or no difference in quality on the display.

Another consideration is the setting for the number of colors. Scanners can produce graphics in black and white, shades of gray, or a wide range of colors. However, if the capture is set at "millions" of colors, the file size can be extremely large. After the image is scanned, it should be saved, or exported, in a format that is compatible with the presentation—in other words, if it is going to be used on a webpage, it should be saved as a GIF or JPG file.

Capturing Digital Images with a Camera

If your students have a photograph and a scanner, they can scan a photograph. However, if they do not already have a photo that has been printed, they may want to use a digital camera to capture the image.

The procedure for using a digital camera is simple: simply point and click. Most cameras have a small preview screen, and you can delete the image if you don't like it. The photos are stored on a small memory card within the camera. To transfer the pictures to a computer, simply connect the camera to the computer with a cable or insert the camera's memory card into the digital memory slot of the computer, open a graphics program, and download the images onto the computer drive. After the images are downloaded, they can be enhanced, resized, or repositioned in an image program and integrated into a multimedia project. Programs such as iPhoto and Picasa can be used to create posters, interactive books, galleries, and slideshows of images created with cameras, scanners, or image editors.

Guideline for Graphics

The following guidelines can help you and your students determine the appropriate use of graphics in multimedia projects.

- Use graphics to enhance the project and illustrate important concepts.

- Do not include graphics that distract from the project.

- If possible, use several simple graphics rather than one complex graphic.

- If complex graphics are required, add arrows or highlight boxes to help focus attention on the relevant areas.

- If graphic icons are used for buttons or other similar elements, be consistent—always use the same icon for the same function.

- Be consistent when placing graphics—designate one part of the screen for graphics and another part for text, title, and so on.

- Keep file sizes as small as possible (by using compression or limiting the number of colors).

- Graphics should be scanned at 72–100 dpi (if they are going to be displayed on a computer screen).

- Check copyright restrictions on all graphics that will be used outside the classroom.

- Graphics that are incorporated into webpages should be less than 50K to minimize transfer time.

- Before editing, cropping, or compressing images, save a copy of the original file.

ANIMATIONS

Animations are graphics that imitate movement. All animations consist of a series of images (with minor changes from one to the next) that are shown in rapid succession and "fool" the eye into seeing motion. Animations help convey and reinforce complex concepts. For example, an animation can be used to depict the flow of electricity, cell division, or a volcano eruption. Although animations can add a wealth of information and excitement to multimedia projects, they can also be time-consuming to develop. This section outlines two types of animations (frame and path), presents resources for locating animations, and provides guidelines for the use of animations.

Frame Animations

Frame animations were popularized by movie and cartoon animators who use them to create the illusion of motion. The first Mickey Mouse cartoon was created by drawing many images with very slight differences between the images. When the images are played in rapid sequence (usually 5–15 frames per second), they blend together, and we see Mickey walking and dancing. Likewise, to create frame animations on a computer, you must draw several frames and play them in rapid succession (see Figure 5.4).

Figure 5.4. Graphics for a frame animation (Addy from HyperStudio).

GIF animations (which are made up of a series of GIF images) are common on the Web. GIF animations are popular because they are small (in file size) and easy to create. For example, if you watch an animation of a small mailbox that opens and closes, you will note that it is made up of three or four images that cycle over and over again. You can locate thousands of GIF animations in clipart galleries on the Web.

You can also create your own GIF animations by producing a series of still images that have slight alterations from one image to the next. Then, using image editors or software tools such as GIF Construction Set (http://www.mindworkshop.com), you can set the play time so that each image will display a split second before the next one appears.

Path Animations

A *path animation* involves moving an object on a screen that has a constant background. For example, a title can "fly in" from the left side, an airplane can fly across the page, or a ball can bounce through a scene. Creating a path animation is much easier than creating a frame animation; you create the object you want to animate, then you move it along a path.

Some programs include features that can easily create path animations. For example, PowerPoint provides numerous predesigned animation schemes (such as "fade in and dim" or "boomerang and exit") for the titles and bullets on the slides. The timing, sequence, speed, and direction of these schemes can be easily modified.

PowerPoint also has a path (called motion) animation option that allows you to specify the path an object (text or graphic) will follow. For example, if you wanted to animate a plane flying across the screen, you would follow these steps (for the 2007 version):

1. Create a slide and insert a picture of an airplane.

2. Select "Custom Animation" from the Animations menu.

3. Highlight (click) the object (airplane) that you want to animate.

4. Click the "Add Effect" button and select "Motion Paths" from the pulldown menu.

5. Select a predefined motion or "Draw Custom Path" and "Freeform."

6. Click the mouse and hold it down as you drag the airplane across the screen to define the path (see Figure 5.5).

7. Double-click the mouse when you reach the end of the path.

8. Select "Play" to see the complete animation.

Figure 5.5. Path animation window.

Flash by Adobe is another popular program for creating animations. Flash is popular for creating Web animations because it uses vector graphics, which are often much smaller than the bitmapped graphics. Flash also offers many sophisticated options, such as key frames and in-betweens. With these features, you can draw a character on frame one, go to frame 10, grab its left arm, and raise it. The software will then calculate the arm's motion for frames 2 through 9 and create the individual images.

Guidelines for Animations

The following guidelines can help you and your students determine how to use animations appropriately.

- Use path animations to move one or two objects on a screen.

- Use frame animation for more complex sequences involving multiple changes.

- Make sure the animation has a purpose. Use animations to illustrate an abstract concept, such as river erosion.

- Do not include animations that distract from the content.

- Keep the animation sequences short, or allow the user an option to interrupt and proceed with the program.

- Avoid animations that loop infinitely—they can be distracting when the viewer is attempting to read the text on the page. If it must loop, limit it to two or three times.

- Test the animations on various computers and different browsers to ensure they display correctly.

- If the animation is designed for the Web, keep the file size small.

AUDIO

Audio refers to sound elements in a program. These elements can include recorded narration, music, and sound effects (such as a bird singing or a telephone dial tone). Audio can assist students' learning, as well as add realism, excitement, and motivation to projects. For example, students can record oral histories, compose music, narrate a presentation, or add sound effects to a project.

There are many ways your students can add audio components to their projects. They can record the audio with a microphone (digital audio), use synthesized speech, create music, post podcasts, or import clip audio (elements that are available for free or for sale).

Digital Audio

Audio can be recorded with a computer and stored in a digital format on computer hard drives, networks, CD-ROMs and other storage devices. The audio files can be accessed and played on a computer or mobile device (such as an iPod or cellphone). A major advantage of this technology is that teachers and students can record their own voices or sounds.

Bringing sound into the digital domain of computer bits and bytes requires a sampling process. At small but discrete time intervals, the computer takes a "snapshot" of the sound. This process is called sampling, and the number of samples taken each second is referred to as the sampling rate. The more samples, the better the sound quality. For example, audio sampled 44,000 times per second (44 kilohertz or kHz) will provide better quality than audio sampled 22,000 times per second (22 kHz).

Selecting a sampling rate is based primarily on two factors: the sound quality needed and the storage space available. The two factors are interrelated: the higher the quality, the more space required, and vice versa. For most educational applications, a sampling rate of 11 kHz is sufficient. For music programs, which require higher quality, higher sampling rates are recommended. Table 5.2 compares the file sizes generated when a 1-second audio clip is recorded at various sampling rates.

Table 5.2. Comparison of File Sizes and Sampling Rates

Sampling Rate	Storage for 1 Second of Sound	Seconds of Sound per 1 MB Storage
44 kHz	44 kilobytes	22 seconds
22 kHz	22 kilobytes	45 seconds
11 kHz	11 kilobytes	90 seconds

Recording Audio with Computers

The recording process for digital audio is not difficult. Most computers have the necessary hardware components built in for recording audio. To digitize audio, follow this procedure:

1. Plug a microphone into the audio input of the computer (or activate the internal microphone.

2. Open an audio recording program (for example, in PowerPoint, select "Insert … Sound … Record Sound").

3. Select a sampling rate and other parameters if they are available.

4. Click "Record."

5. Speak into the microphone.

6. Select "Stop" when you have recorded the segment you want.

7. Test the recording with the "Play" command. If it is acceptable, name the file and save.

8. Digitized sounds can be viewed and edited like text (see Figure 5.6). With the appropriate software program (such as Audacity or GoldWave), sounds can be selected, cut, copied, pasted, and mixed with other sounds. Audio editing is a powerful tool that allows you to rearrange sounds or cut out parts you do not need.

Figure 5.6. Editing an audio wave.

Synthesized Speech

Synthesized speech uses a computer program to translate text into spoken output without any recording process. It simply applies its phonetic rules to pronounce all of the words. The disadvantage of the text-to-speech synthesis method is that it can have an unnatural and mechanical sound. For instance, problems arise with words such as "live" that do not follow consistent rules of pronunciation. Most computer synthesizers cannot accurately differentiate between the use of live in these two sentences: "I live in Florida" and "We are using live bait."

Another problem with synthesized speech is that synthesizers do not have the natural inflections of a human voice; they may not "drop off" to indicate the end of a sentence as we do in natural speech. An example of synthesized speech is the Blabber Mouth II feature of HyperStudio. With this feature, students can type in text and the computer then does its best to read it (see Figure 5.7). Because the only component that the computer has to store is the text, the file size is very small for this type of audio.

Music

There are several options for students who want to compose or play music on a computer. They can record MIDI files from an electronic keyboard or compose original music using a composition software program such as GarageBand.

Musical Instrument Digital Interface (MIDI)

One of the most compact and flexible formats used to store, transfer, and play music is *MIDI* (Musical Instrument Digital Interface). MIDI does

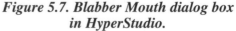

*Figure 5.7. Blabber Mouth dialog box
in HyperStudio.*

not record the actual sounds; instead, it stores the instructions needed to tell the computer (and any connected MIDI devices) which instrument sound to use, which note to play, how loud it should be played, and so on. Similar to sheet music, MIDI files provide the instructions on how to reproduce the music. The computer then interprets the MIDI instructions and produces the music using the sounds that are embedded in the sound card or sound module.

The configuration for the MIDI includes MIDI software, a MIDI-equipped audio card or interface box, cables, speakers, and one or more MIDI instruments. Piano keyboards and other electronic instruments that contain synthesizers can be used to input the musical information to the computer software and to output the recorded songs.

A major advantage of MIDI technology is that it can store complex music in very small files. The MIDI files are a fraction of the size of digital audio files (up to 100 times smaller). This small file size results from the fact that MIDI music is *not* sampled and digitized like digital audio files. Instead, MIDI contains information *about* the sound, not the sounds themselves. Many computer games store music in MIDI files to conserve disk space.

There are many ways to find or generate MIDI files. If you are a musician, you can use sequencing software (such as Cakewalk) that captures everything that you play on a synthesized instrument. The *sequencing* software can record and play back several parts or instruments in perfect synchronization—sort of like an old-fashioned player-piano roll. After the musical information is loaded into the computer, it can be edited or revised in relation to its rhythm, meter, tone, and many other parameters. With MIDI sequencing software, you can experiment with harmonies, record different parts, and play them back as a complete arrangement.

If you are not musically talented, you can still create MIDI files by scanning sheet music. Programs, such as SmartScore, can scan the sheet music and translate the print notation into MIDI commands. Other music recognition software (such as AKoff Music Composer) will allow you to hum, sing, or play music to record a MIDI song. Internet sites also offer access to thousands of MIDI songs that can be purchased and downloaded

Composition Software

Composition software offers a wide variety of options for novice and expert musicians, and the compositions can be saved in a variety of formats, including MP3 and MIDI. For example, GarageBand (which is included in the iLife suite from Apple Computer) is a mini-music studio that provides prerecorded rhythm sections (called loops), solo instruments, and instrumental performances that can be used as backgrounds or can be combined to create "original" compositions. Students can also record music with GarageBand, via a microphone or MIDI synthesizer (such as a keyboard or electric guitar). Final compositions can be saved as individual files or added to playlists to play on iPods, computers, or other devices.

Digital Audio File Formats

Many file formats are used for digital audio, and some can be recognized by one program and not another. For example, .AIFF formats are common on Macintosh computers, and .WAV is the most common format for Windows computers. Some programs (on either platform) can recognize and play files, such as MIDI; others cannot. The following formats are common for audio:

- WAV. The WAV format is the default standard for most Windows-based computers.

- AIFF. The AIFF format is the default standard for most Macintosh computers.

- MP3. MP3 is a compression format that can decrease the size of an audio file, but maintain a high-quality sound. Although MP3 files can be compressed at different ratios, the standard is about a 10:1 ratio. This enables a 3-minute song to be stored on less than 4 MB of disk space. Many of the small, portable audio players, such as iPods, use the MP3 format.

- ASF (Active Streaming Format). ASF is often used for streaming media. It works well with Windows Media Player.

- WMA (Windows Media Audio). An audio format produced by Microsoft to compete with the MP3 and AAC formats.

- QT or MOV. Although QuickTime was originally designed for digital video, it can also be used for a combination of audio and video or for audio-only files.

- AAC (Advanced Audio Coding). ACC is a compressed audio format that can be used on iPods. It competes with MP3.

- SWA. Shockwave Audio is a file format used by Adobe for audio on the Internet.

- MID or MIDI (Musical Instrument Digital Interface). A standard for communicating musical information among computers and musical devices.

If you have an audio file that is not in the correct format, there are programs that will convert files from one format to another. For example, Audacity (available at http://www.audacity.com) will convert to and from .WAV, .MP3, and .AIFF.

Using Existing Audio Files

Audio files in various formats are available from clip media sites and other archives on the Internet. These files can be downloaded, edited, and imported into projects. See, for example, the Florida Museum of Natural History at http://www.flmnh.ufl.edu/natsci/ornithology/sounds.htm.

The fair use portion of the copyright law is generally interpreted as allowing students to use copyrighted music in a classroom situation to fulfill an instructional objective (such as an assignment to create a multimedia project). If students want to use music on their website, however, they must have the rights to record and play the music files. Recording a song from the radio and adding a link to it from a website would definitely violate copyright laws.

Numerous shareware sound files are available on the Web. Prior to incorporating these files into a webpage or an application that will be distributed beyond the classroom, you should carefully read the permission statements. If a permission statement is not associated with the file, send an e-mail message to the site administrator to request permission.

Podcasting Audio

Podcasting is a technique that was been popularized by the iPod. Podcasting allows users to "subscribe" to a series of audio files on the Web and download updates when they are posted. For example, some schools are broadcasting their daily (or weekly) news as podcasts. To do so, they record an audio file of the news each week, save it as an MP3 file, and post it on a Web server (or post it through iTunes or an online blog). Another file, called RSS for Really Simple Syndication is included to allow users to "subscribe" to the show.

Several websites (such as Podbean and MyPodcast) are available that provide free hosting of podcasts, along with the recording tools needed to create them. The list of podcasts shown in Figure 5.8 provides an example of podcasts that are available in the K–12 area of iTunes. For example the children in Room 33 at South Elementary recorded bedtime stories for their parents and the community.

Figure 5.8. K-12 podcasts in iTunes.

After you subscribe to a podcast, you can set the parameters, telling your computer or device to check for new files at a particular site on an hourly, daily, weekly, or other basis. In addition to playing a podcast on a computer, the podcasts can easily be transferred to an iPod, iPhone, or similar MP3 player, and you can listen to them at any time. Imagine the possibilities of having students listen to the stories and news they have downloaded on the bus ride home!

Guidelines for Audio

There are many situations when audio is appropriate in a multimedia program. For example, if the program is designed for nonreaders or students with sight impairments, then audio is definitely required. In addition, audio is a great way to teach someone a different language or to include sound effects (such as heartbeats) and music. However, audio files can be quite large, and students should be cautioned to use them only when necessary. The following guidelines should be considered for audio.

- Use audio only when it is appropriate to the content.
- Record audio at the lowest acceptable sampling rate to minimize file space.
- Use synthesized speech for programs that require a lot of spoken words.

- If possible, use MIDI or MP3 for music—the files are much smaller than digital audio stored in WAV and other formats.

- Do not add audio that will distract from the screen display.

- Check copyright restrictions if the audio will be played outside the classroom environment.

- If your software program does not recognize the audio file format, locate an audio converter program to change the file format.

DIGITAL VIDEO

Digitized video refers to motion sequences that are stored in a digital format; usually it is recorded with a digital video camera and saved as a computer file. Digital video has the potential to add realism to multimedia projects. Students can record school assemblies, document field trips, add video to websites, or create commercials—the possibilities are endless!

Digitizing video, however, is one of the most demanding operations that we ask of a computer. A single digitized image of video requires roughly 1,000,000 bytes or 1 megabyte (MB) for storage and transfer. With 30 images required for each second of full motion video, a digitized stream of motion video requires the flow of 30 megabytes of information per second. A minute of video would then consist of 1,800 megabytes, or 1.8 gigabytes of data, and a 30-minute video would require 54 gigabytes!

Mass storage devices are improving rapidly, but there are still few economical methods for storing 54 gigabytes of data for each half hour of video. An equally challenging issue involves how to move that much data through a computer at a steady 30 megabytes per second to produce the 30 frames per second required to present smooth motion. Even for the most powerful modern desktop computers, this is an astonishing amount of data to process.

Because of the tremendous amount of data, trade-offs are necessary. For example, note that most videos on the Internet are presented in a small window, rather than full screen. In addition, they might appear a bit jerky because they are displayed at less than 30 frames per second, or they might be shown in black and white. All of these techniques can be used to help minimize the size of a digital video.

Digitizing and Editing Video

Digital camcorders, such as the Flip, provide an easy, inexpensive method for capturing video. After video is recorded into the camera, you can attach a cable to the camera and import the video into a computer. Or, in the case of the Flip video camera, simply plug its USB arm into the computer. Digital video software, such as iMovie, Final Cut Pro, Premier, and Movie Maker, provide easy-to-use controls for importing and editing video (see Figure 5.9).

Figure 5.9. Import video controls in Movie Maker.

Digital video software also allows students to sequence video clips, add audio, overlay titles, and experiment with transitions. Through these programs, students can manipulate the video files and other media to tell a story or teach a concept. When the project is complete, they can export it to videotape, save it as a stand-alone computer file, record a DVD, create a podcast, upload to YouTube, or integrate the video into another application, such as PowerPoint.

Although the features and interfaces vary, all of the editing software provides basic functions for editing video. The process consists of these general steps:

1. Import the video into the video editing software.

2. Edit the video clips to the desired length by cropping the unwanted portions.

3. Import other media elements, such as photographs, animations, and audio tracks into the editing software.

4. Place the video clips and still images on a timeline in the desired sequence.

5. Add transitions, such as dissolves and cuts between clips (if desired).

6. Add title slides or textual overlays (if desired).

7. Work with the audio track by adjusting the volume and importing sound effects, music, and so on.

8. Combine the elements into one movie file.

9. Save the movie file in the desired format.

10. Export the movie file to videotape, Web server, DVD, CD-ROM, mobile media, or other device.

11. Test the video, and make adjustments as necessary.

Digital Video File Formats

"RAW" digital video is generally recorded in the DV (digital video) format, and the files are very large. Several common file formats are used to compress and play digital video, including QuickTime, AVI, ASF, and MPEG.

- QuickTime (.MOV and .QT). QuickTime provides both editing and playback interfaces for synchronized video and audio. It works well on both Macs and PCs, and it provides good compression, resulting in smaller file sizes.

- Windows (.AVI, .AFS, .WMF, .WMV). Microsoft introduced a similar but incompatible product called Video for Windows, which uses an .AVI file extension. Since then, Microsoft has introduced other file formats, including .ASF (Advanced Streaming Format), .WMF (Windows Media Format), and .WMV (Windows Media Video).

- MPEG (.MPG, MP3, and MP4). MPEG stands for Motion Pictures Expert Group. It is used as a file format as well as compression technique, and it is popular for high-end video applications.

- FLV (Flash Video Format). Flash video is playable within Flash movies files, which are supported by most browsers on both Macintosh and PC computers.

If you do not have the inclination, equipment, or time to produce your own digital video movies, you may be able to obtain appropriate files through the Web or on a DVD. Be sure you check the copyright restrictions, especially for applications that will be used or accessed outside the classroom.

Guidelines for Video

Digital video files are generally very large; therefore, you must carefully assess whether you want to use video in a multimedia project—especially one for the Web. The following guidelines should be considered for video:

- Use digital video only when absolutely necessary.

- Keep the window size as small as possible (about one-quarter screen) to help improve performance.

- Check the size of the video files after they are recorded, especially if you are going to transfer them via the Internet.

- Make sure there is adequate lighting when recording digital movies.

- Use a tripod for shooting video to minimize extra motion and achieve better compression.

- Shoot close-ups because the video will be viewed in a small window on the computer.

- Experiment with different compression options to obtain the best quality at the smallest file size.

- Check copyright restrictions on video segments, especially for material that will be used outside the classroom.

SUMMARY

Graphics, animations, audio, and video can add life and interest to multimedia projects. They can also be used to illustrate and convey abstract concepts, and they can enhance students' visual literacy and their ability to think, learn, and communicate through visuals and other media. Designing and developing media files allow students to be creative and to investigate the presentation of information from several perspectives. Most students are very enthusiastic about working with sound, graphics, and video.

Creating media files also presents some challenges for educators and students. The media files can be stored in many formats, and problems can arise when students have media files ready to incorporate into a project, but the program will not "see" or open the files. In addition, recording and editing usually require additional software and hardware, which may be in limited supply in classrooms.

This chapter presented a wide array of options for incorporating graphics, animations, audio, and video files. Although each software program will incorporate the media elements in a slightly different manner, almost all software programs (including basic word processors) now have the ability to add graphics, sound, and video. The potential is limited only by the imagination (and hardware) available to the students.

RESOURCES

Graphics and Animation Resources

Adobe (DreamWeaver, Flash, PhotoShop, Acrobat, Illustrator, Premier, etc.): http://www.adobe.com

Apple iLife (iPhoto): http://www.apple.com/ilife

Corel (CorelDraw and Paint Shop Pro, etc.): http://www.corel.com

Flags of the World: http://fotw.vexillum.com/flags

Clipart ETC: http://etc.usf.edu/clipart/index.htm

Clip Media (Art): http://etc.usf.edu/clip/index.htm

Clip Media (Photos): http://etc.usf.edu/clip/photos.htm

GIF Construction Set (Alchemy Mindworks): http://www.mindworkshop.com

GIMP: http://www.gimp.org

Graphic Converter: http://www.lemkesoft.com/content/188/graphicconverter.html

LView Pro: http://lview.com

NASA Images: http://www.nasa.gov/multimedia/imagegallery/index.html

Picasa: http://picasa.google.com

Scanning Tips: http://www.scantips.com/basics01.html

Tux Paint: http://www.tuxpaint.org

Audio Resources

Akoff Music Composer: http://www.akoff.com

Audacity: http://audacity.sourceforge.net

Cakewalk: http://www.cakewalk.com

Classical MIDI Archives: http://www.classicalarchives.com

GarageBand: http://www.apple.com/ilife/garageband

GoldWave: http://www.goldwave.com

Harmony Central: http://www.harmony-central.com/MIDI

MyPodcast: http://www.mypodcast.com

PodBean: http://www.podbean.com

SmartScore: http://www.smartscore.com

Video Resources

Adobe (Premier): http://www.adobe.com

Apple iLife (iMovie, iPhoto, iWeb, iDVD): http://www.apple.com/ilife

Final Cut Studio: http://www.apple.com/finalcutstudio/finalcutpro

Flip Video Camera: http://www.theflip.com

Library of Congress Motion Pictures: http://lcweb2.loc.gov/ammem/browse/ListSome.php?format=Motion+Picture

Microsoft Movie Maker: http://windowslive.com/Desktop/moviemaker

Movie Sounds Page: http://www.moviesounds.com

NASA Video Gallery: http://www.nasa.gov/multimedia/videogallery/index.html

Develop: Multimedia Development Tools

A SCENARIO

The earthquake in Haiti was all over the news. Mr. Wells decided that it would be meaningful for his eighth-grade social studies class to participate in a multimedia project in which they could investigate the causes, patterns, and implications of major earthquakes. Because his students were accustomed to creating both short- and long-term activities with media, he decided to allow them to present their research as a presentation, a movie, or a website. All of these formats were familiar to the students.

The students knew PowerPoint was a presentation program that could be used to produce a linear slide show-type report; however, it also featured Action Buttons that could be used to add branches from one screen to another. Although iMovie and Movie Maker did not provide the same level of interactivity as PowerPoint, they could be used to compile an impressive array of graphics, video clips, transitions, and sound. DreamWeaver was available at their school to create webpages with hyperlinks, graphics, text, and media elements. The difficult part was deciding which tool would be the best for their project about earthquakes.

Anita suggested that her group use PowerPoint because it was easy to use, and they could display charts and graphs related to earthquakes. Pax argued that creating a movie would be best because they could easily incorporate interviews and images downloaded from the Web. If approved, they could even upload the video to YouTube. Sally and Jay both liked the idea of linking together webpages for the project and uploading them to the Web server at the district office.

As the students worked through the DECIDE phase of the project, conducting their brainstorming and research activities, Mr. Wells urged them to concentrate on the content, then decide which tool would be best to present it. In the end, the students decided to use a combination of tools. They created the charts and graphs in Excel, then saved them as GIF images to display on a webpage. They also created a small movie with interviews that they embedded into their website. They were amazed at how many websites with information about earthquakes already existed, and they included links to relevant sites and images. They even located an animation online that showed how the earth's plates move and cause earthquakes. With the focus on the content, it was quite easy for them to select the appropriate development tools.

OVERVIEW

After the media elements are created, they are brought together into a final project with a software program, often called a *development program* or *authoring tool*. There are many affordable software programs that can be used to author and present a multimedia project.

This chapter provides an overview of programs that are commonly available in school environments, such as word processors, spreadsheets, presentation programs, and hypermedia software. It also presents information on developing multimedia webpages with HTML and Web editors, along with image programs and digital video editors, such as iMovie and Movie Maker. All of these options are inexpensive, relatively easy to use, and can include text, graphics, audio, and video.

This chapter includes:

- Multimedia documents and slide shows

    Word processors

    Spreadsheet programs

    Presentation programs

    Image programs

- Hypermedia programs

    HyperStudio

    Flash

- Webpage production

    Text editors

    Web templates

    Application programs

    Web editors

- Digital video programs and editors

    iMovie

    Microsoft Movie Maker

    iDVD

- Selecting a development tool

- Facilitating multimedia projects in the classroom

MULTIMEDIA DOCUMENTS AND SLIDE SHOWS

Almost all application programs (such as word processors, spreadsheets, image editors, and presentation software) can incorporate multimedia components. Most of these programs are inexpensive and available in school environments. In many cases, these tools can be used to create media elements that are later incorporated into a multimedia project. However, students and teachers can also use these applications to combine video, audio, text, and graphics to create multimedia documents, slide shows, and other products.

Word Processors

Word processors, such as Microsoft Word and Pages (part of Apple's iWork program), are important tools for all classrooms. In addition to enhancing students' writing abilities, word processors can be used to create multimedia documents and webpages. For example, in Microsoft Word, several media types can be inserted, including clipart, photographs, animations, and sounds. In addition, it is easy to inscrt and edit WordArt (see Figure 6.1), graphs, charts, tables, organizational charts, and shapes.

Figure 6.1. WordArt in Microsoft Word.

Word processors can also play an important role in multimedia projects by serving as storyboard and flowchart tools. By using the styles and forms features, teachers can create storyboard templates for students to populate with scripts, links, images, and other details. Flowcharts are also easy to create in word processors by using the shape and line drawing features. Alignment and grouping tools can assist in formatting the layouts and locking the elements (see Figure 6.2)

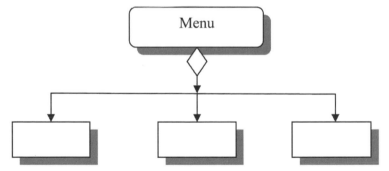

Figure 6.2. Creating a flowchart in Word with shapes and lines.

Spreadsheet Programs

Spreadsheet programs can be great tools for short- or long-term multimedia projects. For example, imagine a project that involves students using a spreadshcct to record the number of calories and the nutritional value of three brands of hot dogs, hot dog buns, and potato chips. For younger students, the teacher could set up a template for the values and formulas; older students could set up the spreadsheet in groups. In addition to entering data, students can add images of the picnic items, generate graphs and charts comparing the different brands, experiment with formulas, and save the worksheet in various formats (including a webpage).

Spreadsheets can also be implemented as a supplement to other tools. For example, charts can be generated in a spreadsheet and then cut and pasted into another program, such as HyperStudio. Charts from spreadsheets can also be embedded directly into a word processor or presentation program.

Presentation Programs

Presentation programs, such as PowerPoint by Microsoft and Keynote by Apple, are popular because they are inexpensive, easy to learn, easy to use, and can incorporate multimedia elements such as graphics, digital video, and digital audio. Presentation programs generally include a variety of predesigned templates with colorful backgrounds and preformatted fonts to make the presentations look professional. These templates are useful for novices who are developing their first multimedia projects. Some templates have a particular theme (such as a beach or party); others are more generic. Remind students to select a design template that offers high contrast between background and text so the words will be easy to read. Presentation software also includes a wide array of clipart and media elements to incorporate into projects.

As the term *presentation* implies, presentation programs are often used for projects that will be presented to a large group, rather than projects designed for individual use. Linear projects, such as lectures and multimedia reports, where one screen automatically follows another, are easy for teachers and students to develop with presentation software. The current version of PowerPoint also includes "action buttons," where hotspots can be created on a screen to branch to a specified slide, Web address, or file. By incorporating action buttons, students can add interactivity, such as menu options and questions.

A nice feature of most presentation programs is that by simply clicking "Insert audio" students can record and test narration directly on the slides. They can also easily control the audio. For example, the sound can be programmed to play automatically when the slide opens or after the mouse is clicked.

Image Programs

Image programs, such as KidPix, TuxPaint, iPhoto, and Picasa are excellent tools for creating multimedia projects. KidPix is an easy-to-use image program that is designed for grades K–8. It provides tools for creating and editing images, and it can be used to inspire creativity in young children. With KidPix, students can also create a slideshow with the built-in tools, and they have the option to save the slideshow as a QuickTime movie.

TuxPaint is another image program that is designed for children (ages 3 to 12). TuxPaint combines an easy-to-use interface, fun sound effects, and an encouraging cartoon mascot who guides children as they use the program (see Figure 6.3). It can be downloaded free of charge from http://www.tuxpaint.org.

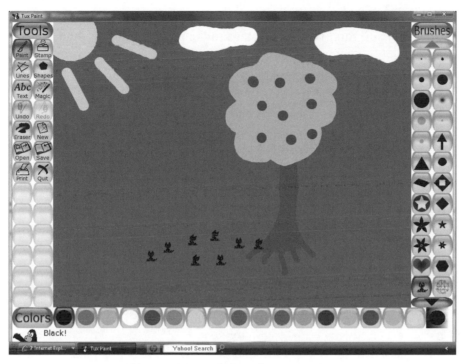

Figure 6.3. Interface for TuxPaint.

Two popular programs for editing, managing, and organizing images include iPhoto (part of the iLife suite by Apple) and Picasa (from Google). iPhoto allows students to import, organize, edit, and share photographs and other graphics. In addition, students can add titles, transitions, and sounds. The images can be displayed in a slideshow, shared on the Web, or made into photo books, cards, or calendars (see Figure 6.4).

Figure 6.4. Creating a photo book in iPhoto.

A similar program, called Picasa, is available from Google. It also helps students organize and share their photos. They can even add geotags to the photos and link them to places on Google Earth (see Figure 6.5).

Figure 6.5. Adding geotags to photos in Picasa.

HYPERMEDIA PROGRAMS

Hypermedia programs are designed so that information stored as text, graphics, audio, video, or animations can be accessed in associative, nonlinear ways. For example, the opening screen of a hypermedia application might contain a menu with four options. Buttons (areas) on the menu can be activated, allowing students to select one of the options and branch to the corresponding screen, audio file, video file, or animation. Hypermedia applications are often used for stand-alone projects (as opposed to class presentations) because they enable users to make their own choices and follow their own paths.

HyperStudio

Although the concept of hypermedia has existed for many years, it has become much more popular because of inexpensive, cross-platform programs such as HyperStudio. The basic structure of HyperStudio consists of stacks and cards (a file is referred to as a *stack*, and a computer screen is called a *card*). Each card can contain text items, buttons, graphics, and other multimedia elements (see Figure 6.6).

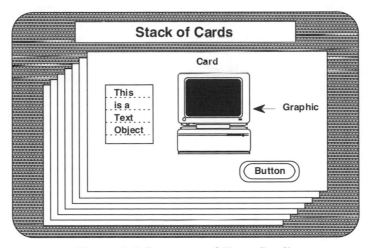

Figure 6.6. Structure of HyperStudio.

Text objects are similar to miniature word-processing blocks and are designed to contain text of various styles and sizes. *Buttons* are designated areas of the screens that can initiate an action, such as moving (branching) to another card or playing an audio, video, or animation. Graphics can be created with paint tools within HyperStudio, or they can be imported from clipart or other graphics programs.

With HyperStudio, a series of pull-down menus and dialog windows are used to develop the applications. HyperStudio is an impressive package that provides built-in links to audio CDs, digital movies, and digitized audio. Animation tools, Web tools, and testing functions that can track correct and incorrect answers are also available. In more recent editions, presentations can be exported to iPod video format, and users can import iTunes playlists, YouTube videos, and more.

Flash

Flash is an Adobe product that has rapidly gained popularity in schools. It is a great tool for creating audio-enhanced, interactive presentations. Finished projects can be stand-alone, or they can be embedded into webpages, presentation software, or other applications.

The workspace in Flash in called the Stage (see Figure 6.7). Flash has a tool palette that can be used to add text, shapes, and color to the Stage. The Stage is associated with a Timeline, which is made up of frames, much like a movie. This makes it relatively easy to create animations.

Figure 6.7. Flash Stage, Timeline, and toolbar.

WEBPAGE PRODUCTION

Access to the Internet provides a great environment for publishing multimedia projects in school. With a simple word processor, students can easily create webpages that can be viewed by people around the world. Even if a school is not connected to the Internet, it is possible for students to use Web technology to publish documents that are available on school networks or stand-alone computers.

All webpages are derived from text files that are interpreted and displayed by Web browsers (such as Firefox, Safari, or Internet Explorer). For example, when the text file shown in Figure 6.8 is displayed through a browser, the student will see the webpage illustrated in Figure 6.9.

```
<HTML>
<HEAD>
<TITLE>Geography Home Page</TITLE></HEAD>
<BODY>
<IMG SRC ="geo.gif">
<BR>
<H2>This page provides links relevant to Freshman Geography</H2>
<P>
Click to see a <A HREF="CA.mov">movie about Central America.</A>.
<BR>
<HR>
<UL>
<LI><A HREF="http://www.geo.gov/">Geography sites</A>
<LI><A HREF="http://www.chs.edu/assign/">Assignments</A>
<LI><A HREF="http://www.chs.edu/reports/">Student reports</A>
</UL>
<HR>
</BODY>
</HTML>
```

Figure 6.8. Text file (HTML) for a webpage.

Figure 6.9. Webpage created from code in Figure 6.8.

The text files used in Web documents adhere to a specific format called the *HyperText Markup Language* or HTML. HTML files use *tags* (words embedded between the < and > characters) to define how information is formatted on the screen. For example, in the line This is bold.</B>, the first tag turns the bold attribute on, and the second one (the one with the /B) turns the bold attribute off. A few common style tags are illustrated in Table 6.1.

Table 6.1. HTML Quick Reference Guide

	Tag	Definition
Essential Parts	<HTML> <HEAD> <TITLE>...</TITLE> </HEAD> <BODY>...</BODY> </HTML>	These tags represent the template or "skeleton" of an HTML document. HTML tags identify the beginning and ending of the document; HEAD tags contain the TITLE tags, which identify the page's bookmark name; and BODY tags contain the text, pictures, headings, etc. of the document
Formatting Text: Headings	<H1>...</H1> <H2>...</H2> <H3>...</H3> <H4>...</H4> <H5>...</H5> <H6>...</H6>	HTML has six levels of headings that are displayed in bolder and separate type than the regular body text. Level 1 is the largest heading; Level 6 is the smallest heading.
Formatting Text: Physical Styles	<B>...</B> <I>...</I> <U>...</U> <TT>...</TT>	Physical style tags tell browsers how to display text. For example, text within the tags <B>...</B> will be **boldface**; text within the tags <I>...</I> will be *italicized*; text within the tags <U>...</U> will be underlined; and text within the tags <TT>...</TT> will be a typewriter font.
Formatting Text: Paragraphs	<PRE>...</PRE> <P>...</P> 	A variety of tags are used to format paragraphs. <PRE>...</PRE> displays text with its original carriage returns and spacing (preformat); <P>...</P> identifies a paragraph; and inserts a carriage return. does not have an ending tag.
Making Lists	<UL> <LI>first item <LI>second item <LI>third item </UL>	<UL>...</UL> creates an unordered list. <LI> tags are placed within the <UL> and </UL> tags to identify each item in the list. Ordered lists that display numbers are created by using <OL> and </OL> instead of <UL> and </UL>. <LI> tags are placed also within the <OL> and </OL> tags.
Displaying an Image	<IMG SRC = "image.gif" ALT = "alternative text"> <HR>	Place the name of the image in "image.gif" and "alternative text." <HR> displays a horizontal line.
Creating Hyperlinks	<A HREF = "http://whereto.dom ">location</A> <A HREF = "MAILTO:name@my .domain">e-mail address</A>	Place the location's address in "http://whereto.dom" and link information in "location." The MAILTO link sends an e-mail message. Insert your e-mail address in both locations.
Playing Movies and Sounds	<A HREF="file_name">i nstructions</A>	Place the name of the sound or movie in "file_name" and directions (such as "click here") in "instructions."

Creating a webpage may appear to be intimidating, but many elementary school students are developing pages every day. In some cases, they learn a few basic HTML tags and then gradually expand their "vocabulary" as they become more experienced. In other cases, they do not learn HTML at all; instead, they use a word processor or Web editor that allows them to create Web documents without typing in any command codes.

There are several ways to create a webpage, including the following:

- Create an HTML page "by hand" by typing HTML code into a text editor.

- Use an online template.

- Use an application program, such as Microsoft Word or PowerPoint, and *Save As . . . webpage*.

- Use a Web editor, such as Adobe DreamWeaver, Apple's iWeb, or products such as KompoZer.

Creating a Webpage with a Text Editor

One of the least expensive methods for creating webpages is to use the free text editors that come with a computer, such as *SimpleText* on Macintosh and *NotePad* on Windows machines. An advantage of creating HTML in these simple text editors is that they save the files in text-only format—exactly the format needed for the webpages.

To create HTML files in a text editor, you type in all of the required codes (as illustrated in Figure 6.8). Then save the file with an .htm or .html extension. Note that the images and media elements will be separate files (usually saved in the same directory). When you are finished, test the file by displaying it through a Web browser.

Keep in mind that no matter how a webpage is created, it is stored in HTML code. Even though there are many other options, it is wise to understand at least the basics of HTML; that way, you and the students will be able to make minor changes to webpages no matter how or where they were created.

Creating a Webpage with a Web Template

Another way to create webpages is to use a template (see Figure 6.10 for an example). These templates use online forms—you simply fill in the forms and a webpage is generated. There are several websites (some are especially designed for teachers) that provide free templates. Many of these websites will also host your pages and store them on their Web server, so you don't have to worry about uploading or storing them on a local Web server.

The following websites offer templates and other tools to allow you to build and store a website easily.

- Google Sites at http://sites.google.com provides a wealth of free templates.

- Weebly at http://www.weebly.com/ provides free Web templates, tools, and hosting.

- Webs.com at http://www.webs.com provides free Web tools, templates, and hosting.

- TeacherWeb at http://teacherweb.com provides a straightforward design. Options are available to create school websites with areas for a calendar, announcements, links, frequently asked questions, and assignments. A small subscription fee is required.

Figure 6.10. Interface for Weebly template.

Creating a Webpage with Application Programs

Webpages have become so popular that many of the standard word processing programs, spreadsheets, presentation programs, and desktop publishing tools include an option to save the file as a webpage (in HTML format). These programs offer a fast, efficient way to create Web documents from existing documents. For example, students could write stories in Microsoft Word, then use the "Save As . . . webpage" to convert it into HTML. At that point, it can be uploaded to a Web server and accessed via a Web browser. Application programs are a great way to get started on large, text-intensive projects.

Creating a Webpage with a Web Editor

Several Web editors are available that provide users with a *WYSIWYG* (what you see is what you get) environment. Some of the most popular programs include DreamWeaver, KompoZer, and iWeb. KompoZer is a free download; iWeb (part of Apple's iLife package) and DreamWeaver are relatively inexpensive for educational use.

These programs allow users to type text on their webpages just as they would in a word processing program. Styles, such as bold, are added by highlighting the text and selecting a style on the menu bar. Users do not see the HTML code; it is generated "behind the scenes" and will be interpreted by the Web browser. It is possible to insert graphics, include lists, create tables, and insert forms with these programs as well (see Figure 6.11).

Figure 6.11. DreamWeaver interface.

After a webpage is created, it (and all relevant media files) must be uploaded to a Web server so the rest of the world can see it. To upload files to a Web server, you may need special permissions and passwords. Most Webmasters and administrators are extremely cautious about granting permission to upload files because of the prevalence of hackers and viruses. You may be asked to send the files to the administrator, and he or she will place them on the server.

DIGITAL VIDEO PROGRAMS AND EDITORS

Producing a video project involves a great deal of planning, organizing, and creative energy. As illustrated in Table 6.2, the phases in a video production project are often referred to as preproduction, production, and postproduction. The video files can be used in a stand-alone mode (as a DVD, for example), or they can be integrated into a hypermedia presentation or Web program.

Table 6.2. Phases of Digital Video Projects

Preproduction	Production	Postproduction
• Select project idea/goal • Outline project • Write scripts and storyboards • Assign roles • Design sets (if necessary)	• Shoot video • Record audio • Create graphics	• Import video into editing software • Edit video clips • Add transitions • Add title slides • Combine the clips into movie file

In the past, editing the video clips into a finished movie was a complex process that involved high-end, expensive equipment, consisting of multiple videotape players, recorders, and control devices. Thanks to advancements in hardware and software, it is now possible to do sophisticated editing with a classroom computer. Popular video editing programs for schools include iMovie by Apple and Movie Maker by Microsoft. If your students need more features, there are several "high-end" editors on the market, such as Adobe Premier and FinalCut Pro. Another tool that should be mentioned is QuickTime Pro. Although this is not a video editor per se (you can't import raw video), it is a powerful tool at a low price. With QuickTime Pro, you have access to simple editing tools (you can shorten a movie or combine two movies) and a wide variety of file formats (you can import numerous file formats and export to QuickTime, AVI, DV, or several other options).

iMovie

iMovie is a digital editor that is a part of the iLife package on Macintosh computers. The ease of use of this application has revolutionized video editing, making it feasible for all of us. Figure 6.12 shows the editing window in iMovie. Note that the clips that have been imported are displayed on the left. A large preview window appears on the right. Students can easily add titles, transitions, and special effects, as well as edit the audio and video clips.

Figure 6.12. Editing digital video in iMovie.

Microsoft Movie Maker

Movie Maker is a similar video editing program that can be downloaded free from the Microsoft site. Figure 6.13 shows the editing window in Movie Maker. Note that the features are basically the same as iMovie, although they are arranged a little differently. Both iMovie and Movie Maker offer tutorials and abundant Help features to get started.

Figure 6.13. Editing digital video in Movie Maker.

iDVD

Although CD-ROMs opened the door for commercial digital video products, the "limited" storage capacity (approximately 900 MB) of CD-ROMs quickly became apparent. However, DVDs can hold up to 17 gigabytes of information, and very high-quality video can be stored on DVDs (usually about 2 hours of full-screen, full-motion video on each side of the disc).

Many computers have the ability to record or "burn" DVDs on DVD discs (called DVD-R for DVD-Recordable). In addition, there are software programs for formatting and organizing the video on the DVD-R discs. Apple has produced two programs (iDVD and DVD Studio Pro) that can be used to create DVDs on Macintosh computers, and there are similar programs available for PCs.

Creating a DVD with iDVD is easy. First, you create and edit your movies in a movie editor, such as iMovie, FinalCut Pro, or Adobe Premier. Before saving the final movie, insert "chapter markers" in the video to designate places where you would like to be able to access a specific point (just like chapters in a book). Next, select a background theme for menus, such as wedding, vacation, memories, or Christmas. Most programs provide built-in themes (with background images, button styles, etc.), or you can create your own interface.

Next, add your movie to the DVD by "dragging" it into the iDVD window (when it is displaying your theme). At this point, iDVD will create two buttons on the Main Menu: "Play Movie" and "Scene Selection." After the DVD is burned, the "Play Movie" button can be used to play the entire movie in a linear fashion. The "Scene Selection" button will offer a list of the chapters that are embedded on the DVD, and the users can branch immediately to any chapter. The menus can also be customized and submenus can be created.

After all of the DVD contents are compiled (which can include video, audio, pictures, and files) and the DVD is previewed, the final step is to "burn" the DVD. Burning a DVD requires a lot of computer resources (be sure you have a powerful computer). Also, before clicking the "Burn" button, you need to close all other programs. Allow plenty of time for the DVD to be recorded—especially the first copy.

SELECTING A DEVELOPMENT TOOL

Each of the development tools described in this chapter has features that are useful for student-created multimedia projects. The following guidelines may help determine which type of tool is best for a particular situation.

- If cost is a factor, application programs or webpages can be the least expensive. Programs such as PowerPoint can be purchased by schools at minimal cost; webpages can be created in text editors or Web creation programs that are free.

- For maximum interactivity, hypermedia programs may be the best. Hypermedia programs are designed to contain hyperlinks to graphics and media elements. In addition, they usually contain question formats and scoring techniques.

- For ease of use, application programs are the best. See Table 6.3 for a comparison of the development tools presented in this chapter.

- Do not use Web programs if a large amount of audio and video must be incorporated into the project.

Table 6.3. Comparison of Development Tools

Attribute	Application	Hypermedia	Webpages	Digital Editors
Learning curve	Low	High	Medium	High
Cost	Low	Medium	Low	Low
Amount of interactivity	Low	High	Medium	Low
Amount of multimedia	Medium	High	Low	High

FACILITATING MULTIMEDIA PROJECTS IN THE CLASSROOM

As the students enter the DEVELOPMENT phase of the project, they compile the media elements based on the information in their flowcharts and storyboards. At this point, the teacher's role is that of a facilitator. This includes the following activities:

- Ensuring that all of the necessary equipment, batteries, software, and so on are available

- Reviewing necessary prerequisite skills related to the technology or concepts related to the content

- Circulating the room, assisting students as they need it

- Monitoring the progress of each group or student, ensuring that students stay on task

- Troubleshooting hardware and software issues

- Conducting formative evaluation and providing ongoing feedback for students' progress

- Being aware of the time allotted for the activity in relation to the progress

- Having a backup plan (or two) in case the technology crashes

- Emphasizing the relationship to the lesson's goals

Multimedia activities in the classroom can be exciting, effective, and motivating. Unfortunately, they also offer opportunities for students to be distracted, off-task, and disruptive. Students may misbehave because they become bored, frustrated, or misdirected. There are, however, several techniques that can assist in keeping students on task and engaged with the activity and the lesson's goals. These techniques include the following:

1. Present clear goals and expectations.

2. Provide adequate structure.

3. Keep students actively involved.

4. Assign "Tech Buddies."

5. Be flexible and ready to adopt.

6. Teach, model, and enforce time management.

Present Clear Goals and Expectations

For some teachers, the thought of having students working cooperatively with multimedia leads to nightmares, as they imagine chaos in the classroom. However, if students are engaged, the discipline problems can actually decrease or disappear entirely! Begin by developing a set of expectations that you and the students can live with—rules that are enforceable. These expectations might include issues such as how to handle the equipment, an appropriate volume level for voices, strategies for seeking help (such as placing a paper cup on the monitor), and so on. Be patient and consistent —you'll be amazed at how captivated the students will become with their activities!

Provide Adequate Structure

Whether your students are first graders or seniors in high school, you must provide a clear framework for them. In other words, "set the stage" in the beginning, telling the students the procedure, exactly what is required (such as writing storyboards), how the activity will be assessed (if you have a rubric, share it with them or let them help you create one), and how much time is allowed for each phase of the activity. If students are working in groups, the roles of the team members should be clear, as well as how the group will be assessed (individually or collectively).

One way to provide structure and assign computer use is by using a Jigsaw cooperative learning approach. For example, each team's graphic artists can work with the graphic artists from other teams to select and review each other's media needs on the class computers. If there are eight groups of students, one person from each group could be designated as the group's graphic artist. These students would form their own group to help create and research each other's graphics on the classroom computers. Similarly, the programmers from each group could work together to produce the templates for the projects.

Keep Students Actively Involved

It has been said that the cure for boredom is curiosity. If students are waiting for their turn with a camera or computer, chances are they may become bored and look for diversions. Multimedia activities must be designed to keep all students engaged at all times. When designing a multimedia project for groups using limited resources, always include supplemental activities that can be completed without hardware. For example, if students are waiting to use a computer, they can conduct research through traditional means (books), work at a learning center that has related manipulatives, evaluate their peers' projects, or write the script for a project.

If limited peripherals (such as a scanner, camera, microphone, etc.) and software are available, you can rotate student groups so that they are assigned a different "station" each day. For example, a scanner might be attached to Computer One; Adobe Photoshop might be installed on Computer Two; a video editor might be installed on Computer Three; and Computer Four can have a connection to the Internet. Rotating assignments allows student groups to plan their time using a scanner, a single copy of Adobe Photoshop, or other limited resources. Students can also use a sign-up sheet to use a particular computer, digital camera, camcorder, or other equipment.

Assign Tech Buddies

Many teachers have found that assigning tech buddies helps to reduce the amount of questions and off-task behavior. By working together, tech buddies can help each other solve problems and troubleshoot. This approach has also been referred to as the "Ask Three Before Me" rule—students must ask three classmates for assistance before seeking the teacher. Student involvement provides valuable assistance for the teacher and helps build students' self-esteem.

Be Flexible and Ready to Adapt

Teachers should accept the fact that technology may not fit neatly into traditional paradigms. For multimedia to foster collaboration, cross-discipline explorations, and complex problem solving, the school schedules may have to be adjusted—some activities may require 30 minutes, others three hours. In addition, Murphy's Law can strike at any time—always have a backup plan (or two).

Teach, Model, and Enforce Time Management

At first, this may seem to be a direct contradiction of the previous guideline (Be flexible and ready to adapt). Flexibility and time management are both important. For example, suppose you have restructured your class schedule to allow three hours for a cross-curricular, multimedia activity. The students, however, are being very creative, and they are experimenting with every font that PowerPoint allows. The three hours are almost over; one group is finished; one is almost done; and the other three groups would need an additional two hours! Possible solutions to this dilemma include setting a kitchen timer to allow specific amounts of time for substeps. For example, you could announce, "You will have 45 minutes to select your background, fonts, and clipart for the project" (assuming that the planning of the project was previously completed). If computers must be shared by various groups and students, computer logs with "time in" and "time out" are also helpful, along with a strict rotational schedule (refer back to Scheduling Computer Time in Chapter 3).

SUMMARY

The final step in the development process is to combine the text, graphics, and media elements with a development tool. There are many alternatives on the market. This chapter focused on several inexpensive options for schools: application programs, hypermedia, webpages, and digital movies. As you are planning the curriculum tools for your classroom, consider these tools and others that will allow your students to produce and deliver their products in a timely fashion.

RESOURCES

Applications and Hypermedia

Adobe (Flash and DreamWeaver): http://www.adobe.com

HyperStudio: http://www.mackiev.com/hyperstudio

iLife: http://www.apple.com/ilife

Movie Maker: http://www.microsoft.com

Multimedia Authoring Web: http://www.mcli.dist.maricopa.edu/authoring

PowerPoint in the Classroom: http://www.actden.com/pp

Digital Video Information on the Web

Adobe Premier: http://www.adobe.com/products/premiere/main.html

DV Magazine: http://www.dv.com

Final Cut Studio: http://www.apple.com/finalcutstudio/finalcutpro

iLife (iMovie, iPhoto, iWeb, iDVD): http://www.apple.com/ilife

Making Movies, A Video Production Guide for Students: http://www.bham.net/bieff/guide1.htm

Movie Maker: http://windowslive.com/Desktop/moviemaker

No Strings Attached (Video Lessons): http://etc.usf.edu/plans/default.htm

HTML Tutorials

An Interactive Tutorial for Beginners: http://www.davesite.com/webstation/html

Free Web Building Tutorials (HTML and CSS): http://w3schools.com

Hypermedia

Flash: http://www.adobe.com

HyperStudio: http://www.mackiev.com/hyperstudio

Image Programs

Adobe (DreamWeaver, Flash, PhotoShop, Acrobat, Illustrator, Premier, etc.): http://www.adobe.com

Corel (CorelDraw and Paint Shop Pro, etc.): http://www.corel.com

Flags of the World: http://fotw.vexillum.com/flags

Clipart ETC: http://etc.usf.edu/clipart/index.htm

Clip Media (Art): http://etc.usf.edu/clip/index.htm

Clip Media (Photos): http://etc.usf.edu/clip/photos.htm

GIF Construction Set (Alchemy Mindworks): http://www.mindworkshop.com

GIMP: http://www.gimp.org/

Graphic Converter: http://www.lemkesoft.com/content/188/graphicconverter.html

iPhoto (Apple iLife): http://www.apple.com/ilife

KidPix: http://www.mackiev.com/kid_pix.html

LView Pro: http://lview.com

NASA Images: http://www.nasa.gov/multimedia/imagegallery/index.html

Picasa: http://picasa.google.com

Scanning Tips: http://www.scantips.com/basics01.html

Tux Paint: http://www.tuxpaint.org

Web Development

DreamWeaver: http://www.adobe.com

Google Sites: http://sites.google.com

iWeb: http://www.apple.com/ilife/iweb

Kompozer: http://kompozer.net

TeacherWeb: http://teacherweb.com

Web.com: http://www.webs.com

Weebly: http://www.weebly.com

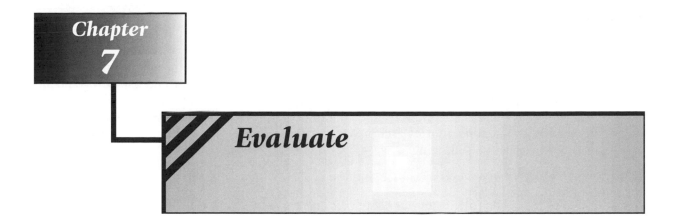

Evaluate

A SCENARIO

Alex enjoyed his chemistry class. His teacher, Ms. Woo, made learning interesting. Instead of daily lectures and individual seatwork, Ms. Woo placed students in collaborate groups and had them work on authentic problems related to the community. One project involved analyzing and reporting on the water quality in a local lake. People swam, fished, and used motor boats in this lake. The results were very interesting! Just as interesting, thought Alex, was the process and final product developed by the students. Ms. Woo continually checked students' progress, was there to answer questions (as well as pose new ones), and ensured students understood her expectations and the objectives of the project. Students were provided with several rubrics that helped outline the expectations. Each group was assigned a particular task related to the overall project, which was later published on the school's website. Each group created webpages based upon its particular task. Ms. Woo had her class conduct this project every semester so data could be compared and analyzed over time. Each class added their results, conclusions and recommendations to an ongoing chart on the website. "It appears as though the water quality is getting worse," Alex commented. "What can we do?" Ms. Woo, who worked closely with the social studies teachers, smiled at Alex and said, "I'm glad you asked. Mr. Redding, your social studies teacher, will ask you the same question. That will be your next project!"

OVERVIEW

To ensure multimedia projects are purposeful, educators need to identify the projects' specific objectives and how these relate to district or state standards. In addition, teachers must correlate the objectives with specific assessment measures to ensure students are learning what has been specified in each objective. Assessment criteria can be clarified and categorized using rubrics. Rubrics can provide feedback about the effectiveness of instruction and provide benchmarks for measuring and documenting students' progress. In addition, rubrics let students know what is expected of them. They serve as a grade contract. Based on the expectations outlined in a rubric, students can plan their time accordingly. For example, if video is not a requirement for a multimedia project, students should not spend time incorporating it into their project unless it is appropriate or they have extra time on their hands. Rubrics can help students set their priorities and better manage their projects, as well as help teachers assess students' progress throughout the development of the multimedia projects.

Poor learning experiences can be avoided through well-planned and frequently assessed projects. Formative assessment provides constructive feedback at each phase of the DDD-E process.

Without it, students may encounter unnecessary obstacles, extra work, frustration, unfinished products, and fragmented learning. Ongoing assessment helps educators teach for understanding and ensures that students are ready to move on to the next step of a project. This chapter defines several assessment techniques and their relationship to multimedia projects. In addition, this chapter provides information on creating rubrics and provides sample rubrics for each phase of the DDD-E process. Topics include the following:

- Alternative assessment techniques

  The role of multimedia in alternative assessment

- Assessment strategies

  Creating a rubric

  Using rubrics

  Additional rubric options

- Assigning grades

  Reflections and future goals

ALTERNATIVE ASSESSMENT TECHNIQUES

There are a variety of ways to evaluate students' learning. Most schools use standardized tests, but critics claim that standardized tests only measure how well a student learns without considering whether he or she can apply what was learned. For example, a student may perform well on a simple mathematics test but still be unable to make correct change. Or a student may score well on a written driving test but be a poor driver. Proponents of alternative assessment claim that a person's capability is found in their ability to produce or perform, not on how well they answer questions on multiple-choice, true or false, or other traditional forms of tests (Ahn 2004; Culbertson and Jalongo 1999; Hersh 2009; Mabry 1999; Rotherham and Willingham 2009). Researchers note that traditional tests tend to reveal only what a student can recall or recognize, often focus on low-level knowledge objectives, and can be culturally biased, distorting student performance. Culture, as well as issues of stereotype, social and psychological factors, poverty, remoteness, access to resources, and health care need to be considered before assumptions can be made about performance on standardized tests (Arbuthnot 2009; Hagie, Gallipo, and Svien 2003; Landau, Greenberg, and Rothschild 2009).

Alternative assessment is assessment in some form other than the true or false, multiple-choice, matching, and fill-in-the-blank responses often associated with standardized tests. Performance-based assessment, authentic assessment, and portfolio assessment are forms of alternative assessment. Many of these terms overlap and are used interchangeably. They are defined as follows.

Performance-based assessment requires teachers to evaluate a student's knowledge and skills by observing the student do something (e.g., participating in a debate, playing an instrument, dribbling a basketball) or create something that results in a tangible product (e.g., a model or drawing, a computer program, a blouse).

Authentic assessment includes performance tests, observations, interviews, exhibitions, and portfolios. The goal of authentic assessment is to involve students in activities that better represent what they are likely to face outside the school setting. The context, purpose, audience, and constraints of the task *must* connect to real-world situations and problems. For example, students might be asked to identify the chemical composition of a given solution by conducting various analyses, or they might take samples from local rivers and lakes and identify pollutants. Both tasks would be performance-based, but the latter would be considered authentic because it involves and addresses a real-world problem.

Portfolio assessment is a systematic collection of a student's best work and may include narrative descriptions, records of observation, test results, student reflections or self-evaluations, and so on. Portfolios show growth over time, focusing on a student's progress rather than on a finished product. A portfolio provides a broad view of a student's achievements. E-portfolios (electronic portfolios) may be used to blend technology, accountability, and assessment. They may be housed online or stored on disc.

Based on the needs of the learner, alternative assessment techniques have the advantage of providing teachers and parents with directly observable products and clear evidence of students' performance. Assessment results are both meaningful and useful for improving instruction. The following guidelines can be used for creating, monitoring, and implementing alternative assessment in the classroom.

- Plan assessment alongside instruction, not as an afterthought. Your assessment plan should represent what is valued instructionally.

- Ensure assessments benefit all learners and inform teaching practices.

- Make expectations clear.

- Collect examples of alternative assessments and activities.

- Include peer assessment techniques. This can enhance students' evaluation skills and accountability.

- Use assessment results to develop learner profiles.

The Role of Multimedia in Alternative Assessment

Creating multimedia projects provides ample opportunities for performance-based assessment, authentic assessment, and portfolio assessment. Table 7.1 identifies project ideas for each of these assessment techniques. Evaluating students on their performance places greater emphasis on comprehension, critical thinking, reasoning, problem solving, metacognitive processes, and the construction of knowledge (Colley 2008; Jonassen 2000; Mabry 1999).

Table 7.1. Multimedia Project Ideas for Various Assessment Techniques

Assessment Technique	Relationship to Multimedia Projects
Performance-Based Assessment	Multimedia projects can be used to demonstrate students' proficiency in specific computer skills; they also serve as a forum for demonstrating and presenting the students' knowledge and skills. For example, using a variety of media elements, students may create a project that demonstrates their knowledge of the water cycle, different body systems, plate tectonics, or other topics.
Authentic Assessment	Multimedia projects may be similar to what students are likely to encounter as professionals. In addition, students may create projects that are designed to gather data for analysis (such as a Webpage that collects information from surveys).
Portfolio Assessment	A multimedia database or e-portfolio can be designed to house digitized samples of a student's work. This includes reading samples (a recording of a student reading aloud), handwriting samples, homework, writing samples, artwork, and performances. Items may be entered into the computer by keyboard, a scanner, microphone, video, or digital camera. Students may also create multimedia resumés.

In addition to evaluating students on the final outcome of their performance, it is important to assess students' progress through each step of the DDD-E process. To create successful multimedia projects, assessment must be ongoing. It begins with the DECIDE process and ends with an evaluation of the final product.

ASSESSMENT STRATEGIES

Checklists, narrative or anecdotal approaches, and rubrics are ways to evaluate a student's performance. Checklists indicate whether certain elements are present, narrative reports consist of a teacher's written notes or documentation of students' progress, and rubrics are used to evaluate designated performance criteria with a rating scale. Each of these can be used to guide students through each step of their project. In addition to teacher observations and anecdotal notes, daily journals (see Chapter 3) can help teachers diagnose each group's progress, problem-solving skills, and social skills. Checklists and rubrics help students know what is expected, leaving the teacher more time to advise and assist students with specific questions.

Creating a Rubric

Before developing a rubric, you must ask yourself the following questions:

- What state or district standards am I addressing?

- What knowledge, skills, or concepts am I trying to assess?

- At what level should my students be performing?

- What criteria should be used to judge students' performance?

After identifying the standards and instructional goals, consider the qualities that need to be displayed in a student's work to illustrate proficient or "top level" performance of these goals. For example, "The student lists and describes the contributions of four people associated with the California Gold Rush." After developing the criteria for the highest level of performance, define the criteria for the lowest level of performance. For example, "The student is unable to list or describe the contributions of anyone associated with the California Gold Rush." After developing the high- and low-level criteria, compare and contrast the two to arrive at the middle level of performance. For example, "The student correctly identifies and describes the contributions of two people associated with the California Gold Rush." If additional distinctions are necessary, make comparisons between the existing criteria to arrive at other score levels.

Moskal and Leydens (2000) discuss the validity and reliability of rubrics. Validity includes the following:

- Content-related evidence—the extent to which the assessment instrument reflects students' knowledge in a particular content area

- Construct-related evidence—the extent to which the assessment instrument measures students' reasoning, problem-solving, or other processing skills

- Criterion-related evidence—the extent the assessment instrument identifies how well a student's performance can be generalized to other, more relevant activities (e.g., how well the student will perform outside of school or in a different situation)

Moskal and Leydens (2000) note that "Since establishing validity is dependent on the purpose of the assessment, teachers should clearly state what they hope to learn about the responding students (i.e., the purpose) and how the students will display these proficiencies (i.e., the objectives)" (p. 4). They list three steps for evaluating the appropriateness of scoring categories to a stated purpose:

1. State the assessment purpose and objectives.

2. Develop score criteria for each objective.

3. Reflect on the following:

    Are all of the objectives measured through the scoring criteria?

    Are any of the scoring criteria unrelated to the objectives?

Teachers should avoid making vague statements such as, "The student covers the topic completely and in depth." What does "in depth" mean? What are the criteria for such an accomplishment? What has the student learned? In addition to validity issues, vague or general statements reduce the reliability of the rubric.

Reliability refers to the consistency of assessment scores. Two forms of reliability are interrater reliability and intrarater reliability. Interrater reliability is based on how well or how closely different evaluators or "raters" assess the same scores. If evaluators come to the same conclusion, then the assessment has "interrater reliability." It is important to have set criteria to guide the rating process. Intrarater reliability focuses on outside factors that may influence the scoring of students' work. For example, a rater's fatigue level, mood, or bias may influence the scoring process if the criteria are too subjective. By establishing a description of the scoring criteria in advance, well-designed scoring rubrics can address this concern (Moskal 2003; Moskal and Leydens 2000).

When designing a rubric, consider the age and ability level of the students. Note the simplicity of the primary rubric at the end of this chapter (see Primary MM Rubric blackline). Encourage student input. This allows students to work toward individual goals and to create their own learning experiences. Keep rubrics short, simple, and to the point. Categorize topic areas or provide separate rubrics for each area, depending on the project's sophistication. For beginning projects, focus on only a few outcomes.

Numbers or words (e.g., deficient, novice, apprentice, intermediate, proficient) may be used as a scale to evaluate learning outcomes. It is important that the criteria for each rating is established and listed on the rubric. For example, expanding upon the Gold Rush example noted earlier, a student would be given a score of "4" if she were able to list and describe the contributions of four people associated with the California Gold Rush; a "3" if she correctly identified and described the contributions of three people associated with the California Gold Rush; a "2" if she were able to list and describe the contributions of two people associated with the California Gold Rush, and given a "1" if she correctly identified and described the contributions of only one person associated with the California Gold Rush. A score of "0" would be assigned if she was not able to do the task. Listing the criteria on the rubric or having it readily available for students provides them with clear expectations and performance standards.

In addition to content, teachers may assess students' multimedia projects according to required media elements, design, and so on. These would be considered in the construction of the rubric as well and are discussed in more detail under "Using Rubrics."

Resources for Creating and Finding Sample Rubrics

Sample rubrics can be found on the Internet at a variety of websites. In addition, there are online tools available to help teachers construct their own rubrics. Examples include the following:

Kathy Schrock's Guide for Educators (assessment and rubric information available at (http://school.discovery.com/schrockguide/assess.html). Lists multiple links to rubric resources, articles, examples, and more.

Midlink Magazine Teacher Resource Room (available at http://www.ncsu.edu/midlink/ho.html). Provides links to rubrics, evaluation resources, and downloadable rubric templates.

Rubistar (available at http://rubistar.4teachers.org). Provides sample rubrics for a variety of topics, as well as an online rubric generator where teachers can create or customize their own rubrics. Both English and Spanish versions are available.

Rubrics allow teachers to clarify criteria in specific forms and make project assessment more objective and consistent. In addition, rubrics allow students to begin their projects with clear and consistent guidelines through which they will be evaluated. Students know what is expected of them and their peers. Rubrics are useful for providing feedback and documenting students' progress.

Using Rubrics

To help students understand how rubrics will be used to evaluate their multimedia projects, review several existing projects. These may be teacher-created for demonstration purposes, samples included with the multimedia program, projects from previous classes, or examples downloaded from the Internet. Review projects that are comparable to your students' ability levels. Encourage students to discuss what they like and dislike about the projects, the projects' strengths and weaknesses, and what they might do to make the project better. Decide what criteria might be used to evaluate the projects. Review sample projects before the DESIGN stage.

As mentioned, rubrics ensure that the students and teacher understand how the project will be evaluated. It is important to provide students with a list of evaluation criteria and standards for the assigned multimedia project at the onset of their projects. Students will know what is expected of them and may put more effort into their projects because of it. Encourage students to use the rubrics to guide them during the learning process and to explain the rubrics to their parents.

Rubrics can be designed to address each step of the DDD-E process and the desired outcome or focus of the multimedia projects. As noted in previous chapters, the steps include:

- DECIDE—Brainstorming and researching

- DESIGN—Planning and designing

- DEVELOP—Gathering and creating media

- EVALUATE—Continual assessment of projects

Figure 7.1 depicts the evaluation stages of the DDD-E process. Each item in the figure is included as a blackline master at the end of this chapter. As previously noted, the teacher reviews daily journals every day to ensure the groups' progress and to help the teacher facilitate instruction. The daily journal entry sheet is in Chapter 3. Additional checklists can be found in Chapter 4.

DECIDE	DESIGN	DEVELOP	EVALUATE
• Research Rubric	• Flowchart Rubric • Storyboard Rubric	• Bug Check	• Self-Evaluation • Group Self-Evaluation • Peer Evaluation • Teacher Evaluation
Daily Journals			

Figure 7.1. Evaluation stages of the DDD-E process.

DECIDE. Assessment begins with the groups' original idea and their ability to define the major sections of their reports, as well as how these sections relate to each other. Students should be able to articulate their research question, explain why it is important, and discuss how they intend to pursue it. Following the students' initial research, the teacher may decide to collect, review, and discuss each group's brainstorming or KWL Knowledge Chart (see Chapter 3), as well as their research findings. Teachers can check the accuracy of the information, ensure that students are using a variety of resources, and verify that the students are addressing the stated questions. Note that the criteria for each score need to be defined by the teacher (and students, if they helped create the rubric). A sample Research Rubric blackline master appears at the end of this chapter.

DESIGN. After their research has been verified, students need to map and define their ideas through flowcharts. After reviewing the flowcharts, the teacher should meet with each group to discuss the anticipated links, sequences, and section relationships identified in their flowcharts. Assessment may be based on the flowchart's structure, links, clarity, symbols, and labels. See the Design Rubric blackline master at the end of this chapter for an example.

Storyboard production can begin after the flowcharts have been approved. Storyboards help students plan how their computer screens will look and relate to each other. Students should make their storyboards as clear and complete as possible. This allows the teacher to provide guidance before the students invest a great amount of time in the final production phase. Teachers may want to provide students with a list of design guidelines (see Chapter 4). The Flowchart Rubric blackline master at the end of this chapter can be used as an example. Again, the criteria for each score need to be defined by the teacher (and students, if they helped create the rubric). The final production phase takes place after the groups' storyboards have been approved.

DEVELOP. In the DEVELOP phase, students construct their final product to meet the standards and criteria set at the beginning of the assignment. Before students submit their projects for final evaluation, projects should go through a review and debugging phase. This is best performed by their peers. Students can check each other's projects to see whether they meet the required criteria, as well as check for programming, spelling, and punctuation errors. A Bug Stops Here blackline master is available at the end of the chapter.

EVALUATE. Self-, peer-, and teacher evaluations occur after the projects are complete. These evaluations provide students with multiple levels of feedback. Self-evaluation encourages students to reflect on what they have learned as well as how it was learned. In addition, it provides students with the opportunity to elaborate on what went well and what they might have done differently. Peer evaluation offers students another audience for their projects. It allows students to measure the extent to which they were able to explain their work and ideas successfully to each other. In addition, peer evaluations allow students to practice their evaluation skills, provide ideas and constructive feedback, and help each other with the projects. Peer evaluations may also be used within groups (intragroup evaluation) to evaluate each member's cooperative efforts. (See Group Self-Evaluation blackline master at the end of this chapter.) Teacher assessment provides ongoing support and guidance, as well as a final evaluation of the project. The teacher's evaluation should reflect the criteria established during the beginning stages of the project.

The project's final evaluation may be based on one or more of the following: content learning, technology skills, design skills (see Additional Rubric Options section), as well as media appropriateness, social skills, or self-reflection, depending on the purpose of the project. The depth and scope of the evaluation should be consistent with the students' age and ability level. Sample evaluation forms are reproduced at the end of this chapter.

Additional Rubric Options

Depending on the project's goal and the students' ability level, teachers may wish to employ multiple rubrics to evaluate various outcomes. For example, a content rubric may be used to evaluate the students' understanding of a particular topic, as well as how well they communicated their knowledge. A technical rubric may review defective links, inoperative media (e.g., video or audio clips), and so on. A design rubric may critique the clarity and consistency of the layout, purpose of the media and navigation options, contrast between text and background, text readability (including fonts, sizes, colors, and styles), types of feedback, and whether the students followed their storyboards and flowchart. A presentation rubric may provide students with feedback on their speaking skills, appearance, organization, professionalism, ability to capture and hold the audience's attention, and so on.

One or more of these rubrics may be provided to the students and attached to the teacher's final evaluation form to aid in the summative evaluation of the students' projects. Examples of each of these rubrics are available at the end of this chapter.

ASSIGNING GRADES

Groups may receive a grade based on the combined, averaged scores of the teacher and peer evaluations (see Figure 7.2). Sample teacher and peer evaluation forms appear at the end of this chapter.

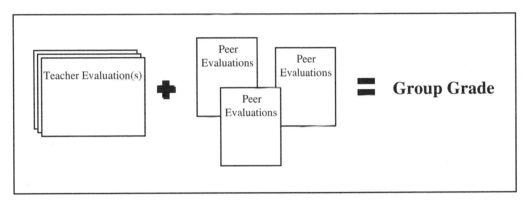

Figure 7.2. Assigning group grades.

Teacher evaluation forms may include an overall rating of a group's journal entries and bibliography information, as well as the average rating of the group's storyboard, design, content, and mechanics rubrics. For example, using the sample teacher evaluation form located at the end of this chapter, a group may have averaged a rating of 2 on their storyboards, design, and technical rubrics, and the teacher may have rated the group's content, journal entries, and bibliography information as 3s (see Figure 7.3). The teacher's evaluation equals 15 points, or an average score of 2.5.

Teacher Evaluation

CRITERIA	0 to .99	1 to 1.99	2 to 2.99	3
Storyboards (see Storyboard Rubric)			2	
Design (see Design Rubric)			2	
Content (see Content Rubric)				3
Technical (see Technical Rubric)			2	
Daily journal entries				3
Bibliographical information				3

Good job! You effectively organized your project and demonstrated excellent teamwork! You averaged 2.5 on your project.

Total __15__

Figure 7.3. Sample teacher evaluation form.

Teachers may choose to insert their own categories for final evaluation. In addition to the sample form presented in Figure 7.3, a blank form is included at the end of this chapter.

Using the Peer Evaluation blackline master, students can evaluate each other's projects. The sample form available at the end of this chapter provides space for students to comment on a project's content and design. It also asks that students rate the project on a scale of 0 to 3. Teachers can evaluate the students' comments and weight them appropriately, transferring the students' average rating to the final grades evaluation form (see Final Grades blackline master). For example, if three groups evaluated a project, and groups 1 and 2 gave the project a 3 and group 3 gave the project a 2, the average score transferred to the final grades sheet would be 2.67. Figure 7.4 shows the final grade sheet with transferred scores from the teacher's evaluation and average peer evaluation. In this example, the group grade equals 2.59, the average of the teacher and peer evaluations. The letter grade depends on the teacher's grading scale.

Final Grades				
CRITERIA	0 to .99	1 to 1.99	2 to 2.99	3
Group Self-Evaluations				
Self-Evaluation				
Peer Evaluations			2.67	
Teacher Evaluation			2.5	

Group Grade __2.59__   Individual Grade _____

Figure 7.4. Final grade sheet with two transferred scores.

Individual grades may be based on the combined and averaged scores of students' self-assessment, the group's self-evaluations, and the group grade (see Figure 7.5). This ensures individual accountability within groups. Sample self-evaluation and group self-evaluation forms appear at the end of this chapter.

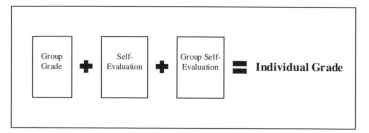

Figure 7.5. Assigning an individual grade.

Using the Self-Evaluation blackline master, students reflect on what they learned. The teacher uses the student's comments to rate the evaluation on a scale of 0 to 3 and adds his or her rationale for the score on the back of the evaluation. For example, if a student is specific and notably reflective on each of the questions, the teacher may score the evaluation a 3. This score is transferred to the final grade sheet.

The Group Self-Evaluation blackline master provides group members with the opportunity to rate the participation and contributions of their teammates, as well as their own. The average score of each student is transferred to his or her final grade sheet. For example, if Samantha received ratings of 3, 2, and 2 from her teammates and rated herself a 3, her average group self-evaluation score would be 2.5. The average of the self-evaluation, group self-evaluation, and group grade determine an individual's final grade. In Figure 7.6, the self-evaluation and group self-evaluation scores have been transferred to the final grade sheet, along with the scores from Figure 7.4. The final individual grade equals 2.70: the average of the group self-evaluation (2.5), self-evaluation (3), and the group grade (2.59). Again, the letter grade depends on the teacher's grading scale.

Final Grades

CRITERIA	0 to .99	1 to 1.99	2 to 2.99	3
Group Self-Evaluations			2.5	
Self-Evaluation				3.0
Peer Evaluations			2.67	
Teacher Evaluation			2.5	

Group Grade __2.59__   Individual Grade __2.70__

Figure 7.6. Final grade sheet with transferred scores.

Teachers are encouraged to make their own evaluation forms designed to meet the needs and ability levels of their students. Teachers can determine the point scale (0–3, 5–10, etc.) and decide how to weigh the various scores for final evaluation. This chapter provides several examples of various rubrics; teachers may pick and choose those that are applicable to their students and multimedia projects. Additional forms for specific projects are included in Chapters 8, 9, 10, and 11.

REFLECTIONS AND FUTURE GOALS

Learning does not end with a grade. Teachers need to provide time for students and themselves to reflect on what went well and how they would change or improve upon the assignment in the future. Students have an opportunity to assess their own learning and contributions on the self-evaluation form, but their feedback about the learning experience may help teachers improve the organization, management, timelines, and so on for the next project. Teachers are encouraged to solicit feedback from students, having them write or discuss what helped them complete the project, where they may have encountered confusion or frustration, and what changes they would recommend for the next project. Student feedback as well as the teacher's own reflections and analyses of student learning should be used to improve future learning experiences associated with the development of multimedia projects.

SUMMARY

The multifaceted nature of multimedia project development encourages many types of assessment. Assessment is ongoing and determines whether a group is ready to proceed to the next stage of development. Checklists, rubrics, and other assessment tools ensure that students know what is expected of them. In addition, rubrics allow teachers to clarify criteria in specific forms and make project assessment more objective and consistent. Teachers need to ensure the validity and reliability of their assessment tools, including rubrics.

The DDD-E model poses several levels of assessment. In the DECIDE stage, students should be able to articulate their research question, explain why it is important, and discuss how they intend to pursue it. Next, they should demonstrate their ability to gather, organize, and synthesize information through brainstorming activities and research. In the DESIGN stage, students need to display how they intend to map and link their ideas together. In addition to examining the project flowcharts, students can explain the anticipated links, sequences, and section relationships identified in their flowcharts with the teacher. Afterward, students can begin producing their project's storyboards. The completed set is assessed by the teacher before the students continue to the DEVELOP stage. The DEVELOP stage includes review and debugging by the students' peers. Final projects include self-, peer, and teacher evaluations. Daily journal entries (see Chapter 3) that assess the group's progress and ability to work together can be collected and submitted with the group's final project. Groups may receive a grade based on the combined scores of the teacher and peer evaluations, and a final individual grade may be based on students' self-assessment, group self-evaluations, and group grade. Rubrics ensure that both students and teacher understand how each step of the project will be evaluated. At the end of the project, student feedback, teacher reflection, and analyses of student learning can be used to improve future multimedia project assignments and learner outcomes.

BLACKLINE MASTERS

This chapter includes an assortment of blackline masters designed to help teachers and students review and evaluate multimedia projects. Blackline masters include:

- Research Rubric: used in the DECIDE phase to ensure that students are ready to move on to the DESIGN phase

- Flowchart Rubric: a form used to evaluate a group's flowchart before the students proceed to the storyboard stage of the DESIGN phase

- Storyboard Rubric: a final evaluation form for a group's storyboards; a storyboard checklist is provided in Chapter 4

- The Bug Stops Here: a review sheet used to help students debug projects during the DEVELOP phase, before the projects are submitted for final evaluation

- Self-Evaluation: one way in which students can reflect on their participation and learning at the end of a multimedia assignment

- Peer Evaluation: one way in which student groups can evaluate other groups' work

- Group Self-Evaluation: a sample of how students may evaluate their own group's performance (intragroup evaluation)

- Teacher Evaluation: a sample of how teachers may evaluate a group's project

- Blank Evaluation: a template for creating your own rubrics

- Content Rubric: a sample rubric for evaluating the content of a project (Note: Educators will need to fill in the objectives and list the performance criteria.)

- Technical Rubric: a sample rubric for reviewing defective links, inoperative media (e.g., video or audio clips), the use of technology (scanners, digital camera, video camera)

- Design Rubric: a sample rubric for evaluating a project's design

- Presentation Rubric: a sample rubric for evaluating project presentations

- Primary MM Rubric: a simple rubric designed for young children

- Final Grades: an accumulating score sheet for determining an individual's final grade, as well as a group grade

REFERENCES

Ahn, J. 2004. Electronic portfolios: Blending technology, accountability and assessment. *Technological Horizons in Education Journal* 31(9): 12, 16, 18.

Arbuthnot, K. 2009. The effects of stereotype threat on standardized mathematics test performance and cognitive processing. *Harvard Educational Review*, 79(3): 448–473.

Colley, K. 2008. Performance-based assessment. *The Science Teacher* V75(8): 68–72.

Culbertson, L. D., and Jalongo, M. R. 1999. But what's wrong with letter grades? Responding to parents' questions about alternative assessment. *Childhood Education* 75(3): 130–135.

Hagie, M., Gallipo, P., and Svien, L. 2003. Traditional culture versus traditional assessment for American Indian students: An investigation of potential test item bias. *Assessment for Effective Intervention* 29: 15–25.

Hersh, R. 2009. A well-rounded education for a flat world. *Educational Leadership* 67(1): 51–53.

Jonassen, D. H. 2000. *Computers as mindtools for schools: Engaging critical thinking* (2d ed.). Upper Saddle River, NJ: Prentice-Hall.

Landau, M. J., Greenberg, J., and Rothschild, Z. 2009. Motivated cultural worldview adherence and culturally loaded test performance. *Personality and Social Psychology Bulletin* 35: 442–453.

Mabry, L. 1999. *Portfolios plus: A critical guide to alternative assessment.* Thousand Oaks, CA: Corwin Press.

Moskal, B. M. 2003. Recommendations for developing classroom performance assessments and scoring rubrics. *Practical Assessment, Research & Evaluation* 8(14). Available at: http://PAREonline. net/getvn.asp?v=8&n=14. Accessed on August 2, 2010.

Moskal, B. M., and J. A. Leydens. 2000. Scoring rubric development: Validity and reliability. *Practical Assessment, Research & Evaluation* 7(10). Available at: http://pareonline.net/getvn.asp? v=7&n=10. Accessed on August 2, 2010.

Rotherham, A., and Willingham, D. 2009. 21st century skills: The challenges ahead. *Educational Leadership* 67(1): 16–21.

Research Rubric

CRITERIA	0	1	2	3
Clarity of research question	There is no research question stated.	Question is vague and hard to understand.	Question is somewhat clear, but could be more precise.	Question is clear and specific.
Supportive answers	There are no answers to the stated question.	Few of the answers support the research question.	Most of the answers support the stated question.	The answers directly support the stated question.
Resources	No or only one reputable resource is used.	Two reputable resources are used.	Three reputable resources are used.	Four or more reputable resources are used.
Accuracy	Information is lacking and is inaccurate.	The information contains more than one inaccurate statement.	The information contains one inaccurate statement.	The researched information is accurate.
Bibliographical information	Information is lacking and is inaccurate.	The information contains more than one inaccurate statement.	The information contains one inaccurate statement.	The information is correct.
Brainstorm (or KWL Knowledge Chart)	Activity was not started.	Activity is missing more than one required element.	Activity is missing one required element.	The information is complete.
				Total _____

From *Multimedia Projects in Education: Designing, Producing, and Assessing, Fourth Edition* by Karen S. Ivers and Ann E. Barron. Santa Barbara, CA: Libraries Unlimited. Copyright © 2010.

Flowchart Rubric

CRITERIA	0	1	2	3
Structure	The flowchart is incomplete or missing.	The flowchart does not have any structure.	Structure is not aligned with the project's goals and content.	Structure is aligned with the project's goals and content.
Branching	There is no branching.	Branching is incomplete.	Branching is complete, but it is not clearly depicted.	Branching is complete and clearly depicted.
Labels	None of the elements of the flowchart are labeled.	More than one of the elements is not labeled.	All elements are labeled, but not easy to understand.	Each element is clearly labeled and easy to understand.
Symbols	No symbols are used.	More than one incorrect symbol is used.	One incorrect symbol is used.	All symbols are correct.
Ease of use	Flowchart cannot be followed.	Flowchart is difficult to follow; it's easy to get lost.	Flowchart is somewhat easy to follow; it could be clearer.	Flowchart is easy to follow and understand.
				Total _____

From *Multimedia Projects in Education: Designing, Producing, and Assessing, Fourth Edition* by Karen S. Ivers and Ann E. Barron. Santa Barbara, CA: Libraries Unlimited. Copyright © 2010.

Storyboard Rubric

CRITERIA	0	1	2	3
Screens	More than two of the required screens are not included.	Two of the required screens are not included.	All but one of the required screens are included.	All required screens are included.
Links	No links are indicated or described.	More than one link or description is incomplete.	One link or description is incomplete.	All links are indicated and described.
Content	Content is missing or incomplete.	Content is complete, but inaccurate.	Content is complete, but difficult to read and understand.	Content is complete, factual, interesting, and easy to understand.
Layout	The design is inconsistent in more than one area.	The design is inconsistent in one area.	The design is consistent, but not clear.	The design is consistent and clear.
Media elements	Media elements are not included.	Some of the media elements are included and described.	All media elements are included, but not all are described.	Required media elements are included and described.
Font, background, and transition	Font, background, and transition information is incomplete.	Two of the requirements are incomplete.	One of the requirements is incomplete.	All font, background, and transition information is provided.
				Total _____

From *Multimedia Projects in Education: Designing, Producing, and Assessing, Fourth Edition* by Karen S. Ivers and Ann E. Barron. Santa Barbara, CA: Libraries Unlimited. Copyright © 2010.

The Bug Stops Here

Name of group being reviewed: _____

Project title: _____

Reviewed by: _____

Spelling Corrections

Word	Page		Word	Page
_____	_____		_____	_____
_____	_____		_____	_____
_____	_____		_____	_____

Punctuation and Grammar Corrections

Problem	Page	Problem	Page
_____	_____	_____	_____
_____	_____	_____	_____
_____	_____	_____	_____

Link and Media Corrections

Problem	Page	Problem	Page
_____	_____	_____	_____
_____	_____	_____	_____
_____	_____	_____	_____

List design and content comments on back.

Self-Evaluation

Name of group: _____

Project title: _____

Group member: _____

How did you contribute to the project?

What did you learn about your topic in the process of developing this project?

What did you learn about multimedia development in the process of developing this project?

What did you learn about yourself in the process of developing this project?

Teacher's Rating: _____   (Comments on back)

From *Multimedia Projects in Education: Designing, Producing, and Assessing, Fourth Edition* by Karen S. Ivers and Ann E. Barron. Santa Barbara, CA: Libraries Unlimited. Copyright © 2010.

Peer Evaluation

Name of group being reviewed: _____

Project title: _____

Reviewed by: _____

Content

What did you learn about this topic that you did not know before?

In terms of content, what are the strengths of this project?

How might the presentation of information be improved?

Design

What are the strengths in the design of this project?

What improvements in the design would you suggest?

On a scale of 0 to 3 (3 being the highest),
how would you rate this project? _____

Group Self-Evaluation

Name of group being reviewed: _____

Project title: _____

Group member: _____

What were your group's strengths?

What were your group's weaknesses?

What are some of the things that you learned about working with others?

What would you do better the next time your group works together?

On the back of this form, list yourself and your group members. Rate yourself and each of your group members' level of participation in the project. 0 = not enough, 1 = fair, 2 = a lot, 3 = did most of the work. Explain your ratings.

From *Multimedia Projects in Education: Designing, Producing, and Assessing, Fourth Edition* by Karen S. Ivers and Ann E. Barron. Santa Barbara, CA: Libraries Unlimited. Copyright © 2010.

Teacher Evaluation

CRITERIA	0 to .99	1 to 1.99	2 to 2.99	3
Storyboards (see Storyboard Rubric)				
Design (see Design Rubric)				
Content (see Content Rubric)				
Technical (see Technical Rubric)				
Daily journal entries				
Bibliographical information				
				Total _____

	CRITERIA	0	1	2	3
					Total _____

Content Rubric

CRITERIA	0	1	2	3
Objective:				
Objective:				
Objective:				
Structure: Begins with an introduction, uses students' own words, and ends with a conclusion.	Does not use students' own words.	Uses students' own words, but intro and conclusion are missing.	Uses students' own words, but intro or conclusion is missing.	Meets all of the requirements.
Flow: Chunks information in a meaningful way, text is easy to follow and understand.	Information is scattered and difficult to understand.	Information is somewhat organized, but difficult to understand.	Information is somewhat organized and easy to understand.	Meets all of the requirements.
Mechanics: Spelling, grammar, and punctuation are correct.	More than four spelling, grammar, or punctuation mistakes are made.	Three or four spelling, grammar, or punctuation mistakes are made.	One or two spelling, grammar, or punctuation mistakes are made.	Meets all of the requirements.
			Total _____	

Technical Rubric

CRITERIA	0	1	2	3
Navigation links	More than two of the links do not work correctly.	Two of the navigation links do not work correctly.	One of the navigation links does not work correctly.	All links work correctly.
Menu links	More than two of the menu links do not work correctly.	Two of the menu links do not work correctly.	One of the menu links does not work correctly.	All links work correctly.
Media elements	More than two of the media elements are not working.	All but two of the media elements are working.	All but one of the media elements are working.	All media elements operate correctly.
Text boxes	More than four text boxes aren't "read-only" or locked where appropriate.	All but three or four text boxes are "read-only" or locked where appropriate.	All but one or two text boxes are "read-only" or locked where appropriate.	All text boxes are "read-only" or locked where appropriate.
Use of different technology tools (e.g. digital camera, scanner, video camera, microphone, etc.)	Project is lacking more than two of the necessary tools.	Project incorporates all but two of the necessary tools.	Project incorporates all but one of the necessary tools.	Project incorporates all of the necessary tools.
				Total _____

From *Multimedia Projects in Education: Designing, Producing, and Assessing, Fourth Edition* by Karen S. Ivers and Ann E. Barron. Santa Barbara, CA: Libraries Unlimited. Copyright © 2010.

Design Rubric

CRITERIA	0	1	2	3
Continuity	Project does not follow storyboards or flowchart.	Project follows some of the storyboards.	Project follows the storyboards but not the flowchart.	Project follows the storyboards and flowchart exactly.
Layout	The layout is not clear and is inconsistent.	The layout is clear but is not consistent.	The layout is somewhat clear and is consistent.	The layout is very clear and consistent.
Purpose of media elements	More than two media elements are not meaningful.	All but two of the media elements are meaningful and add to the project.	All but one of the media elements are meaningful and add to the project.	All media elements are meaningful and add to the project.
Text clarity	Text is not easy to read and doesn't contrast with the background.	The text is not easy to read but contrasts with the background.	The text is easy to read but doesn't contrast with the background.	All text is easy to read and contrasts with the background.
Navigation buttons	None of the navigation buttons are easy to understand.	Some of the navigation buttons are easy to understand.	Most of the navigation buttons are easy to understand.	Navigation buttons are clearly marked and identified.
Feedback	Feedback is not consistent or appropriate.	Feedback is consistent but not appropriate.	Feedback is not consistent, but it is appropriate.	Feedback is consistent and appropriate.
				Total _____

Presentation Rubric

CRITERIA	0	1	2	3
Clarity	Presenter(s) did not speak clearly and did not speak loud enough.	Presenter(s) spoke loud enough, but did not speak clearly.	Presenter(s) spoke clearly but not in a loud enough voice.	Presenter(s) was articulate and spoke in a loud enough voice.
Attire	Presenter's attire was not appropriate.	Most of the presenter's attire was appropriate.	Presenter's attire was appropriate, but not well kept.	Presenter(s) was well groomed and dressed for the presentation.
Professionalism	Presenter(s) was rude and disrespectful.	Presenter(s) seemed indifferent and not attentive to the audience.	Presenter(s) acted professional most but not all of the time.	Presenter(s) was polite, professional, and attentive to the audience.
Organization	Presenter(s) was very disorganized, distracting the presentation.	Presenter(s) was somewhat organized but needs to improve a lot.	Presenter(s) was well organized most of the time.	Presenter(s) was well organized throughout the presentation.
Appeal	Presenter(s) did not captivate or hold my attention.	Presenter(s) held my attention for a short period of time.	Presenter(s) held my attention for most of the time.	Presenter(s) captured and held my attention the whole time.
Outcome	I did not learn anything from this presentation.	I did not learn that much from this presentation.	I learned a lot, but I feel more could have been presented.	I learned a lot from this presentation; it was very thorough.
				Total _____

From *Multimedia Projects in Education: Designing, Producing, and Assessing, Fourth Edition* by Karen S. Ivers and Ann E. Barron. Santa Barbara, CA: Libraries Unlimited. Copyright © 2010.

Primary MM Rubric

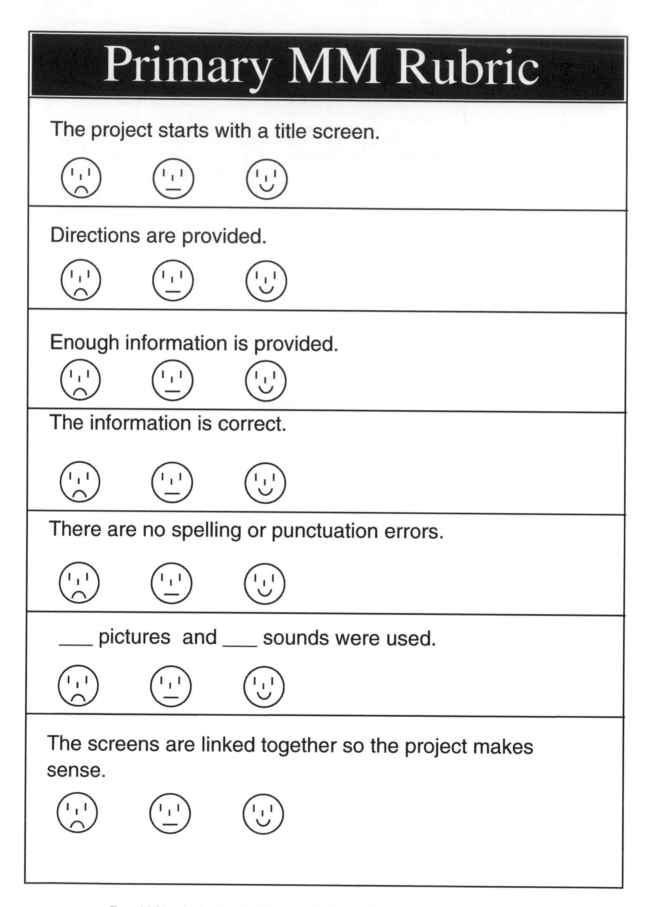

The project starts with a title screen.

Directions are provided.

Enough information is provided.

The information is correct.

There are no spelling or punctuation errors.

___ pictures and ___ sounds were used.

The screens are linked together so the project makes sense.

Final Grades

CRITERIA	0 to .99	1 to 1.99	2 to 2.99	3
Group Self-Evaluations				
Self-Evaluation				
Peer Evaluations				
Teacher Evaluation				

Group Grade _____   Individual Grade _____

Multimedia Projects: Hypermedia

A SCENARIO

Images and discussion of the latest oil spill prompted Ms. Tinder and her students to develop a multimedia project designed to raise awareness of alternative energy. Students worked in pairs to research alternative energy sources. Findings were listed, and the class voted on which energy sources they would like to investigate more thoroughly. Each group was assigned to report on the benefits, costs, barriers, current use, efficiency, research and development, and other factors associated with the use of its alternative energy source. Students were assigned to groups based on interests. Huzaifah, Jamal, Yulisa, Carlos, Paige, and Carrie each expressed solar energy as one of their top interests, so Ms. Tinder assigned them to the "solar group." The students worked together to determine roles and assignments within the group. Jamal and Carlos recently had solar energy panels installed on their homes, so they volunteered to research the cost, bring pictures, and video tape an interview with representatives from the companies that installed the panels. Paige and Huzaifah agreed to examine the efficiency and the research and development of solar energy, and Yulisa and Carrie volunteered to investigate the current use and barriers. Each pair also made notes concerning other factors associated with solar energy.

The planning, design, and development of multimedia projects was common for Ms. Tinder's students. She began the school year with each student creating an "all about me" project, inviting students to express and share their interests, likes, dislikes, and so on in a format of their choice. She knew that the creation of multimedia projects enhanced her students' communication and collaboration, creativity, and critical thinking and problem-solving skills. She also knew that multimedia was a natural part of her students' world and wanted to connect learning in school to students' lives.

"Ms. Tinder," Jamal interjected, "One of the solar reps we interviewed wanted to know if our group would be willing to present our project to the company president!"

"Why not?" smiled Ms. Tinder. "It sounds like a great opportunity to share what you have learned and let the company know you are twenty-first-century learners!"

OVERVIEW

Ideas for multimedia projects are endless, limited only by the imagination of teachers and students. Multimedia projects can be integrated across the curriculum, and they can help students share their knowledge in many ways. In addition to engaging students as they learn specific content standards, multimedia projects may be designed to focus on specific student skills (learning how to use a particular authoring tool), selected media formats (animation), or social skills (cooperative learning).

As with any other curricular unit, planning is an essential part of successful multimedia projects. Limited computer resources may require educators to facilitate several activities at once. This idea is not new; many educators find themselves managing multiple activities in the classroom on a daily basis. For example, during a social studies unit on the Gold Rush, some students may be panning for gold, others may be working on a model of a mining camp, some may be working on written reports, and more may be weighing and evaluating the value of gold nuggets. During multimedia projects, the only difference is that some students may be working on computers while others are working on non-computer-related activities. The computer provides the students with yet another mode of learning—one that provides new insights into organizing, synthesizing, evaluating, and presenting information. This chapter presents several ideas for multimedia projects that can be created with hypermedia tools such as HyperStudio by Roger Wagner (MacKiev.com), Flash by Adobe (www.adobe.com), and others. The tool is not as important as the process. A lesson description, the DDD-E process, and ideas for concurrent activities are provided for each project.

SAMPLE PROJECTS

The following projects address various areas of the curriculum and can be created with most authoring tools. Students should be familiar with the chosen tool before engaging in the multimedia project. The sample projects are designed for classrooms with four computers and 32 students; however, adjustments can be made to meet other conditions. Design teams consist of four students and periods may consist of 30 to 45 minutes. See Chapter 3 for computer scheduling options. Wikis, blogs, Google Apps, learning management systems (e.g., Blackboard, Moodle, etc.), and other online tools may be used for group collaboration, journal entries, sharing of information, and so on.

All About Me

Lesson Description: This project is designed for beginners to provide them with the opportunity to focus on planning, design issues, and the authoring tool. It also addresses standards related to reading and writing. The content of the project is information about the students. Each student team creates an eight-screen (or card) project consisting of the following screens: title, information, main menu, student 1, student 2, student 3, student 4, and credits. (All About Me blackline masters are provided at the end of this chapter).

DECIDE. Assign student teams as described in previous chapters. As a class, brainstorm what makes people interesting, what information students might find in an autobiography, and other related questions. Generate a class list of 10 items (e.g., name, date and place of birth, hobbies, and favorite books, among other things). Assign each student the responsibility of providing information about himself or herself for each of the 10 items.

DESIGN. The next period, provide student teams with a copy of a flowchart (see the All About Me: Flowchart blackline master). Discuss the flowchart's layout and how the screens will be connected. Next, distribute copies of the All About Me: Storyboard Templates (see the blackline masters at the end of this chapter). Explain how the students should complete the storyboards, and how they will use them to create the computer screens of their multimedia projects. Discuss design issues (e.g., contrasting background and text, consistency), and, if possible, show some sample All About Me projects. These sample projects may be created by the teacher or be projects from previous classes. Use the projects to show good and bad examples of design, and let the students discuss what they observe. For example, a bad example might have navigation icons in inconsistent places on the screens, unreadable text, links that do not work, and spelling mistakes. Following the class discussion, provide students with a list of design guidelines (see Chapter 4) and a checklist of expectations (see All About Me: Project Checklist blackline master). During the next period, students work on their team's storyboards, including the storyboards about themselves. Each self-storyboard should contain a paragraph describing the 10 items that the student has answered about him or herself. Teams' storyboards should be assessed and approved by the teacher before students are allowed to work on the computers. Students can track their progress by using the journal entry forms discussed in Chapter 3.

DEVELOP. After the students' storyboards have been approved, teams take turns at the computer stations. If teams are not working on the computers or on their storyboards, the students can be:

- Reading an autobiography or biography of a famous person of their choice and working with a Venn diagram to compare differences and similarities between the person they are reading about and themselves

- Creating a self-portrait using pastels, papier-mâché, clay, or other medium

- Creating a three-dimensional, life-size body cutout of themselves using two sheets of butcher paper and paper scrap stuffing

- Using a life-size cutout of a member of their team to study and illustrate the skeletal system, muscles, and so on

- Researching, gathering, and organizing information for a class newspaper or magazine that describes what occurred during the year most students were born

- Researching information about their place and date of birth, hobbies, or the like, for a possible extension activity that adds more cards or screens to their project

As students complete their multimedia projects, another team reviews the project for problems or errors (see Chapter 7). The corrected project, along with the group and self-evaluations and journal entries, is submitted to the teacher. It may take students four to six periods to finish their project.

EVALUATE. In addition to the teacher's evaluation, peers may be asked to evaluate each other's projects (see the All About Me: Teacher Evaluation and All About Me: Peer Evaluation blackline masters). The students receive a group grade based on the teacher and peer evaluations. Students receive an individual grade based on their group, self, and intragroup evaluations. The two grades can be averaged for a final score. A class Jeopardy game or quiz may be provided to see how well students know their classmates.

Pollution Solution

Lesson Description: This project focuses on the students' ability to research, synthesize, and present information about the hazards of pollution. Other topics are possible, based on the grade level and science standards that need to be addressed. In this example, students are required to use a variety of media formats to help them emphasize the importance of finding solutions to pollution. For instance, they may incorporate digitized photographs and video segments into their projects to illustrate the outcomes of pollution or animations that illustrate a recycling process.

DECIDE. Assign student teams as described in previous chapters. As a class, brainstorm what students already know about pollution and what they want to learn about it (see the KWL Knowledge Chart in Chapter 3). For example, they may know that pollution is harmful, but they may not know the extensive effects of pollution on the environment, what regulations are in effect to help stop pollution, what causes smog, how and what items are recycled, the dirtiest cities in the world, and steps they can take to help stop pollution. Assign or have each group select a different topic to research. Distribute and explain the BrainStorm activity sheet and the Bibliography sheet (see Chapter 3). Before groups brainstorm and begin research about their specific topic, stipulate that groups need to incorporate photos, video segments, or animations to illustrate their points. Ask the students why pictures are important when discussing a topic like pollution. Discuss (or demonstrate) how a picture of dead fish in a river has a stronger impact on people than the text "dead fish in a river" has by itself.

DESIGN. Students may take two or three class periods to research their specific topic. As students are finishing their research, discuss the concept of flowcharts and storyboards. Students need to examine their research findings and organize the information by chunks and meaningful links. Students may want to use index cards to create and manipulate a rough draft of their flowchart and storyboard ideas. Discuss the design issues explained in Chapter 4. View sample projects that contain video, animations, and photographs and have students discuss what makes the projects effective or ineffective. Provide groups with a list of design guidelines; a storyboard template (see Chapter 4); and the journal entry form, project checklist, and bibliography sheet available in Chapters 3 and 4. Explain each form. In addition, provide groups with the storyboard, design, content, and technical rubrics available in Chapter 7. Groups should keep these forms in a binder. Multiple copies of the journal entry form and the bibliography form should also be available. Students may take three to five class periods to complete their flowchart and storyboards.

DEVELOP. After the students' flowchart and storyboards have been approved, teams take turns at the computer stations (see Chapter 3 for a computer schedule). If teams are not working on the computers or on their storyboards, students can be:

- Creating a brochure that lists local recycling centers and ways that people can help stop pollution

- Writing and illustrating a creative story, performing a skit, or creating an audio story (with sound effects and music) about a superhero who helps prevent pollution, a boy (or girl) who always threw trash on the ground until the ground fought back, a container's question as to whether there is life after trash, and other ideas

- Working on a classroom mural of the trash collected from the school yard

- Creating and videotaping a show in which the students demonstrate or create products made from other things, such as bird feeders made from pinecones, peanut butter, and bird seed

- Writing a poem or song about pollution

- Creating and solving math problems related to money earned by recycling

- Developing quiz questions about their project for other students

As students complete their multimedia projects, another team reviews the project for problems or errors (see Chapter 7). The corrected project, along with the project's rubrics, group and self-evaluations, bibliography sheets, and journal entries, is submitted to the teacher.

EVALUATE. Following the teacher's evaluation of the projects, peers need to evaluate each other's projects, too (see Chapter 7). The students receive a group grade based on the teacher and peer evaluations. Students receive an individual grade based on their group, self-, and intragroup evaluations.

When the grading is complete, a main menu can be developed that links the projects together (see Figure 8.1). Students can view the entire multimedia presentation and answer each other's quiz questions for additional content evaluation. The remaining column on the KWL Knowledge Chart can now be completed.

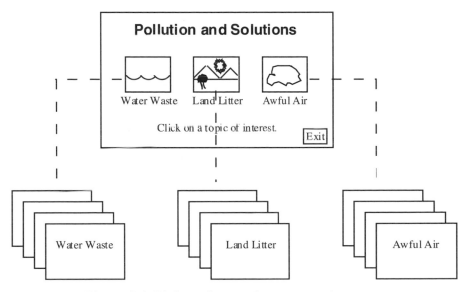

Figure 8.1. Link student projects to a main menu.

Community Concerns

Lesson Description: This project focuses on the students' ability to develop and issue a survey, organize and interpret the collected information, discuss issues with members of the community, and participate in an authentic learning experience. Students are required to research and address community concerns by reading the local newspaper, watching the local news, and interacting with members of the community. Findings are presented in a multimedia project. Authentic learning experiences are the result of conducting interviews, making video recordings and audio tracks of community members, and compiling the data. Multiple standards across different subject areas can be addressed through this and similar activities.

DECIDE. Assign student teams as described in previous chapters. As a class, discuss the concept of a community and what issues their community may be facing. Topics may include the homeless, curfews, the elderly, crime, education, and other concerns. Assign or have each group select a different topic to research. Explain that their research should include local newspaper articles and television news, as well as interviews with community members. Distribute the BrainStorm activity sheet (see Chapter 3) to help students organize the possibilities of their topic. During the next two or three class periods, discuss how to construct a survey and, if possible, distribute sample surveys. Students should think about questions that are important to their particular topic. For example, students researching the concerns of the elderly may ask the elderly questions regarding health care, social security, transportation, recreation services, and family concerns. This student group may contrast and compare answers they receive from the elderly with answers they receive from other age groups. All of the data are accumulated, synthesized, and evaluated. The teacher should approve the surveys before students begin their interviews. During the interviews, students should ask for written permission to record, video, or photograph the person being interviewed. Students can keep track of their sources using the Bibliography sheet (see Chapter 3).

DESIGN. Discuss the concept of flowcharts and storyboards. Students need to examine their research findings and organize the information by chunks and meaningful links. Students may want to use index cards to create and manipulate a rough draft of their flowchart and storyboard ideas. Discuss the design issues explained in Chapter 4. View sample projects that contain audio tracks, video, and photographs, and have students discuss what makes the projects effective or ineffective. Provide groups with a list of design guidelines, a storyboard template (see Chapter 4), and the journal entry form and project checklist available in Chapters 3 and 4. Explain each form. In addition, provide groups with the storyboard, design, content, and technical rubrics available in Chapter 7. Groups should keep these forms in a binder. Multiple copies of the journal entry form and the bibliography form should be available. Students may take three to five class periods to complete their flowchart and storyboards. Remind students to complete daily journal entries (see Chapter 3).

DEVELOP. After the students' flowchart and storyboards have been approved, teams take turns at the computer stations. If teams are not working on the computers or on their storyboards, students can be:

- Proposing a club or fund-raising campaign that supports their specific topic

- Developing quiz questions about their project for other students

- Working on a model of their community

- Creating a travel brochure about the benefits of their community

- Writing letters to their local representatives about their findings and concerns

- Composing letters to classes in other communities, encouraging them to conduct the same surveys and share their results (e-mail or regular mail)

- Researching and constructing models or pictures of historical places, events, or people tied to their community

- Creating an interesting facts or trivia game about their community to play with other students

As students complete their multimedia projects, another team reviews the project for problems or errors (see Chapter 7). The corrected project, along with the project's rubrics, group and self-evaluations, bibliography sheets, and journal entries, is submitted to the teacher.

EVALUATE. Students may choose to share their projects with local community members. Peers and teachers can also evaluate the projects. Students may receive a group grade based on the average score of their peer, teacher, and community evaluations. Individual grades are calculated by the group grade, self-, and intragroup evaluations.

All That Jazz

Lesson Description: This project focuses on the students' ability to research, synthesize, and present information about different styles of music. In addition to standards related to reading and writing, students have the opportunity to address standards related to the historical and cultural context of music. Students are required to incorporate audio clips of a selected music style into their projects to help teach other students about music. For example, students creating a project about ragtime could include audio clips of *The Entertainer* and the *Maple Leaf Rag* while discussing the contributions and history of Scott Joplin. Each team chooses or is assigned a specific music style and generates a multimedia project that reports assigned information about that style. Educators may choose to impose a specific layout and style for student storyboards and flowcharts; hence, the projects will contain the same topics and can be connected at the end of the project.

DECIDE. Assign student teams as described in previous chapters. As a class, generate a list of different types of music (e.g., rock-and-roll, ragtime, classical, jazz, country-western). Discuss what students already know about certain types of music and what they would like to learn about the types of music (see the KWL Knowledge Chart in Chapter 3). For example, they may know that Elvis Presley is considered the King of Rock and Roll, that Beethoven wrote classical music, and that ragtime was popular during the 1920s. Students may want to learn the origins of country music or find out more about New Age music. In addition to their topics of interest, ask students to research the following information: the music's history and peak(s) of popularity, at least three musicians and their history and contribution to the music style, and additional music titles and interesting facts. Randomly assign or let students choose a music style from the list. Distribute the BrainStorm activity sheet from Chapter 3. To adhere to a specific project format, explain that each group's BrainStorm sheet should contain the following information: the music type should be placed in the Main Idea bubble, and Related Idea bubbles should contain music history, musicians, music titles, and interesting facts. Students can create additional Related Idea bubbles for other topics. Branches from the Related Idea bubbles will contain more specific information about the topic. Allow students three to five periods for research, reminding them that audio clips are required for the project. Assist students with their research by bringing in a variety of music recordings on CDs or audio clips.

DESIGN. As students are finishing their research, discuss the concept of flowcharts and storyboards. As a class, discuss how the gathered information might best be organized, chunked, and linked together. Create a flowchart for everyone to follow (see Figure 8.2).

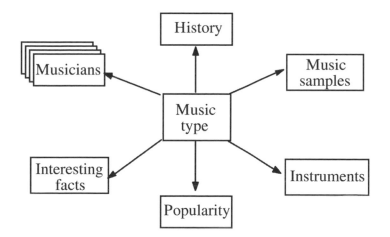

Figure 8.2. Sample flowchart.

Next, discuss the design issues explained in Chapter 4. View sample projects that contain music clips and have students discuss what makes the projects effective or ineffective. Discuss storyboard designs and decide on a standard layout for everyone to use. Distribute the journal entry form and project checklist available in Chapters 3 and 4. Explain each form. In addition, provide groups with the storyboard, design, content, and technical rubrics available in Chapter 7. Students may take three to five class periods to complete their flowchart and storyboards.

DEVELOP. After the students' flowchart and storyboards have been approved, teams take turns at the computer stations. Ensure students are familiar with various audio formats and compression techniques (see Chapter 5). If teams are not working on the computers or on their storyboards, students can be:

- Writing a persuasive report for a future debate explaining why their music style is the best

- Developing quiz questions about their project for other students

- Developing a board game about the life of a composer

- Reading a biography of a composer and designing a diorama depicting and explaining an important event in the composer's life

- Learning and interpreting the lyrics to a particular song

- Creating a watercolor or acrylic painting that depicts the mood or feelings associated with a particular piece of music

- Learning to play a music selection

- Creating a composition of their own

As students complete their multimedia projects, another team reviews the project for problems or errors (see Chapter 7). The corrected project, along with the project's rubrics, group and self-evaluations, bibliography sheets, and journal entries, is submitted to the teacher.

EVALUATE. Both students and teachers evaluate the projects. The students receive a group grade based on the teacher and peer evaluations. Students receive an individual grade based on their group, self-, and intragroup evaluations. When the grading is complete, a main menu can be developed that links the projects together. The remaining column on the KWL Knowledge Chart can now be completed. Teachers may want to create a quiz or short essay exam that assesses students' knowledge of the presented projects.

Sherlock Project: A Problem-Solving Adventure

Lesson Description: This project focuses on the students' ability to solve problems, research, and develop interdependent clues to produce a multimedia project that demonstrates their processing skills. In addition, graphics and pop-up text boxes can be required components of the project. Students are required to create a mystery that is solved by finding and deciphering the various clues within the project. For example, a group may use the theme of a haunted house and tell the story of how the only way out of the house is to enter the correct combination into the passageway door. Throughout the project, students create mathematical and logic problems that will help users determine the correct code. For example, in the first room of the house, the following clue could be discovered when users click on a ghost (see Figure 8.3):

It happened on a scary night,
One I know was full of fright;
Yet Joey Jones, as calm as could be,
Said, "Divide 800 by the answer in Room 3."

A text box may appear, the clue may be recorded audio, or both. Room three's clue might appear when users click on a book (see Figure 8.4):

Weary travelers visit here;

Guess how many times a year?
(7 * 8) – (10 + 21)

By combining the clues in rooms one and three, the answer to room one is 32. Room six's clue may indicate that this is the first number in the combination. For example, upon visiting room six, the users may find the following scrawled on the wall (see Figure 8.5):

Room 1 = 1st number to combination

Projects can be made much more complex and sophisticated by integrating current areas of study, incorporating outside research into the answers to the clues, making answers to clues dependent on more than one other clue, and incorporating different media that become part of the clues. To begin, limit students to six clues in the puzzle.

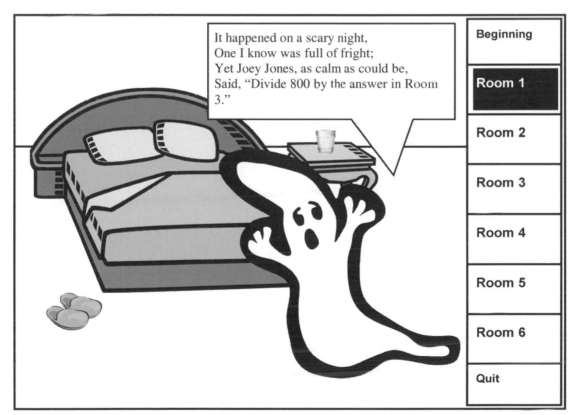

Figure 8.3. Sample screen design for room one.

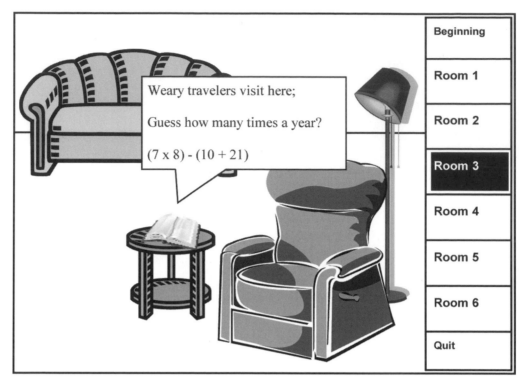

Figure 8.4. Sample screen design for room three.

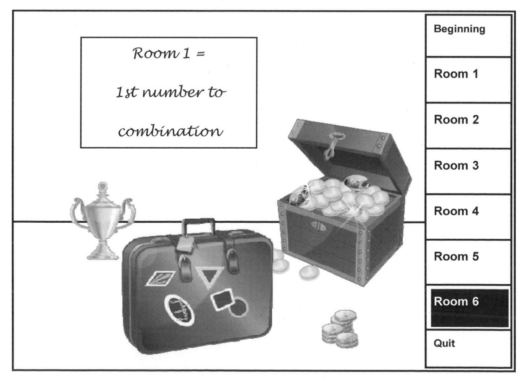

Figure 8.5. Sample screen design for room six.

DECIDE. Assign student teams as described in previous chapters. As a class, discuss the different strategies students can use when solving a math problem, as well as the basic problem-solving steps: (1) understanding the problem, (2) devising a plan, (3) carrying out the plan, and (4) looking back. Discuss the importance of gathering all information before coming to a conclusion about a problem. Illustrate this by distributing one puzzle clue to each different student group (see the Introductory Puzzle blackline master at the end of this chapter). Ask the students if they can solve the puzzle. Obviously, they cannot, because they each hold only one piece to the puzzle. Randomly select groups to read their puzzle pieces aloud, while everyone else takes notes. Inquire whether students can solve the puzzle after each clue. Note that some clues may not make any sense until other clues are read, and that some clues are interdependent (they rely on other clues for additional information). Some clues may have to be repeated. After all of the clues are read, discuss the answer and how students arrived at it. Reflect on the interdependent puzzle pieces and the importance of gathering and understanding all the clues.

Explain that students are going to create a multimedia project based on the puzzle example. Their project should contain a theme (e.g., a haunted house, a pirate's treasure, outer space, the jungle) and their clues should be hidden (pop-up text boxes) or part of the graphic environment. Users should experience traveling from room to room or place to place.

Let student teams brainstorm about a specific theme and a mystery to go along with it. For example, using an outer space theme, the story might involve the crash of a spaceship on an unknown planet; the clues might spell the name of the planet or give its position from the sun. Or, using a pirate theme, the story might involve the location of a buried treasure; the clues could provide the x and y coordinates to a location on a treasure map. After a theme and a story have been decided, students can discuss the solution to their mystery and create clues that users will need to solve the mystery. Remind students to make some of their clues interdependent. Provide students with two or three periods to complete this first step.

DESIGN. Once student teams have finished their puzzles, review the concepts of flowcharts and storyboards. Each clue should have its own storyboard, and the flowchart should show the navigation possibilities throughout the project. Clue cards or screens may be linked to a central location, be accessible from every clue card, or found attached to another clue card. Discuss the design issues explained in Chapter 4. If possible, view sample problem-solving projects for additional design ideas. Provide groups with a list of design guidelines, a storyboard template (see Chapter 4), and the journal entry form and project checklist available in Chapters 3 and 4. Explain each form. Also provide groups with the storyboard, design, and technical rubrics available in Chapter 7 and the Puzzle Rubric blackline master at the end of this chapter. Groups should keep these forms in a binder and complete daily journal entries.

DEVELOP. After the students' flowchart and storyboards have been approved, teams take turns at the computer stations. If teams are not working on the computers or on their storyboards, students can be:

- Working on problem-solving puzzles provided by the teacher or brought in by other students

- Creating a record-keeping sheet for users to keep track of their notes as they attempt to solve their completed project

- Researching and contributing to a class book on mathematical magic tricks

- Reading and acting out a mystery on video

- Playing problem-solving games like Master Mind and chess

- Researching and reporting on famous (fictional or nonfictional) detectives

- Writing a mystery and creating puppets for its production

As students complete their multimedia projects, another team reviews the project for problems or errors (see Chapter 7). The corrected project, along with the project's rubrics, group and self-evaluations (see Chapter 7), and journal entries, is submitted to the teacher. Provide the students with at least 10 class periods on the computer to finish a 10-card or screen project, especially because some of the students will spend their development time creating and researching different pictures for their project's theme. Clip art libraries should be made available to the students.

EVALUATE. Following the teacher's evaluation of the project, peers need to evaluate each other's projects as well (see Chapter 7), remembering that specific content may or may not be an integral part of the project. Emphasis should be placed on the clarity of information, sophistication of the puzzle, use of graphics, and overall design. For alternative evaluation forms, see the puzzle rubric and Peer Puzzle Evaluation blackline masters at the end of this chapter. Each Sherlock project should be shared and solved by the different groups.

SUMMARY

The possibilities for multimedia projects are endless, and emphasis on student learning outcomes can be placed in a variety of areas. This chapter presented sample multimedia projects that focus on different areas of the curriculum and learning outcomes. It also provided a variety of ongoing activities for students not working on computers. Extension activities for the projects presented in this chapter include sharing projects with peers over the Internet or with the school and community at local conferences. Projects may also be recorded to DVDs for student distribution and archival purposes.

BLACKLINE MASTERS

This chapter contains variations on several blackline masters presented in other chapters, providing teachers with additional ideas for creating their own checklists and evaluation forms that are specific to the students' projects and ability levels. Specific forms have been designed for the All About Me and Sherlock projects. References are also made to the checklists and evaluation forms in other chapters. Blackline masters in this chapter include:

- All About Me: Flowchart: a flowchart for All About Me projects

- All About Me: Storyboard Template: an alternative storyboard layout

- All About Me: Project Checklist: a specific checklist for All About Me projects

- All About Me: Teacher Evaluation: a simplified evaluation sheet for All About Me projects

- All About Me: Peer Evaluation: a specific evaluation sheet for All About Me projects

- Introductory Puzzle: a story problem containing independent clues

- Puzzle Rubric: one way of evaluating problem-solving adventure projects

- Peer Puzzle Evaluation: an alternative peer evaluation form for problem-solving adventures.

All About Me: Flowchart

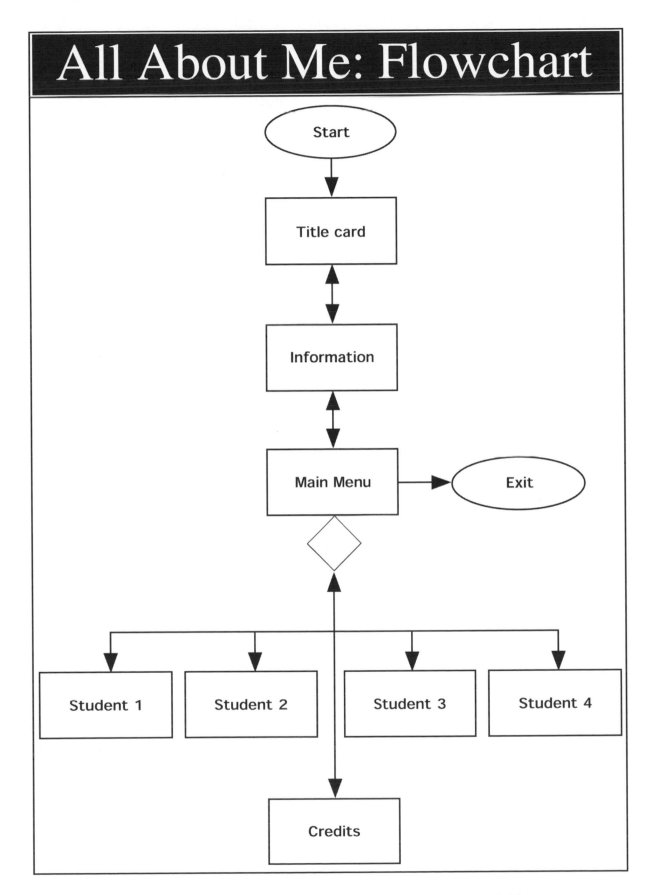

From *Multimedia Projects in Education: Designing, Producing, and Assessing, Fourth Edition*
by Karen S. Ivers and Ann E. Barron. Santa Barbara, CA: Libraries Unlimited. Copyright © 2010.

All About Me: Storyboard Template

	Font	Size	Style	Justification	Color
Title					
Text					

Button	Go to	Transition	Other

Background: _____

Border: _____

Pictures: _____

All About Me: Project Checklist

Team Name _____

Before developing your project at the computer, complete the following:

☐ Flowchart   ☐ Storyboards

Make sure your project has:

☐ A minimum of _____ pages (or cards).

☐ A maximum of _____ pages (or cards).

☐ A Title page (or card).

☐ An Information page (or card).

☐ A Main Menu.

☐ A page (or card) with a paragraph description for each member in your group.

☐ A Credits page (or card).

☐ Appropriate navigation options.

☐ Text that is easy to read and is accurate.

☐ Complete sentences with correct punctuation, grammar, and spelling.

☐ The assigned media requirements:

_____ Clip art

_____ Original drawings (use of paint tools)

_____ Audio

☐ Other: _____

From *Multimedia Projects in Education: Designing, Producing, and Assessing, Fourth Edition*
by Karen S. Ivers and Ann E. Barron. Santa Barbara, CA: Libraries Unlimited. Copyright © 2010.

All About Me: Teacher Evaluation

CRITERIA	0	1	2	3
Continuity	Project does not follow storyboards or flowchart.	Project follows some of the storyboards.	Project follows the storyboards but not the flowchart.	Project follows the storyboards and flowchart exactly.
Content and mechanics	Project does not contain paragraphs about each team member.	Project contains paragraphs about each team member but there are many errors.	Project contains paragraphs about each team member with one or two errors.	Project contains paragraphs about each team member without any errors.
Media elements	None of the media elements have been incorporated.	Two or more media elements don't work, or few are incorporated.	All media elements are incorporated, but one does not work.	All media elements are incorporated and work.
Navigation buttons	None of the navigation buttons are functioning correctly.	Some of the navigation buttons are functioning correctly.	Most of the navigation buttons are functioning correctly.	All navigation buttons are functioning correctly.
Design	None of the design guidelines were followed.	Some of the design guidelines were followed.	Most of the design guidelines were followed.	All design guidelines were followed.
Daily journal entries	Journal entries are missing for three or more days.	Journal entries are missing for two days.	Journal entries are missing for one day.	No journal entries are missing.
				Total _____

All About Me: Peer Evaluation

Name of group being reviewed: _____

Project title: _____

Reviewed by: _____

What are the strengths of this stack?

How might the presentation be improved?

What improvements in the design would you suggest?

On a scale of 0 to 3 (3 being the highest), how would you rate this project? Why?

Introductory Puzzle

Help Mr. Alfonzo calculate the average number of pages read in one week by a group of his students: Fred, Ethel, Lucy, Ricky, Wilma, and Betty.

Both Fred and Ethel read two books with 70 pages each. In addition, Fred read a 20-page book about frogs.

Lucy read the same frog book as Fred, the same cat book as Barney, and half of the dog book that Ricky read.

Ricky read a 20-page book about dogs.

Barney read a 60-page book about cats and two 30-page books.

Both Wilma and Betty read the same books as Ethel.

Answer: 115 pages. [Fred: (2x70) + 20 = 160; Ethel: 2x70 = 140; Lucy: 20 + 60 + (20÷2) = 90; Ricky: 20; Wilma: 140; Betty: 140] Divide total pages by 6.

Extension Activities:
- Calculate each student's average number of pages read in one week.
- Determine the range, mode, and medium of the group. Compare and contrast this to the group mean.
- Track and calculate the average number of pages read in one week by individuals and the class. Compare this with other classes and age groups.
- Create a bar graph that illustrates the favorite genre of the class. Compare this with other classes and age groups.

Puzzle Rubric

CRITERIA	0	1	2	3
The project presents users with the goal(s) and objectives of the puzzle.	Project does not have goals or objectives stated.	Project presents a goal, but no objectives.	Project presents objectives, but no clear goal.	Project presents clear goals and objectives for the puzzle.
The group uses several interdependent clues.	The project does not have interdependent clues.	The project has one interdependent clue.	The project has two interdependent clues.	The project has three or more interdependent clues.
The group includes all of the necessary info to solve the puzzle, and the design of puzzle is appealing.	Not enough information is included, and the design is not appealing.	Not enough information is included, but the design is appealing.	Enough information is included, but the design is not appealing.	Enough information is included, and the design is appealing.
The puzzle challenges the user's thinking skills, yet it isn't too difficult to complete.	The puzzle is too simple.	The puzzle is too difficult to complete.	The puzzle is somewhat challenging, but not challenging enough.	The puzzle is challenging, but not too difficult to complete.
It is easy to navigate through the puzzle - buttons are easy to understand and work.	Buttons are not easy to understand and some do not work.	Buttons are easy to understand, but some do not work.	Buttons are not easy to understand, but they all work.	Buttons are easy to understand, and they all work.
				Total _____

Peer Puzzle Evaluation

Name of group being reviewed: _____

Project title: _____

Reviewed by: _____

What are the strengths of this stack?

How might the presentation be improved?

Explain why you were able or unable to solve the puzzle.

On a scale of 0 to 3 (3 being the highest), how would you rate this project? Explain your answer.

Multimedia Projects: Webpages

A SCENARIO

The students in Mr. Romano's class speak a language that didn't exist a few short years ago. Terms like Google, tweet, blog, wiki, podcast, YouTube, MySpace, and Facebook are common and very familiar to the students. Most of the students have a FaceBook or MySpace account that they monitor frequently. Social networking is a part of their daily life.

With this in mind, for their next science project, Mr. Romano wanted his students to focus their online knowledge to create an informational website about forensic science. Most of the students were well versed in TV shows such as NCIS, and they knew that science could be used to solve crimes—new or "cold" cases. What they needed, however, was a better understanding of how fingerprints, DNA, and trace evidence could be used to solve crimes.

As the students worked through the DDD-E process, they conducted research via Google and other databases and located resources (such as images and charts) on the Web. Mr. Romano also arranged for a speaker to visit from the state's crime lab, along with a police detective. While the visitors were available, Kevin recorded an interview with questions that had been scripted. Throughout the process, they were reminded that their final projects should be accessible for everyone on the Web—even with a "slower" modem. Therefore, they were careful about the file size of their photos and the length of the audio clips.

When the projects were ready for testing, Mr. Romano uploaded the files to a Web server, and each student contacted a friend or relative for an online review. When the projects were finished, the students added their school's e-mail address for feedback in the footer of each page. Proud of their work, many of the students also added a link to the website from their MySpace pages.

OVERVIEW

The World Wide Web is a powerful resource for K–12 education. Never before has the educational community had such an inexpensive, easily accessible method of communicating and distributing information. It opens doors to multicultural education, establishes real-world learning experiences, promotes higher-order thinking skills, enables social networking, and helps increase motivation and writing skills.

The Web offers a wonderful environment for students to create and publish multimedia projects. These projects can reside on a local hard drive (for individual use), they can be shared on an intranet (for internal viewing only), or they can be placed on the Internet (for the whole world to see).

There are many reasons for students to create websites. Besides sharing their artwork and stories with others, students can collect data for original research projects and produce reports that are linked to authentic, dynamic information sources. They can also post school news for the community, establish online homework assignment centers, create subject guides with links to the Internet, or produce interactive lessons or WebQuests (see http://www.webquest.org).

The projects outlined in this chapter are examples of school-based activities that involve Web-based development. The first (School Newsletter) and second (Our Town) projects require that the students interact with others to acquire the information needed.

The Web is also a great place for students to publish reports on a variety of topics that they can share. By creating a Web-based report, they can include links to resources available at other sites. The "Sailing the Internet with Magellan" project is an example of a report that incorporates many sites but also includes original material that has been synthesized by student groups.

The final project in this chapter focuses on creating instructional materials to be distributed on the Web. Similar to interactions designed in hypermedia programs, students can provide information on a webpage and then embed questions to test the knowledge of the users.

SAMPLE PROJECTS FOR WEB-BASED DEVELOPMENT

The following projects can be created with tools ranging from text editors and word processors to sophisticated Web creation programs (such as KompoZer, iWeb, or DreamWeaver). Online Web editors with multiple templates and free hosting are also available at Weebly, Google Sites, and other resources. Teachers should choose the most appropriate tool for their students and ensure that their students are familiar with the tool before beginning the project (see Chapter 6 for more information on Web authoring tools).

The sample projects can be designed and developed by individual students or by groups of up to six students. In all cases, it is important to maintain a thorough review cycle before uploading the pages, particularly if they will be accessible through the Web.

School Newsletter

Lesson Description: The School Newsletter project is similar to a personal homepage; however, it includes information about the entire student body rather than just individual students. This project is ideal for student groups. Each group can be assigned one particular aspect of student life, such as sports, clubs, drama, scheduling, faculty profiles, upcoming events, and so on.

The online school newsletter can supplement a print newsletter, or it can be developed separately. If the students are in a journalism course, or if the school newspaper is interested in establishing an online presence, the project can serve as an extension and integration of other school activities. If there is already an online newspaper at your school, this project can have a narrower focus, such as a newsletter for an individual class or club.

DECIDE. As a class, brainstorm potential topics that could be included in an online newsletter. Allow time for the students to investigate resources available at the school, such as statistics for sports, electronic files of school history, photographs, or other archival information. Research and discuss different layouts for the newsletter. Microsoft Office provides numerous newsletter templates to help students get started (see Figure 9.1).

Figure 9.1. Sample Microsoft Office newsletter templates.

Assign student teams that will focus on one particular aspect of student life. Allow plenty of time for the students to review other school websites and investigate the format of other online newspapers. Ask them to conduct a search and visit other school newsletters and websites.

DESIGN. Discuss the overall flow of the lesson with the entire class. Emphasize the need for a consistent interface for the entire online newsletter, as well as the need for each section to be unique. Discuss navigation options and whether the project should incorporate frames or tables. Other ideas might include the following:

- Using the school mascot and colors as a theme

- Including audio clips with interviews

- Podcasting audio and/or video news

- Creating a visual tour of the school

- Linking to the district website

- Including information about the community

Remind the students that they must be careful not to include personal information (such as photos or home addresses) about individual students. Also, emphasize the need to involve the school's administrators in the review cycle.

DEVELOP. After the students' flowchart and storyboards have been approved, teams take turns at the computer stations (see Chapter 3). Other activities that the students can work on include the following:

- Reviewing hardcopy newsletters from the school

- Taking pictures of the school and community

- Reviewing video from sports events for possible inclusion in the project

- Recording greetings, speeches, and other narratives for the project

- Experimenting with alternate ways to display statistics and other data.

EVALUATE. As students complete their portion of the online newsletter, another team reviews the pages for problems or errors. If possible, the pages should be tested on different computers and operating systems (Macintosh and PC), as well as with different browsers. Be sure to include as many administrators, teachers, coaches, and students as possible in the review cycle. The club's president and faculty sponsor should authorize all content that relates to a particular club or organization before being uploaded to the Internet or intranet.

Our Town

Lesson Description: This project focuses on research, interactions with community members, and students' ability to organize and interpret collected information. Students are required to create a website for the community or nonprofit organization. If possible, they should collect or create photographs, video, and audio samples that reflect the flavor of the community and focus on its unique attributes.

DECIDE. As a class, discuss the community and possible topics for a website. Allow time for students to search for local organizations that already have websites. Brainstorm in small groups to generate as many ideas as possible for consideration. For example, they might create a website for the local park, or conduct research on the air or water quality and post the results on the Web. Other possibilities include creating a website to attract tourists or producing a site that presents a local, historical event, or person.

As the students conduct their field research, they should ask for written permission to record, video, or photograph anyone whom they want to include on the website. If existing graphics are used, they should seek permission to scan the images. Students can keep track of their sources using the Bibliography sheet in Chapter 3.

DESIGN. Allow time for the students to review websites that have similar content to what they are targeting. As they outline their intended content, remind them that they must keep the scope within the constraints allowed. In other words, if this is a short-term project, they may be limited to creating only a few pages. Ask them to consider the target audience for the website—it might include local people or a worldwide audience. They should also think about including words and phrases that would optimize the possibility of finding the website via a search engine.

DEVELOP. Teams can alternate between data collection, media production, and the creation of their webpages. The focus should be on community involvement and focus. In addition to working on the computer, students can be:

- Creating a printable travel brochure for tourists

- Researching the town's history

- Interviewing senior community members about the community's evolution

- Photographing community groups and historical sites

- Recording unique sounds and videos

- Interviewing the mayor or other elected officials.

EVALUATE. As students complete their webpages, the teacher, other students, the community members who were involved, and the administration should review the projects. It is important that each page be thoroughly reviewed before it is uploaded to the Internet. In addition, the copyright releases for all media elements should be documented and filed for future reference.

Sailing through the Internet: A Research Project about Ferdinand Magellan

Lesson Description: This research project encourages students to use resources on the Internet as integral parts of the report. The project requires students to locate relevant information and integrate the resources into a report with links at appropriate places throughout the report. Before assigning such a project, teachers should conduct Internet searches to verify that appropriate material exists for the topic areas assigned. Internet filters should be used to prevent students from accessing inappropriate information as they conduct their searches. The example focuses on a report on Ferdinand Magellan (see Figure 9.2). Because so many topics already have related websites, it is important to assign topics that are unique in some way and will require either a synthesis of existing websites or the creation of a unique approach/topic.

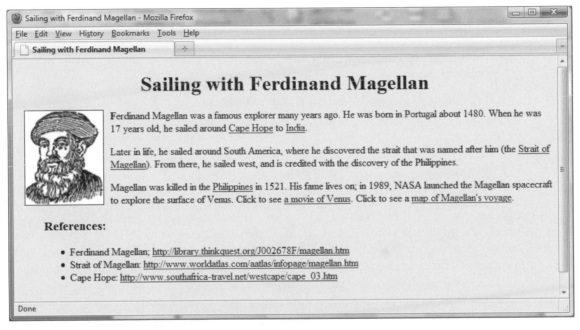

Figure 9.2. Ferdinand Magellan report.

DECIDE. Provide an overview of the project's goals. Assign teams and allow the students to select a topic from a prepared list (in this case, a list of explorers). As a class, brainstorm what students already know about their assigned explorer and what they need to know (see the KWL Knowledge Chart in Chapter 3). For example, they may know that these persons are famous explorers but not the exact dates or routes of their explorations. Next, have the students speculate about the information they might find about the explorers on the Web. They can also speculate about how the information was added to the Internet and by whom. For example, if the research centers on contemporary artists, they may have developed their own personal home pages. If the research centers on a historical character (such as Magellan), someone else must have been responsible for creating the resource. As students conduct their searches, emphasize that they need to ascertain the validity and accuracy of the content. Ask them to fill out a Fact or Fiction sheet (see the blackline master at the end of this chapter) when they are analyzing the reliability of the sources.

DESIGN. Students may take two or three class periods researching their specific topic, depending on the number of Internet connections available for student use. If connections are limited, have the students print out potential sites (along with the URL) so they can read and evaluate the information offline.

As students complete their research, they should write the reports, linking to the Web at appropriate places. Flowcharts and storyboards are extremely important to help students map out their ideas and provide a structure for their reports.

Discuss using media elements in the projects. Point out that graphics that are not optimized for the Web (as far as size, resolution, etc.) may be slow to load. Encourage them to locate electronic maps that can be modified to depict trade routes and other geographic points of interest. Provide copies of the Web design guidelines and a storyboard template.

Remind students of copyright restrictions. Publishing on the Web is different from producing a multimedia project that will be used only within the classroom. All graphics, music, text, and video should be original or should be part of the public domain. If students locate a graphic or another media element on the Web, they should read the copyright statements to make sure that they can place that element on a webpage that will be accessible through the Internet.

DEVELOP. After the students' flowchart and storyboards have been approved, teams take turns at the computer stations (see Chapter 3 for a computer schedule). If teams are not working on the computers or on their storyboards, students can be:

- Conducting research about the topic in textbooks, videos, and encyclopedias to continue verifying the content found on the Web

- Building a model of Magellan's ship with paper or cardboard

- Reviewing maps that were available at Magellan's time

- Charting Magellan's journeys on a contemporary world map

- Writing a comparison of Magellan's journey to that of John Glenn (or another contemporary figure).

As students complete their Web-based reports, another group reviews them. If some of the links do not work, the reviewers should note them so they can be corrected. If possible, student review teams should also note any graphics or media elements that take too long to download, and they should test the site with different browsers and computers. The content of the report should be original and should access other resources as supporting documentation.

EVALUATE. Follow the general procedure for project evaluations (teacher evaluation, peer evaluation). If the projects are going to be uploaded to a Web server (and therefore accessible throughout the world), an additional review-and-revision cycle may be necessary. After the teacher has noted changes, students should revise the content as necessary before uploading the projects to the server. All class reports can be linked via a class page that explains the project and the parameters.

A Lesson in Life

Lesson Description: After your students master the basics of designing and developing a website with HTML and other tools, they can focus on more advanced interactions on the Web. There are various programs and techniques (such as JavaScript) that can produce interactions. Some tools, such as DreamWeaver, can automatically generate JavaScript interactions, such as feedback on questions. In addition, there are many websites that provide free access to game and quiz-generating programs (see Table 9.1).

This project focuses on the students' ability to design a lesson that teaches about a concept they are currently studying. Interactions should be included whereby users can test their knowledge of the subject and receive meaningful feedback.

Table 9.1. Game and Quiz Generating Programs on the Web

Website	Address
Quiz Center	http://school.discovery.com/quizcenter/quizcenter.html
QUIA	http://www.quia.com
TestMaker	http://www.testmaker.com
Easy Test Maker	http://www.easytestmaker.com
Quiz Game Master	http://cybertrain.info/quizman/qmhome.html
APTE Puzzle Center	http://www.apte.com/puzzles
Hot Potatoes	http://web.uvic.ca/hrd/halfbaked

DECIDE. Before beginning the project, demonstrate several websites that are designed to deliver instruction and interactivity. Table 9.2 provides many examples of online courses. Prior to the demonstrations, review the sites and show the students examples based on student age, site content, and programming expertise required.

Table 9.2. Instructional Sites on the Web

Website	Address
Explorelearning (Math/Science)	http://www.explorelearning.com
FunBrain	http://www.funbrain.com
Foreign Languages for Travelers (Learn over 35 languages)	http://www.travlang.com/languages
InterActivate	http://www.shodor.org/interactivate
Interactive Websites	http://jc-schools.net/tutorials/interactive.htm
I Like 2 Learn	http://www.ilike2learn.com/ilike2learn
Blue Web'n	http://www.kn.pacbell.com/wired/bluewebn
Kids Know It	http://www.kidsknowit.com
Read Write Think	http://www.readwritethink.org/index.asp
Knowledge Bears	http://www.kbears.com
Kids Educational Websites	http://kidsedwebsites.com

Assign student teams as described in previous chapters. As a class, generate a list of possible topics about life that could be taught on the Internet. The topics could include such areas as AIDS, life management skills, health, sex education, reproduction, air quality, and so on. Allow plenty of time for the students to generate possible topics and areas of investigation.

Demonstrate techniques for incorporating interaction on the Web. Discuss the advantages of delivering Web-based education, including access to a worldwide audience, ease of distribution, and ease of updates and maintenance. Allow the students to work through several sites on the Internet that deliver instruction.

DESIGN. After each group has selected or been assigned a topic, the groups can begin developing the flowcharts and storyboards. Most of this project should take place within a confined set of webpages, without branches to external sites. Caution the students to flowchart the lesson carefully so that the navigation is easy and intuitive. After the storyboards are complete, the teacher should review them carefully to make sure the content is chunked and presented in a logical manner. Questions and feedback should be checked for accuracy and relevance.

DEVELOP. After the students' flowchart and storyboards have been approved, teams can begin the production phase by creating the graphics, text, and interactions. The integration of interactive exercises (questions, puzzles, etc.) can create issues between different platforms (Mac vs. PC) and different browsers (Firefox, Internet Explorer, Safari, etc.). Extensive testing is required to ensure that the project will operate correctly on different delivery systems. If teams are not working at a computer, they can be involved in the following activities:

- Reviewing books and articles about the latest developments in Web authoring tools

- Taking pictures or drawing graphics that can be incorporated into their lesson

- Constructing questions or quizzes and pilot testing them with other students

EVALUATE. Following the reviews and evaluations by the teacher and peers, the students should be encouraged to pilot test their programs with other classes. The classes may be within the same school or located elsewhere in the world. After the program has been thoroughly tested, it can be uploaded to the Internet. Students should be encouraged to include e-mail feedback forms on the program to solicit responses from other students and teachers who implement the lesson.

SUMMARY

The possibilities for multimedia projects on the Web include informational pages, instructional sites, and worldwide research. This chapter presented sample Web projects focusing on students, schools, local communities, and instruction. As the Web continues to proliferate in our homes and schools, the development of Web-based programs will become an increasingly important tool for students.

BLACKLINE MASTERS

The Web is an invaluable resource for sharing and researching information. This chapter described several activities and two blackline masters for assisting students with their Web projects. Blackline masters in this chapter include:

- Web Design Guidelines: a list of guidelines specific to Web projects

- Fact or Fiction: a means to record and analyze information on the Web

Web Design Guidelines

The following guidelines can help make your Web pages more user-friendly for the visitors to your site.

General

Carefully plan your pages before you create them.
Place a descriptive title on the top of all pages.
Include the date of the last revision on the pages.
Limit the length of Web pages to three screens.
Test the pages with several different browsers and computers.
Check all pages for correct spelling and grammar.

Graphics

Make sure the graphics are relevant to the page.
Limit the file size of the graphics to less than 30K each.
Limit the number of graphics on each page.
Use GIF graphics for line drawings and simple graphics.
Use JPG graphics for photographs.
Limit the width of graphics to less than 470 pixels.

Text

Make sure there is high contrast between background and text.
Limit the length of text lines.
Include blank space between paragraphs.
Limit the use of blinking text.

Media: Audio and Video

Use audio and video only when necessary.
Include information about audio and video file sizes.
Include information about format (e.g., wav, avi, quicktime)

From *Multimedia Projects in Education: Designing, Producing, and Assessing, Fourth Edition* by Karen S. Ivers and Ann E. Barron. Santa Barbara, CA: Libraries Unlimited. Copyright © 2010.

Fact or Fiction

Because anyone can create a Web page, it is important to try to determine if the information presented there is true or not. Fill out this form for Web sites that you are including in your project.

Web Site #1

Title of Site _____

Address (URL) _____

Author _____

Date last modified _____

Clues that help to determine if the information is Fact or Fiction

_____

Web Site #2

Title of Site _____

Address (URL) _____

Author _____

Date last modified _____

Clues that help to determine if the information is Fact or Fiction

_____

Web Site #3

Title of Site _____

Address (URL) _____

Author _____

Date last modified _____

Clues that help to determine if the information is Fact or Fiction

_____

From *Multimedia Projects in Education: Designing, Producing, and Assessing, Fourth Edition* by Karen S. Ivers and Ann E. Barron. Santa Barbara, CA: Libraries Unlimited. Copyright © 2010.

Multimedia Projects:
Presentation Tools

A SCENARIO

Service learning was an integral part of Ms. Ponder's social studies curriculum. Each year, her students chose a community issue or concern and worked together to address the problem. This year, her class decided to address the health consequences of poor nutrition and lack of exercise. This seemed to be a common problem in the community, as well as around the country. Students were placed in groups, based on their interest in the topic, and prepared their research and recommendations for inclusion in a class presentation that was shared with community leaders, families, and their fellow students. Students took turns speaking to the different groups. Students helped to create the overall goals of the project, as well as the criteria for which they were to be assessed. One student commented to Ms. Ponder that this project didn't seem like school; where was the test? "I feel like I'm doing something for real," said the student, "I mean, this is real life, not a textbook." Ms. Ponder couldn't agree more. "Life is not a textbook," she replied, "It's an experience. And we never know what experiences life will bring us. That's why learning from and with each other is so important. Textbooks and other materials provide us with knowledge, but what we do with the knowledge is what counts. That's life." Based on their research and the support they received from their presentation, the students conducted health fairs, published a healthy cookbook on the Web, started a morning exercise class, and opened a fresh fruit and vegetable stand for the school and community.

OVERVIEW

Designing and presenting multimedia projects provide students with invaluable real-world learning experiences; presentation and public-speaking skills are necessary in many occupations. In addition, presentation projects can be used to address a variety of standards, including those related to listening and speaking skills, writing, and so on. Students learn to work together, apply their research skills, plan and organize content, select appropriate media and layouts, and deliver professional-looking presentations.

Although professional-looking presentations can be created with authoring and Web tools, there are several tools on the market especially designed for creating large group presentations. Microsoft PowerPoint is probably the most common. Keynote, part of Apple's iWork package, is available for Macintosh users. Scholastic Keys provides elementary students with a kid-friendly interface for Microsoft PowerPoint, as well as Word and Excel. Most presentation programs provide the option of using predesigned templates. Some programs also have "wizards" or other guides that prompt users through the design process.

This chapter presents several ideas for multimedia projects that can be created with presentation tools. A lesson description, the DDD-E process, and ideas for concurrent activities are provided for each project.

SAMPLE PROJECTS FOR PRESENTATION TOOLS

The following projects can be created with most presentation tools. Teachers should choose the most appropriate tool for their students and ensure that they are familiar with the tool before beginning the project. Students should also be familiar with guidelines for presentations (see the Presentation Guidlines blackline master at the end of this chapter). The sample projects describe classrooms with four computers and 32 students; however, adjustments can be made to meet other conditions. Design teams consist of four students. See Chapter 3 for computer scheduling options.

Persuasive Automotive

Lesson Description: The goal of this lesson is to engage older students in persuasive speaking and writing strategies. Students structure ideas and arguments in a sustained, persuasive, and sophisticated way and support them with precise and relevant examples. In this lesson, students research, compare, and analyze real-world considerations of purchasing an automobile. Each group of students is assigned a different automobile (e.g., a sports utility vehicle—SUV) from different manufacturers. As part of their research assignment, student groups must try to persuade classmates that their assigned automobile is the best. For example, students researching a Subaru Forester would create a presentation highlighting what they believe are its benefits—gas mileage, price, warranty, options, aesthetics, safety, buying options (current percentage rates and leasing options), and so on. Audience members would have the chance to ask questions and debate the presented issues. Other topics for persuasive speaking include school rules, laws, best places to eat or shop, the most influential person who ever lived, and so on. For younger students, teachers can have them try to persuade one another of Goldilocks's guilt or innocence in trespassing, what makes the best pet, and so forth. Students have the opportunity to state a clear position in support of a proposal, support a position with relevant evidence, follow a simple organizational pattern, and address reader concerns.

DECIDE. As a class, determine what students know about buying an automobile (use the KWL Knowledge Chart in Chapter 3). Ask students what they know about their own or their parents' cars and why they purchased them. Complete the second column of the KWL Knowledge Chart by asking students what they would like to know about purchasing cars. Introduce the project by assigning students to teams as described in previous chapters. Explain that groups will randomly choose an SUV to research and share with the class. As part of the assignment, explain that they will be required to present an overview and the benefits of the SUV via a presentation tool. Continue to explain that the purpose of the presentation is to persuade classmates that their SUV is the best. Groups must be prepared to answer questions and to debate the presented issues. As a group, design an evaluation form for the presentation. For an example, see the Persuasive Presentation Evaluation blackline master at the end of this chapter.

Provide student groups with the opportunity to brainstorm and research topics about their SUV. Check their progress and Bibliography sheets (see Chapter 3) before letting them move on to the DESIGN phase.

DESIGN. After the students' research has been approved, provide class time to create flowcharts and storyboards. To expedite the process, teachers may provide the students with a standardized template (see Figure 10.1). A limit of 15 screens could be imposed, if desired. Remind students of the purpose of bulleted text and the printout options available in the presentation tool.

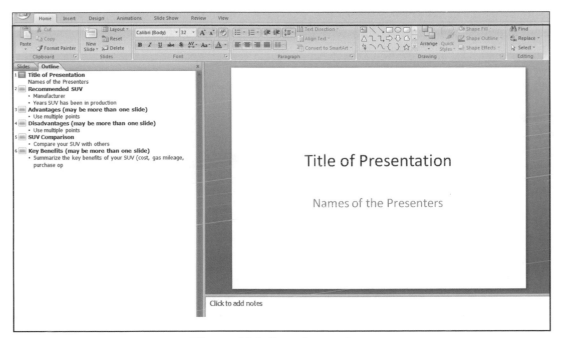

Figure 10.1. Sample template.

DEVELOP. After the students' flowchart and storyboards have been approved, teams take turns at the computer stations (see Chapter 3 for a computer schedule). If teams are not working on the computers or on their storyboards, students can be:

- Conducting additional research about their SUV

- Locating and charting where the majority of their SUV is sold

- Creating a brochure about their SUV

- Comparing and contrasting their SUV with other SUVs

- Creating a model, drawing, or collage of their SUV

Team members should review and practice their presentation before presenting it to the class.

EVALUATE. Teachers and students use the evaluation form created during the DECIDE phase of the project. Students may be evaluated on the effectiveness of their presentation, its organization and structure, its content and accuracy, their speaking skills, and so on. The evaluations are collected and averaged by the teacher. Students may also choose to conduct self- and intragroup evaluations (see Chapter 7).

Famous People in History

Lesson Description: The goal of this lesson is to engage students in an informative presentation about a famous person in history, a common requirement across grade levels, addressing social studies and language arts standards. Student groups have the opportunity to choose a famous person and to share their findings with the class. Media elements can be added to the presentations to highlight certain aspects of the famous person. For example, if students choose to do a presentation on Scott Joplin, music can be added to demonstrate his work. If Neil Armstrong were chosen, students might opt to include an audio segment of his first words on the moon. In any case, the goal of the presentation should be to inform viewers about a particular person in history. Presentations should be clear, well organized, and interesting and should address the content criteria established by the teacher.

DECIDE. Assign student teams as described in previous chapters. Ask what makes a person famous. Students may discuss current celebrities. Ask them what makes these people different from others or debate whether they really are different. Discuss how celebrities or famous people of today compare with famous people of yesterday. Discuss what made people in history famous.

Following this discussion, have the groups decide on a famous historical person to research and present to the class. Ensure that each group chooses a different person. After their selection is approved, students conduct research on the person they have chosen. Evaluate their research before letting students continue the DESIGN phase.

DESIGN. Students need to examine their research findings and organize the information for their presentation. Make sure they understand the importance of flowcharts and storyboards. Provide groups with a list of design guidelines, a presentation storyboard template (see Chapter 4), and the journal entry form and project checklist. Explain each form. In addition, provide groups with the storyboard, design, content, and technical rubrics (see Chapter 7). Groups should keep these forms in a binder. Multiple copies of the journal entry form and the bibliography form should be available. Remind students of the purpose of bulleted text and the printout options available in the presentation tool (see Chapter 6). Teachers may choose to set a minimum and maximum number of screens in the presentation.

DEVELOP. After the students' flowchart and storyboards have been approved, teams take turns at the computer stations. If teams are not working on the computers or on their storyboards, students can be:

- Creating a Venn diagram that compares the life of their famous person to their own lives
- Designing a booklet about the career of their famous person
- Drawing a portrait of their famous person
- Creating a timeline of their famous person's life.

EVALUATE. Peers and the teacher can evaluate group presentations by using the content, technical, and presentation rubrics in Chapter 7. The students receive a group grade based on combined scores. Students receive an individual grade based on their group, self-, and intragroup evaluations. The teacher may present a whole-class quiz to assess what was learned from each presentation.

Scientific Follow-Up

Lesson Description: The goal of this lesson is to engage students in reporting their scientific findings. This is one way to assess students' knowledge of what they have learned and can be applied to science projects across grade levels.

Following small-group science experiments, organize student groups into design teams to present their findings to the whole class. Talk about how they think such presentations might relate to real life. Discuss the importance and purpose of presentations in the business world, in the scientific community, and in education.

DECIDE. In the DECIDE phase, student groups must decide how to best represent and discuss their findings by reexamining their data and methods. Students should organize their ideas with a planning sheet (see Chapter 4) before continuing to the DESIGN phase.

DESIGN. Depending on the experiment, students may want to incorporate a variety of media (e.g., charts, photos, animations) into their presentations to illustrate their methods and findings (see Figure 10.2).

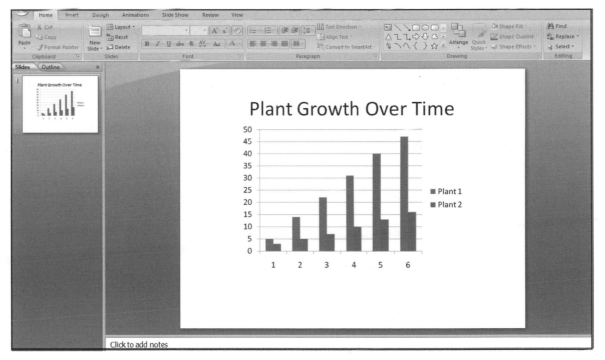

Figure 10.2. Chart example.

Make sure students understand the importance of flowcharts and storyboards. Provide groups with a list of design guidelines, a presentation storyboard template (see Chapter 4), and the journal entry form and project checklist available in Chapters 3 and 4. Explain each form. In addition, provide groups with the storyboard, presentation design, content, and technical rubrics available in Chapter 7. Remind students of the purpose of bulleted text and the printout options available in the presentation tool (see Chapter 6). Teachers may choose to set a minimum and maximum number of screens in the presentation.

DEVELOP. After the students' flowchart and storyboards have been approved, teams take turns at the computer stations (see Chapter 3 for a computer schedule). If teams are not working on the computers or on their storyboards, students can be:

- Conducting further research on their scientific investigation

- Conducting a similar experiment and comparing the results

- Creating a newsletter about the implications of their experiment

EVALUATE. Peers and the teacher can evaluate group presentations (see Chapter 7). The students receive a group grade based on the teacher and peer evaluations. Students receive an individual grade based on their self- and intragroup evaluations. The two grades can be averaged for a final score (see Final Grades in Chapter 7).

How To

Lesson Description: The goal of this lesson is to encourage students to teach each other how to do something and addresses standards related to listening and speaking skills. For example, students need to be able to give precise directions and instructions, restate and perform multiple-step instructions and directions, and so on. There are many advantages to using a presentation tool for instruction: step-by-step instructions can be bulleted, enlarged photographs can show procedures close up, video and animation can show a sequence of events, and learners can be provided with screen-by-screen handouts to assist them in the learning process.

DECIDE. Assign student teams as described in previous chapters. Introduce the project, explaining that the goal of the presentation is to teach their classmates how to do something. You may begin by asking the students to tell you how to make a peanut butter and jelly sandwich. Have a loaf of bread, a jar of peanut butter, a jar of jelly, a plate, and a spoon on a table in front of you. Depending on the age of the students, this can be quite funny. Do exactly as they say. For example, if the students say, "Put the peanut butter on the bread," pick up the jar of peanut butter and place it on the loaf of bread. Students will quickly discover the importance of precise and properly sequenced directions. Discuss different strategies for communicating how to do something and the advantages of using different media elements. Following the discussion, let groups decide on something to teach. Next, students should brainstorm different ways to teach the procedure to the class.

DESIGN. When students are ready to move on to the DESIGN phase, make sure they understand the importance of flowcharts and storyboards. Discuss the design issues explained in Chapter 4 and, if possible, show the students samples of "how-to" presentations. Again, review the significance of certain media elements. Once the students' flowchart and storyboards are approved, they can begin developing their presentations.

DEVELOP. After the students' flowchart and storyboards have been approved, teams take turns at the computer stations. If teams are not working on the computers or on their storyboards, students can be:

- Conducting further research on their how-to activity

- Practicing their presentation through their storyboards

- Researching and evaluating how-to books

- Creating a how-to commercial

EVALUATE. How-to presentations may be evaluated by the rubrics in Chapter 7 or by a customized rubric designed by the class. For an example, see the How-to Evaluation blackline master at the end of this chapter.

SUMMARY

In addition to planning and organizational skills, presentation tools provide students with the opportunity to practice speaking in front of a group and conveying their ideas verbally. Presentation tools can help support a presenter's train of thought, as well as provide visual cues for learners. Creating and delivering presentations through presentation tools provides students with valuable real-world and authentic learning experiences.

BLACKLINE MASTERS

Presentation projects provide students with opportunities to practice their speaking and presentation skills. This chapter includes additional evaluation forms for assessing specific student projects. Blackline masters in this chapter include:

- Presentation Guidelines

- Persuasive Presentation Evaluation: a rubric designed to rate the presenter's ability to persuade his or her audience

- How-to Evaluation: a rubric designed to rate the presenter's ability to teach members of the audience a procedure

Presentation Guidelines

These guidelines can help you make effective presentations.

Computer Display

Keep the presentation simple and easy to follow.
Make sure the text is readable to everyone (about 24 pt font).
Mix upper- and lowercase letters for the bullets.
Keep consistent headings (titles) and subheadings.
Provide plenty of space between bullets.
Use a maximum of five colors.
Include a maximum of six bullets.
Each bullet should only have about six words.
Include key phrases in bullets -- not the entire presentation.
Use high contrast between the text color and the background.
Do not place text on a highly textured/patterned background.
Make sure your graphics are large enough for everyone to see.
If you include charts, make large labels and legends.

Media: Audio and Video

Use audio and video only when necessary and appropriate.
Test the speakers and projection unit before the presentation.
Make sure everyone can hear and see the media.

Presentation Techniques

Rehearse the speech before presenting it.
Make notes to yourself on cards or on the computer.
Face the audience -- not the projection screen.
Start with a brief introduction and overview of the topic.
Don't read the bullets to the audience; expand on them.
Always plan a little extra in case you talk too fast.
Don't talk too fast -- pause and let the audience reflect.
Stand tall and speak directly to the audience (don't slouch)!
Don't fidget with keys, coins, pens, pencils, etc.
End the presentation with a summary and conclusion.
Smile!

From *Multimedia Projects in Education: Designing, Producing, and Assessing, Fourth Edition*
by Karen S. Ivers and Ann E. Barron. Santa Barbara, CA: Libraries Unlimited. Copyright © 2010.

Persuasive Presentation Evaluation

CRITERIA	0	1	2	3
Clarity	Presenter(s) did not speak clearly and did not speak loud enough.	Presenter(s) spoke loud enough, but did not speak clearly.	Presenter(s) spoke clearly but not in a loud enough voice.	Presenter(s) was articulate and spoke in a loud enough voice.
Supporting facts	Presenter(s) did not provide facts to support his or her opinion.	Presenter(s) provided one or two facts to support opinion.	Presenter(s) provided three or four facts to support opinion.	Presenter(s) provided five or more facts to support his or her opinion.
Viewpoints	Presenter(s) did not consider other opinions and didn't provide compelling reasons for own opinion.	Presenter(s) did not consider other opinions, but provided compelling reasons for own opinion.	Presenter(s) considered other opinions, but didn't provide compelling reasons for own opinion.	Presenter(s) considered other opinions and provided compelling reasons for own opinion.
Organization	Presenter(s) was very disorganized, distracting the presen-tation.	Presenter(s) was somewhat organized but needs to improve a lot.	Presenter(s) was well organized most of the time.	Presenter(s) was well organized throughout the presentation.
Appeal	Presenter(s) did not captivate or hold my attention.	Presenter(s) held my attention for a short period of time.	Presenter(s) held my attention for most of the time.	Presenter(s) captured and held my attention the whole time.
Persuasiveness	Presenter(s) did not change my opinion; he or she reinforced my other beliefs.	Presenter(s) did not change my opinion.	Presenter(s) changed my opinion, but I'm not completely convinced.	Presenter(s) changed my opinion; I'm completely convinced.
				Total _____

From *Multimedia Projects in Education: Designing, Producing, and Assessing, Fourth Edition*
by Karen S. Ivers and Ann E. Barron. Santa Barbara, CA: Libraries Unlimited. Copyright © 2010.

How-to Evaluation

CRITERIA	0	1	2	3
Clarity	Presenter(s) did not speak clearly and did not speak loud enough.	Presenter(s) spoke loud enough, but did not speak clearly.	Presenter(s) spoke clearly but not in a loud enough voice.	Presenter(s) was articulate and spoke in a loud enough voice.
Directions	Presenter(s) did not provide clear or step-by-step directions.	Presenter(s) provided step-by-step directions, but they were not clear.	Presenter(s) provided clear directions, but they were not step-by-step.	Presenter(s) provided clear, step-by-step directions.
Organization	Presenter(s) was very disorganized, distracting the presentation.	Presenter(s) was somewhat organized but needs to improve a lot.	Presenter(s) was well organized most of the time.	Presenter(s) was well organized throughout the presentation.
Instructional approach	Presenter(s) did not use a variety of instructional approaches.	Presenter(s) used two different instructional approaches.	Presenter(s) used three different instructional approaches.	Presenter(s) used four or more different instructional approaches.
Appeal	Presenter(s) did not captivate or hold my attention.	Presenter(s) held my attention for a short period of time.	Presenter(s) held my attention for most of the time.	Presenter(s) captured and held my attention the whole time.
Outcome (Fill in the blank based on the topic.)	I did not learn anything about how to _____.	I learned a little about how to _____.	I learned a lot about how to _____.	I successfully learned how to _____ and I could teach someone else.
				Total _____

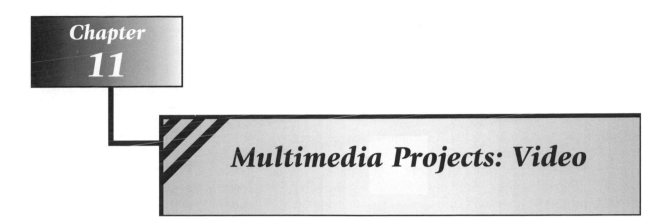

Multimedia Projects: Video

A SCENARIO

Mrs. Guillaume checked out 10 Flip video cameras and 10 laptops from the school media center. She made sure the cameras had new batteries and the laptops where charged. She demonstrated how to use the camera to her students. Students were assigned to groups of three, and each group received a Flip camera, laptop computer, a sand dollar, and a teacher-created brochure on sand dollars. Props and art supplies were available, too. Mrs. Guillaume went over the assignment. Students had 30 minutes to learn as much as they could about sand dollars, using their prior knowledge, the brochure, and the Internet, and to report what they had learned in a video format. Students were encouraged to be creative, making their report as interesting as possible. Mrs. Guillaume had invited the principal to observe and judge the most interesting and educational video presentation.

Students went to task immediately, brainstorming their strategies; conducting, evaluating, and synthesizing their research; and planning for the video presentation. Presentations could be recorded in the next room or outside the classroom. Thirty minutes passed quickly, and the students returned to their seats. The presentations began. Groups took turns plugging in their Flip camera into the classroom computer's USB drive to show their videos. The principal, Ms. Norman, was amazed at the creativity and learning that occurred. One group took the perspective of the sand dollar to share information; another group wrote a song. The students laughed and applauded each other's presentations. "What fun!" smiled Ms. Norman. "I'm not sure I can pick a winner. I think you all deserve an 'A' for talent, scholarship, collaboration, and presentation. Your teacher deserves an 'A,' too, for giving you the tools to learn and to demonstrate your knowledge."

OVERVIEW

Students live in a visual world, watching television, going to movies, playing video games, and logging on to the Internet. Video is everywhere—even in grocery store checkout lines. It is a "natural" part of today's world, accessible on mobile devices, in automobiles, and more. Creating a video project can help make learning more meaningful to students because it is a part of their everyday life—how they play, interact, and learn. Now, thanks to video editing programs that are inexpensive and easy-to-learn, video projects are feasible for students in all grades. As discussed in Chapters 5 and 6, today's technologies make it easy to capture video. Video can be captured on cell phones, digital cameras, smartphones, computer Webcams, and inexpensive video cameras such as the Flip (http://www.theflip.com).

Video projects can be created from either analog or digital sources with popular, easily available programs such as iMovie on the Macintosh and Movie Maker on Windows computers. HyperStudio and other programs make it easy to convert projects into podcasts. Projects can be shared on the Web, including YouTube (http://www.youtube.com), TeacherTube (http://www.teachertube.com), and iTunes U (http://www.apple.com/itunes/whats-on).

Integrating video production into classroom activities has many benefits for students. Similar to other multimedia projects, video production encourages collaboration and requires students to be active and constructive (Bohot and Pfortmiller 2009; Bruce 2009; Jonassen, Howland, Marra, and Crismond 2008; Ranker 2008). It also has social benefits, such as improving students' self-confidence and providing public relations opportunities for school and other events (Hamilton and Flanagan 2007; Loveland and Harrison 2008; Valmont 1994). Written and oral communication skills have always been important in academics. Now, we have the tools to enhance students' understanding of and aptitude with visual communications (Hoffenberg and Handler 2001; Ranker 2008; Siegle 2009).

SAMPLE PROJECTS FOR VIDEO-BASED DEVELOPMENT

Video Projects can range from a simple, one-shot video of a demonstration, interview, or event to a complex, multiple-edit production. For example, students may take a camera on a field trip to record their experiences, they can create video yearbooks, or they can produce the school news programs. Some view video as "the ideal format for the culminating product of a project-based learning experience" (Hoffenberg and Handler 2001); others see it as another tool that can be used on a daily basis to document and supplement the curriculum.

The sample projects included in this chapter offer a variety of approaches for video. Video may be recorded or imported using digital cameras, television, DVDs, or websites. After editing the video in a digital format, final products may be recorded on a DVD or displayed on a computer.

Before assigning a video product, carefully analyze the skills and experiences of your students. Obvious differences in requirements and outcomes should be expected based on students' understanding of the technical and design aspects of video production (video scripting guidelines are presented at the end of this chapter). Remember, however, that although the quality of the finished product may be higher with a high school media production class than an elementary class, the learning benefits can be the same or even greater.

As with other multimedia projects, you'll want to assess your resources. If you have three computers in your classroom, one of which is set up for video editing, the others may be used to design graphic logos or other elements that can be incorporated into the students' videos. Scheduling and rotation lists will depend on the number of computers and video cameras available in the classroom. As groups take turns shooting their video segments, other groups can be using the computers for research, graphics, or digital editing. Those who are not working with computers or cameras can be assigned other tasks that are related to the project. The following projects are designed to give you ideas of how to incorporate digital video into your classroom.

Welcome to Our World

Lesson Description: A good, introductory video project is one in which the students can concentrate on the process rather than new content. This project focuses on compiling a video overview of a familiar environment, such as the students' classroom, school, or community. Innovative approaches could include assuming the perspective of a dog, cat, or bug.

Depending on the amount of video recording and editing equipment available, the parameters of the project should be constrained to a reasonable limit. In other words, teachers may encourage compiling a limited number of video clips—one that establishes the setting of the "world," one that includes close-ups of the "inhabitants," and still frames or graphics of some of the objects in the "world." Audio can be limited to a single voice-over track that describes the world as the video plays.

DECIDE. As a class, discuss the possible topics for the "worlds," emphasizing that it can be as broad as the earth or as narrow as their classroom. In addition, they may choose to take a unique perspective, such as ants in an anthill, bees in a beehive, or a cell in the body. Brainstorm in small groups to generate as many ideas as possible for consideration.

After a list of topics is generated, help students filter the list by discussing issues that may facilitate or complicate the shooting. For example, would it be easier to create a "world" from a student's, dog's, or an ant's point of view? In which cases might props or special graphics be required? Does the project timeline allow sufficient time to improvise and create scenery?

Divide the class into groups of four or five students, based on their interest in various topics. Be sure that at least one student in each group is proficient with a digital camera and editing software. Discuss criteria for the project and conduct any research that may be relevant.

DESIGN. Assist students in the pre-production phase: outlining their project, creating a shot list, and writing the narration. Recommend that they include a title screen to set the stage and an initial still frame or video that establishes the setting and the perspective. Emphasize that they should use a variety of shots—some close-up and some wide angle—to add interest and variety.

DEVELOP. When it is time to shoot the video, team members should assume various roles, such as actors, lighting technicians, camera operators, and producers. After the video is imported into an editing program, ensure that all students have input into the appropriate cuts and transitions. If a team is waiting for a camera or computer, other members can be:

- Researching related information about their assumed perspective (e.g., ant)

- Practicing the narration

- Locating background music or sound effects

- Analyzing, comparing, and identifying the various perspectives of newspaper or magazine articles regarding a particular topic (e.g., movie reviews, policies, world events)

- Writing about why it is important to value and understand different perspectives

EVALUATE. When the projects are complete, display them for the entire class. Have students discuss the different interpretations and perspectives. Which of the videos are the most similar or the most different? Why?

If this is an initial video project, have students discuss lessons learned by answering the following questions:

- Which part or parts of the project were easier than originally thought?

- Which part or parts of the project were more difficult to complete?

- How did the video contribute to the effectiveness of this project? In other words, could a PowerPoint presentation have been as effective?

- What are two "lessons learned" that you would like to share with your classmates?

Creating a Convincing Commercial

Lesson Description: Students are very familiar with commercials on television. However, have they ever stopped to analyze commercials and consider the persuasive tactics that are employed? This project involves student groups in creating a short commercial that could be used to convince others to purchase a specific product.

DECIDE. Begin the assignment by showing examples of television commercials. You may have access to prerecorded commercials on DVD or the Web. Websites with commercials can be located at the following addresses:

- Classic TV Ads at http://www.roadode.com/classicindex.shtml

- Advertisement Ave at http://www.advertisementave.com

- ClipLand at http://www.clipland.com/index_tvc.shtml

- TV Commercials at http://www.specialweb.com/tv/commercials.html

- SongTitle (music from commercials) at http://www.songtitle.info

As the commercials are being viewed (either individually or as a group), have the students note the following:

- The length of time each ad runs

- How many edits (different scenes) are used in each commercial

- Where and how the commercials "imprint" the company—either by logo, by jingle, or by words and actions

- The emotions that are evoked by the commercial

- The targeted audience—children or adults; males or females; local, national, or international audiences

Form groups of four to six students, and have them continue the discussion by brainstorming possible products that they could target for the commercials. These products can be real or fictional; however, do not allow them to target a product that is already being advertised on television. Ask each group to generate at least 20 ideas of possible content items. Help them select a product that is feasible, based on their interests and the availability of props, images, and resources. Encourage innovation, creativity, and fun.

DESIGN. Discuss general design issues for commercials. Emphasize the need to convey a persuasive position in a short period of time. Encourage them to search the Web for information about producing commercials and possible lessons learned by marketing companies.

Students should create storyboards or video scripts, or both, that detail the types of video shots needed, along with the narration. Continually remind them of the short length of the final video; encourage them to brand the product with a logo, a jingle, or a phrase. Review the following design guidelines that apply to commercials:

- The most important portion of the commercial is the visual aspect. Even if the sound is turned off or down, a message should be conveyed.

- Commercials aim to motivate viewers and to touch their emotions. Concentrate on one or more emotions.

- Grab the viewer's attention quickly. Within a couple of seconds, the viewers may decide (consciously or unconsciously) to leave the room if they are not "hooked" by the commercial.

- Keep the message simple and visual. Include the name of the company and logo visually on the screen.

- Be repetitive. Repeat the product name several times in the commercial.

- Keep it short. Commercials are often designed for 30-second slots; however, many are only 10 or 20 seconds.

At this time, it may be a good idea for the class to design a rubric for evaluating their commercials. Criteria may include the appeal of the commercial (how well it motivates or touches the viewer's emotions), how well the message is conveyed and remembered, how well it grabs the viewer's attention, whether it convinced one to purchase the product, and so on.

DEVELOP. When it is time to shoot the video, team members should assume various roles, such as actors, lighting technicians, camera operators, and producers. After the video is imported into an editing program, ensure that all students have input into the appropriate cuts and transitions.

If a team is waiting for a camera or computer, members can be:

- Researching and comparing the cost of time slots for commercials (e.g., advertising during the Super Bowl versus advertising at 3:00 a.m.)

- Analyzing and comparing the commercials of different time periods (e.g., 1950s vs. 2010)

- Practicing the narration (if applicable), as well as rehearsing for the commercial

- Locating background music or sound effects, if appropriate

- Surveying other students about their favorite or worst commercials, including why they are their favorite or worst and what makes them remember the commercials

- Analyzing and comparing commercials aired during different shows and time slots throughout the day (these may be videotaped for use during class time).

EVALUATE. Record the projects to videotape for class evaluation. Students use the rubric designed in the DESIGN phase to evaluate and discuss each group's commercial. A sample rubric appears at the end of this chapter.

Digital Storytelling

Lesson Description: The term "digital storytelling" can be used to refer to many approaches and content areas. For example, in the literal sense, students write a story and "act it out" via video. This is one method for integrating video projects into the language arts curriculum and meeting standards addressing speaking, reading, writing, and other skills. Video storytelling can also refer to producing documentaries. Whether the video story is fiction or nonfiction, it provides students with a means to act out or convey what they know through an interactive environment.

Depending on the grade level and topic to be addressed, select or have your students create a story to act out on video. For example, students may act out a play about the famous ride of Paul Revere or write the script themselves based on research. Students may reenact the Boston Tea Party or other historical event; act out fairy tales, nursery rhymes, or chapters of books they are reading; or create and act out a story of their own. They may document the day of a teacher, a student, or school custodian; document the growth of a plant over time, the life cycle of a butterfly, and so on.

DECIDE. Make sure the selected topic is relevant and is aligned with your state or district standards. For example, if you are a fourth-grade teacher in California, you may want to design a timeline of the events that led up to the California Gold Rush and group your students to research and act out one of the events. The recorded events can be imported, edited, combined, and sequenced inside the computer and burned onto a DVD about the California Gold Rush.

Students can work in teams toward one topic, as described earlier, or perhaps work on different documentaries or stories that will be made accessible through a CD-ROM or DVD. For example, younger students may act out and record short nursery rhymes, and the teacher may link these within PowerPoint. Older students may be assigned to document specific concerns relative to their community and produce a community-based DVD to share with city council members. Whichever approach you decide to take, make sure your students understand what will be required of them (define the criteria) and assign them to appropriate teams.

DESIGN. Assist students in the preproduction phase: outlining their project, creating a shot list, and writing the narration. Emphasize that they should use a variety of shots—some close up and some wide angle to add interest and variety. Define the evaluation criteria for the design of their project.

DEVELOP. When it is time to shoot the video, team members should assume various roles, such as actors, lighting technicians, camera operators, and producers. After the video is imported into an editing program, ensure that all students have input into the appropriate cuts and transitions.

If a team is waiting for a camera or computer, members can be:

- Constructing a picture, diorama, or brochure related to their topic

- Practicing the narration (if applicable), as well as rehearsing for their video

- Locating background music or sound effects, if appropriate

- Reading books related to their topic

EVALUATE. The evaluation of the selected project will be based on the criteria defined during the DECIDE and DESIGN stages. Projects can be presented during Open House or shared with other classes studying the same topics.

Historical Movie

Lesson Description: Digital storytelling can also be used to illustrate historical documents or recreate historical events. Several examples can be found at http://digitalstorytelling.coe.uh.edu/social_studies.html. In this lesson, students create a digital story using images of the Civil War to support their narrative of the Gettysburg Address.

DECIDE. Introduce the topic and provide background information for the students. Use a KWL chart to list what students know and want to learn about the document and the related historical events. Have students brainstorm ideas of where to locate information about the Gettysburg Address and the history of the Civil War. Create a rubric for the project, based on desired content or facts and the project design. Give students time to conduct the necessary research.

DESIGN. Divide the class into pair groups and assign a section of the Gettysburg Address to each group to memorize and recite. Have students choose pictures from a Civil War website that can be used to illustrate the document. Students should have enough pictures to cover their narration, with each picture displaying no more than 8 seconds. Such criteria should be added to the rubric for evaluation.

DEVELOP. Have each group read and record its assigned section of the document into Apple's iMovie or Window's Movie Maker. Team members can take turns reciting or they can recite their part together. Import and combine all of the audio clips into a master file. Distribute the master file to all groups. Each group will then add the photographs to the sound track to create their final movie. Encourage students to add transitions and titles where appropriate.

If a team is waiting for a computer, members can be:

- Rehearsing for narrative for the video

- Searching the Web for relevant photographs to include in the video

- Locating background music to serve as an introduction to the movie

- Creating maps or diagrams that could be incorporated into the movie

EVALUATE. Record the projects to DVD for class evaluation. Evaluate the projects based on the rubric created in the DECIDE and DESIGN stage. Optimize the videos for the Web and post them on the school website (using student initials only).

Show and Tell

Lesson Description: Students record segments that demonstrate how to do a particular task. For example, students could create video shots that demonstrate different tennis swings and shots. The digital video segments are made accessible through a program like iDVD so viewers can pick and choose which swings or shots they would like to see demonstrated, the order in which they would like to see them, and how often they want to see each segment.

DECIDE. Have students explain what is meant by" "a picture is worth a thousand words." Discuss the advantages and disadvantages of text, pictures, and video. Have students share experiences of how they learned something by watching someone else or give examples of how they could learn something by watching someone else. Discuss what makes it easy or difficult to learn by watching someone.

Place students in groups and have them brainstorm ideas of what could be learned by watching someone do something. For example, how to swing a bat, dribble a basketball, tie a knot, make a balloon animal, overhand shuffle a deck of cards, and so on. Remind students that learning is the first step before doing—just because someone *knows* how to ride a bike (get on the seat, balance oneself, and pedal), does not mean he or she can do it without practice! Some learning tasks are more difficult than others.

Have student groups select a multistep task (like making a balloon animal) or variations of a single task (e.g., multiple ways to shuffle a deck of cards, different tennis swings, and so on). Have students share what would make a" "how-to" video useful—types of shots (e.g., close-up, angles), pace, clarity, and so on. Create a rubric based on the criteria defined by the class.

Discuss how text and pictures may be used to enhance or support the video clips. Create a rubric with the students that includes the important elements of the assignment. See the How-to Evaluation blackline master in Chapter 10 for more ideas.

DESIGN. Assist students in the preproduction phase: outlining their project, creating a shot list, and writing the script (if applicable) for the video. If the videos will be incorporated into a PowerPoint presentation, website, or other program, students will also need to develop a flowchart and storyboards. These should indicate the placement of the video clips. Flowcharts, storyboards, and the video outline and shot list are reviewed before teams are allowed to go to the next stage.

DEVELOP. When it is time to shoot the video, team members should assume various roles, such as actors, lighting technicians, camera operator, and producer. After the video is imported into an editing program, ensure that all students have input into the appropriate cuts and transitions.

If a team is waiting for a camera or computer, members can be:

- Practicing the narration (if applicable), as well as rehearsing for their video

- Locating background music or sound effects, if appropriate

- Researching interesting facts or the history of their particular topic

- Researching and identifying experts related to their particular topic

- Listing what they want to learn how to do and why

- Viewing similar videos on YouTube

EVALUATE. Use the class-created rubric(s) to evaluate the projects. Superior class projects may be uploaded to YouTube or iTunes (after review by the teacher and permission from the parents).

SUMMARY

Today's technologies make it easy and relatively inexpensive to create, edit, and produce video. Video projects may be recorded to DVD or made into podcasts for viewing or they be incorporated into other multimedia projects (e.g., PowerPoint presentations or webpages). Creating videos is a powerful addition to a student's arsenal of learning tools, creating opportunities for high-level thinking, organization, planning, and management skills that can be applied in the" "real world." Developing digital videos encourages creative thinking, multiple perspectives, and teamwork. They can be implemented across the curriculum for meaningful learning and provide a real-world way to engage actively students in the learning process.

BLACKLINE MASTERS

Blackline masters in this chapter include:

- Video Guidelines: a list of guidelines specific to writing video scripts

- Commercial Evaluation: a sample rubric for evaluating student commercials

REFERENCES

Bohot, C., and Pfortmiller, M. 2009. Technology connection: Motivational videos and the library media specialist: Teachers and students on film: Make 1. *Library Media Connection* 28(3): 52–53.

Bruce, D. 2009. Writing with visual images: Examining the video composition processes of high school students. *Research in the Teaching of English* 43(4): 426–450.

Hamilton, C., and Flanagan, C. 2007. reframing social responsibility within a technology-based youth activist program. *American Behavioral Scientist* 51: 444–464.

Hoffenberg, H., and Handler, M. 2001. Digital video goes to school. *Learning & Leading with Technology* 29(9): 10–15.

Jonassen, D., Howland, J., Marra, R. M., and Crismond, D. 2008. Meaningful learning with technology (3rd ed.). Upper Saddle River, NJ: Pearson Merrill/Prentice-Hall.

Loveland, T., and Harrison, H., III. 2008. Producing television commercials in high school technology education: An authentic standards-based project. *Technology Teacher* 68(3): 5–12.

Ranker, J. 2008. Composing across multiple media: A case study of digital video production in a fifth grade classroom. *Written Communication* 25: 196–234.

Siegle, D. 2009. Literacy in the 21st century: The fourth R—video recording. *Gifted Child Today* 32(2): 14–19.

Valmont, W. J. 1994. Making videos with reluctant learners. *Reading and Writing Quarterly: Overcoming Learning Difficulties* 10(4): 369–378.

Video Guidelines

The following guidelines can improve your digital videos.

Pre-Production

Make sure you have charged batteries or an electrical connection.
Obtain talent and copyright releases.
Label all tapes and log all shots.
Record with the best possible camera -- digital, if possible.
Use external microphones instead of built-in camera microphones.
Target the scripts at the intended audience.
Carefully plan your shots to tell a story.
Keep the script simple -- include only one or two main points.
Create a shot list and use it to sequence the recording.
Consider impact of distribution media (videotape or DVD vs. Web).

Production

White-balance the camera before shooting.
Shoot with your back to the light.
Use natural lighting; avoid fluorescent lighting.
Beware of cluttered backgrounds and excess movement.
"Set the stage" for the video with a wide shot of the area.
Shoot people interacting with each other, not the camera.
Use a tripod (or stand still and keep the camera very still).
Minimize panning, tilting, tracking, and other movements.
Shoot excess footage at both ends of a shot (to be edited out later).
Continue recording until the audio portion ends.
Carefully frame your shots and "lead" the eye of the viewer.
Use over-the-shoulder shots to draw the audience into the action.
Minimize harsh, close-up shots of people.
Maintain a continuous time code.

Post-Production

Minimize special effects and transitions.
If in doubt, leave it out.
Smooth sound is more important than smooth video.
Keep an archival copy of the source video.

From *Multimedia Projects in Education: Designing, Producing, and Assessing, Fourth Edition* by Karen S. Ivers and Ann E. Barron. Santa Barbara, CA: Libraries Unlimited. Copyright © 2010.

Commercial Evaluation

CRITERIA	0	1	2	3
The commercial's length was appropriate.	Commercial's length was way too short.	Commercial's length was way too long.	Commercial's length was almost appropriate.	Commercial's length was appropriate.
The commercial struck a variety of my emotions.	Commercial did not strike my emotions.	Commercial struck one of my emotions.	Commercial somewhat struck a variety of my emotions.	Commercial struck a variety of my emotions.
The commercial's message was clearly conveyed and is rememberable.	Commercial's message was not conveyed.	Commercial's message was somewhat conveyed, but it is not something I will remember.	Commercial's message was clearly conveyed, but it is not something I will remember.	Commercial's message was clearly conveyed and is something I will remember.
The commercial motivated me to purchase or support its product.	It made me not want to purchase or support this product.	It did not motivated me to purchase or support its product.	I'm unsure whether or not I will purchase or support this product.	It motivated me to purchase or support this product.
The commercial captured and held my attention.	Commercial did not captivate or hold my attention.	Commercial held my attention for a short period of time.	Commercial held my attention for most of the time.	Commercial captured and held my attention the whole time.
The commercial included the company logo and repeated the product names several times.	Commercial excluded logo and didn't repeat product name.	Commercial included logo but didn't repeat product name.	Commercial excluded logo but did repeat product name several times.	Commercial included logo and repeated product name several times.
				Total _____

From *Multimedia Projects in Education: Designing, Producing, and Assessing, Fourth Edition* by Karen S. Ivers and Ann E. Barron. Santa Barbara, CA: Libraries Unlimited. Copyright © 2010.

Glossary

alternative assessment. A form of assessment other than the true or false, multiple-choice, matching, and fill-in-the-blank responses that are often associated with standardized tests. Performance-based assessment, authentic assessment, and portfolio assessment are forms of alternative assessment.

analog video. Video that is stored as an electrical signal with a continuous scale. Videotape is generally used to store analog video.

authentic assessment. A method of evaluating a student's performance based on observations, performance tests, interviews, exhibitions, or portfolios. The context, purpose, audience, and constraints of the task must connect to real-world situations and problems.

authoring system. A computer program designed specifically to create computer-based instruction.

AVI. A Microsoft video file format that stands for Audio Video Interleave. This format is used extensively on the Windows platform, especially for download and play files.

bandwidth. The transmission capacity of a telecommunications system. The greater the bandwidth, the greater the amount of digital information that can be transmitted per second.

bitmapped image. A computer image that consists of individual dots or picture elements (pixels).

bits per second (bps). A common method of measuring the speed of a modem. Most telephone modems transfer information at 56,600 bps (also referred to as 56K). DLS and cable modems are faster.

Blackboard. A course management system (CMS).

blog. An online journal or communication tool that is updated frequently and intended for a specific group or the general public. Entries are posted to a single page, usually in reverse-chronological order.

branch. To move from one location of a program to another. For example, if a button initiates a video file, it is said to *branch* to video.

bug. An error in a program.

button. An object or area of the screen used to initiate an action, such as a branch to another card.

byte. Eight bits working together. A single byte can have any value from 0 to 255.

capture. The process of collecting and saving text or an image data.

card. The basic unit of HyperCard and HyperStudio, equivalent to one screen of information.

CD-audio (compact disc-audio). High-quality audio stored on a compact disc in a linear format. Each compact disc can store 74 minutes of sound with no degradation of quality during playback.

CD-R. A recordable compact disc, allowing users to write to the disc one time (see CD-RW).

CD-ROM (compact disc-read only memory). A prerecorded, nonerasable optical storage disc that stores approximately 650 – 700 MB of digital data.

CD-RW. A recordable compact disc that allows users to write to the disc many times.

clip. A short video segment.

clip art. Graphics that are commercially distributed for use in product development.

compression. Reduction of data for more efficient storage and transmission; saves disk space, but may also reduce the quality of the playback.

constructivism. The belief that learning takes place through the construction of knowledge.

cooperative learning. A way of structuring student-to-student interaction so students are successful only if their group is successful. Students are held accountable for their individual learning, they receive specific instruction in the social skills necessary for the group to succeed, and they have the opportunity to discuss how well their group is working.

Course Management System (CMS). A comprehensive software package that facilitates the design, delivery, assessment, and management of online courses. A CMS is also called an LMS **DDD-E.** A model for the systematic design of multimedia projects, consisting of four phases: DECIDE, DESIGN, DEVELOP, and EVALUATE.

debug. The process of correcting problems (e.g., code, grammar, and spelling) in a program.

dialog box. A window that asks a question or allows users to input information.

digital camera. A camera that records images in true digital form. The images are usually downloaded directly into a computer through a USB or FireWire connection.

digital video. Video that is stored in bits and bytes on a computer. It can be manipulated and displayed on a computer screen.

digitizing. The process of converting an analog signal into a digital signal.

disc. Usually refers to a videodisc or compact disc. Computer diskettes are generally referred to as *disks* (with a *k*), and compact discs are referred to as *discs* (with a *c*).

DPI (dots per inch). Refers to printing resolution of an image. Most printers can print 300–1200 dpi.

DV. Digital video. Often used to refer to the format used by a digital camcorder with "DV" tapes. Also used to refer to the compression type used by DV systems.

DVD (digital video disc). A second generation of the original CD-ROM format. It provides up to two layers of digital information on a single-sided compact disc. It stores up to 4.7 gigabytes for one layer; 8.5 gigabytes for two layers. Advanced digital video and audio features are specified.

DVD-R. A recordable video disc.

DVD-RW. A recordable video disc that allows users to write to the disc many times.

e-portfolio. A meaningful collection of student work in an electronic format.

FireWire. The Apple Computer trace name for the IEEE 1394 standard that enables direct transfer of digital video between devices, such as a camcorder and computer.

flash memory. Flash memory is used to record photographs in a digital camera. The flash memory space (usually on a memory card or stick) can be erased and used again.

Flip video camera. A handheld digital camcorder by Flip Video that plugs into a computer's USB port to transfer video.

flowchart. A visual depiction of the sequence and structure of a program.

fps. Frames per second. Describes the frame rate—the number of frames displayed each second.

frame. One complete video picture.

frame rate. The number of video frames displayed each second.

freeware. Software, often available for download on the Internet, that is free for anyone to use.

frequency. The number of times per second that a sound source vibrates. Frequency is expressed in hertz (Hz) or kilohertz (kHz).

full-motion video. Video frames displayed at 30 frames per second.

GIF (Graphic Interchange Format). A file format for Web graphics that allows for 256 colors. It uses a lossless compression and is best used for line art and graphics with solid areas of colors. GIFs also support interlacing, transparency, and animation. GIF89a is another name for transparent or animated GIFs.

Google Apps. Free Web-based applications supported by Google designed to encourage communication and collaboration.

Group Investigation. A cooperative group technique similar to the Jigsaw method except that students do not form "expert groups." Student teams give class presentations of findings.

hertz (Hz). Unit of frequency measurement; numerically equal to cycles per second.

HTML (HyperText Markup Language). Coding language used to create hypertext documents to be posted on the Web. HTML code consists of embedded tags that specify how a block of text should appear or that specify how a word is linked to another file on the Internet.

HTTP (HyperText Transfer Protocol). The protocol for moving hypertext files across the World Wide Web.

HyperStudio. A hypermedia development program for Windows and Macintosh computers, developed by Roger Wagner Publishing, Inc.

icon. A symbol that provides a visual representation of an action or other information. An icon or an arrow is often used to denote directional movement in hypermedia.

image. A graphic, picture, or one frame of video.

iMovie. A free desktop video editing program developed and distributed by Apple Computer, Inc.

Internet. A group of networks connecting governmental institutions, military branches, educational institutions, and commercial companies.

Internet Service Providers (ISPs). Organizations that provide connections to the Internet. They may be universities or private companies.

iPod. A combination portable digital media player and hard drive from Apple Computer.

Jigsaw. A method of cooperative group learning that assigns each of its members a particular learning task. Team members meet with members of other groups to form "expert groups" to discuss and research their topic. Following research and discussion, the students return to their own teams and take turns teaching their teammates about their topic.

JPEG (Joint Photographic Experts Group). A common format for storing images (especially photographs) on the web.

kilohertz (kHz). Unit of frequency measurement; equal to 1,000 hertz.

Learning Management System (LMS). See Course Management System.

Learning Together. A method of cooperative group learning that incorporates heterogeneous student groups that work on a single assignment and receive rewards based on their group product.

link. A connection from one place or medium to another. For example, buttons contain the linking information between cards.

liquid crystal display (LCD) panel. A panel that connects to a computer to display the computer screen when the LCD panel is placed on top of an overhead projector.

MIDI (Musical Instrument Digital Interface). A standard for communicating musical information among computers and musical devices.

Moodle. An open source course management system.

movie file. The file that is created by combining audio, video, and images.

Movie Maker. A free video editor available on Windows Millennium and XP systems.

MPEG (Moving Picture Experts Group). A common format for storing digital video files.

MP3. An audio-only compression format that can decrease the size of an audio file but maintain a high-quality sound.

multimedia. A type of program that combines more than one media type for disseminating information. For example, a multimedia program may include text, audio, graphics, animation, and video.

object-oriented drawings. Graphics that are composed of separate geometric objects that can be layered one atop the other to create images. Also known as Vector drawings or simply drawings.

objects. In hypermedia, generally refers to elements that are placed on the screen, such as buttons, fields, and graphics. Objects are components that can be manipulated and can contain links to other objects.

open source. A development methodology that allows users to access and modify a program's content and source code free of charge and for free distribution.

performance-based assessment. An assessment method through which teachers evaluate students' skills by asking them to create an answer or product that demonstrates their knowledge or skills.

pixel. A single dot or point of an image on a computer screen. *Pixel* is a contraction of the words *picture element*.

plug-and-play. A device that is automatically recognized and accessible when plugged into a computer.

PNG (Portable Network Graphics). PNG is a lossless format that supports interlacing and transparency.

podcast. Digital files that can be distributed over the Internet and played back on computers and portable media devices (e.g., cell phones, MP3 players, Apple's iTouch). A podcast can be syndicated, subscribed to, and downloaded automatically when new content is added via RSS feeds.

portfolio assessment. An estimation of a student's abilities based on a systematic collection of the student's best work, records of observation, test results, and so on.

postproduction. The phase of a video project that includes editing the video.

PowerPoint. A presentation program developed by Microsoft.

PPI (pixels per inch). Refers to image resolution. Most monitors can display 60–120 ppi.

preproduction. The planning phase of a video project—includes setting a goal, writing scripts, etc.

production. The phase of a video project that consists of shooting the video and compiling the media.

QuickTime. A file format that allows computers to compress and play digitized video movies.

RealAudio. A compression and transfer technique that allows audio files to play over the Internet as they are transferring.

resolution. The number of dots or pixels that can be displayed on a computer screen. Higher resolutions create sharper images. Also refers to the sharpness or clarity of a computer screen. Displays with more lines and pixels of information have better resolution.

sampling rate. The number of intervals per second used to capture a sound when it is digitized. Sampling rate affects sound quality; the higher the sampling rate, the better the sound quality.

scanner. A hardware peripheral that takes a picture of an item and transfers the image to a computer.

scripting language. A set of commands that is included in some icon- and menu-based development systems. The scripting language allows complex computer instructions to be created.

scripts. A series of commands written in a language embedded in a hypermedia program.

sequencer. A device that records MIDI events and data.

slide show (electronic). Computer screens designed in a sequence for projection purposes.

sound module. A peripheral for MIDI that uses an electronic synthesizer to generate the sounds of musical instruments.

stack. A group of cards in the same HyperStudio file, usually based on the same theme.

storyboard. A visual representation of what will be placed on a computer screen. In addition, storyboards contain information that helps the programmer and the production specialists develop media components.

streaming. Files that can be played as they are sent over the Web.

Student Teams Achievement Divisions (STAD). A cooperative group technique: Students learn something as a team, contribute to their team by improving their own past performance, and earn team rewards based on their improvements.

synthesizer. A musical instrument or device that generates sound electronically.

Team-Assisted Individualization (TAI). A cooperative group technique that combines cooperative learning with individualized instruction. Students are placed into groups but work at their own pace and level.

Teams Games Tournament (TGT). A cooperative group technique similar to STAD except that weekly tournaments replace weekly quizzes. Homogeneous, three-member teams formed from the existing heterogeneous groups compete against similar ability groups to earn points for their regular, heterogeneous group.

text-to-speech synthesis. Sounds created by applying computer algorithms to text to produce spoken words.

theory of multiple intelligences. A theory proposing that there are multiple ways of knowing, suggesting that people possess several different intelligences.

timeline. A method for organizing the video clips in sequential order.

transition. Visual effects, such as dissolves or wipes, that take place as a program moves from one image or screen of information to the next.

Uniform Resource Locator (URL). URLs are the exact location (address) of an Internet resource, such as a webpage.

upload. The process of sending a complete file to the host computer.

vector image. A computer image constructed from graphic formulae. Images that are made up of lines, boxes, and circles (such as charts) usually are vector images.

.WAV. The extension (last three letters) for sound files saved in Microsoft wave format.

Web 2.0 Tools: A new generation of tools that support using the Web for creativity, collaboration, social networking, video and photo sharing, and other forms of information distribution. Web 2.0 tools include wikis, blogs, and podcasts.

Web browser. A software program that can display webpages.

WebQuest. A Web-based project designed to guide learners as they research a specific issue and to incorporate the results of the research into an authentic product or project.

wiki. A server program that allows users to work collaboratively to create and edit the content of a website using a regular Web browser.

window. An area on a computer screen that displays text, graphics, messages, or documents.

Windows Movie Maker. A software editing program that can be used to create digital movies. Is included with Windows Millennium Edition and XP.

World Wide Web (WWW). Hypermedia-based Internet information system. Graphical user interfaces allow users to click a mouse on desired menu items, accessing text, sound, pictures, or even motion video from all over the world.

Index

About the Authors

KAREN S. IVERS is professor and associate dean in the College of Education at California State University, Fullerton. Her published works include *A Teacher's Guide to Using Technology in the Classroom and Technologies for Education: A Practical Guide*. She was awarded CSUF's first Outstanding Teaching Innovations with Electronic Technology award and was the 2006 Distinguished Faculty Marshall for the College of Education.

ANN E. BARRON is professor of Instructional Technology in the College of Education at the University of South Florida, Tampa, FL. Dr. Barron has authored or coauthored over 100 journal articles, conference papers, and books. She was the recipient of the President's Award for Excellence in 2003, the Online Teaching Award in 2002, and the Jerome Krivanek Distinguished Teaching Award in 2000.

CUT AND MAKE
NORTH AMERICAN INDIAN
MASKS IN FULL COLOR

A. G. Smith and Josie Hazen

DOVER PUBLICATIONS, INC., New York

FOR DUSTIN

Cut and Make North American Indian Masks in Full Color is a new work,
first published by Dover Publications, Inc., in 1989.

International Standard Book Number: 0-486-26088-7

Manufactured in the United States of America
Dover Publications, Inc., 31 East 2nd Street, Mineola, N.Y. 11501

INDIAN MASKS were used in connection with traditional religion: in dance ceremonies, to honor or make contact with ancestors or supernatural beings; in curing the sick; and in teaching the traditions of the tribe to its young members.

These bizarre faces, made from a variety of natural materials, continue to inspire wonder in those who see them today. They are considered to be valuable artifacts of the ancient cultures of Native American peoples, are studied widely by anthropologists, and are preserved in many museums for public viewing.

This book contains eight masks based on authentic Indian designs. They are easy to assemble and, with the addition of just a piece of string, can be either worn or displayed on a wall in your home.

GENERAL DIRECTIONS

Tools. The tools you will need to make the masks are (1) scissors; (2) an X-ACTO knife with a #11 blade, for cutting out eyes and other openings inside the mask pieces; (3) white glue, such as Elmer's or Sobo; (4) a sharp or pointed tool, for scoring fold lines and punching out holes for string; (5) a spoon or other burnishing tool, for pressing pieces together after they have been glued; (6) a ruler; (7) a tissue or damp sponge; and (8) some string.

Visual aids. On the book's covers, you will find a color photograph of each mask as it looks when fully assembled. Before assembling a mask, you should examine the photograph of it to familiarize yourself with the way the pieces will look when fitted together. The line diagrams that accompany the directions for each mask identify the pieces by key. Pieces are keyed by the same letters and numbers that are used in the directions and on the color plates.

Cutting out the pieces of a mask. Use scissors to cut along the black outline of each piece. Use an X-ACTO knife to cut out eyeholes and all inside areas marked "cut out," and to remove slivers of paper from outer nooks and crannies that your scissors cannot reach into. If you have never used an X-ACTO knife before, be careful; the blade is extremely sharp! Your work surface (especially if it is a wood table or floor) should be protected from the blade by a thick layer of newspaper or cardboard.

DO NOT cut any pieces from the plates before you are ready to use them! The keys that identify the pieces are printed *next to* them, not *on* them. So if you cut out all the pieces for a mask at once, you may later be forced to guess their positions or rely completely upon the cover photograph as an assembly guide.

Fitting and gluing pieces together. Tabs, to which glue is applied, appear on at least one of the pieces of each mask. They do one of two things: connect one piece to another, or close up seams that make a single flat piece three-dimensional. Tabs are always white and marked with a single black dot.

As soon as you have cut out a piece that has tabs, *score* along the black border lines between the tabs and the outer edges of the piece. Do this by tracing along the lines with a sharp or pointed tool, using a ruler as a guide. Press hard enough to score a groove in the paper, but not hard enough to cut through it. You will find that the scored lines make the tabs easier to manipulate at crucial moments (such as the moments just after you have applied glue to them).

Before applying glue to the tabs, make sure that all the eyeholes and inside areas marked "cut out" have been cut from the pieces, and try the pieces for fit. Put glue *only* on the surface of the tab marked with a dot; never apply glue to a surface that will receive a tab. Do not use too much glue—the excess will seep out and spoil the printed surface. Keep a tissue or damp sponge handy so that you can quickly wipe away excess glue before it has a chance to run or harden. Use a spoon or other burnishing tool to press down areas that have just been glued.

Allow glued sections to dry thoroughly before handling them. If you have a main piece that needs to have more than one attachment glued to it, glue the attachments *one at a time*, letting each one dry thoroughly before gluing on the next.

Attaching string for hanging and wearing. Places where string should be attached are indicated by a dot (black or white) on the left and right sides of a mask. Carefully punch a hole in each of these two dots with a sharp or pointed tool; then push the two ends of a long piece of string through the holes from the back of the mask, so that the ends hang down in front and the middle of the string hangs behind. (Use a piece at least 2 feet long; you can always cut off any excess later.) Knot one end of the string in front.

For hanging up the masks on a wall, leave only an inch or two of slack in the string behind the mask, and you have your proper length. To adjust the string for wearing, place the mask on your face, holding it up with one hand, and use your free hand to pull the *un*knotted end of the string forward until it is taut enough around your head to support the mask.

Once the string is adjusted to the appropriate length, knot the other end in front and cut off any excess string that is dangling from the knots. Your mask is now ready to wear or hang.

If you wish to hang a mask in between the times that you wear it, you can shorten the string without cutting it by doubling the excess into a loop and wrapping a few layers of masking tape or transparent tape around the base of the loop. When you are ready to wear the mask again, you can restore the string to its original length by simply removing the tape.

THE INDIVIDUAL MASKS

Aztec Turquoise Mask: Xiuhtecuhtli, the Fire God (Plate 1). The Aztecs of Mexico made beautiful mosaic masks for use in their ceremonies. Often the skull of a human sacrifice was covered with tiny bits of turquoise and used as a mask. This mask represents the god of fire, who resides at the center of the cosmos. His name means "turquoise lord," turquoise being a symbol of fire.

The 2 pieces of this mask are keyed AT. Cut out AT-1 and the eye and nose holes. Insert the nose (AT-2) from behind AT-1 into the space you have cut for it, allowing it to become curved; then glue the tabs flat against the back of AT-1. After the nose has dried, close the four seams (two at the top and two at the bottom) of AT-1 and glue the seam tabs in place. Attach a string.

Aztec Turquoise Mask

Eskimo Tunghak Mask (Plates 2–4). Although the Eskimos of Alaska had little time and few raw materials for art, they celebrated their hunting successes and enlivened cold nights with masked dancing. Their driftwood masks show remarkable carving skill and ingenious use of available materials. This mask depicts a tunghak, a mythical being who controlled the supply of game, in this case, probably seal.

The 24 pieces of this mask are keyed ET. Cut out ET-1 and the black centers of the eyes, the nose opening and the forehead opening. Close the two seams at the bottom of ET-1 and glue the

(Continued after color plates.)

AT-2

cut out

cut out

cut out

AT-1

PLATE 1. Aztec Turquoise Mask: Xiuhtecuhtli, the Fire God

PLATE 2. Eskimo
Tunghak Mask

ET-10

ET-10

ET-9

ET-9

ET-8

ET-8

ET-2

ET-6

ET-5

ET-7

ET-7

ET-7

ET-7

cut out

cut out

ET-1

PLATE 3. Eskimo
Tunghak Mask

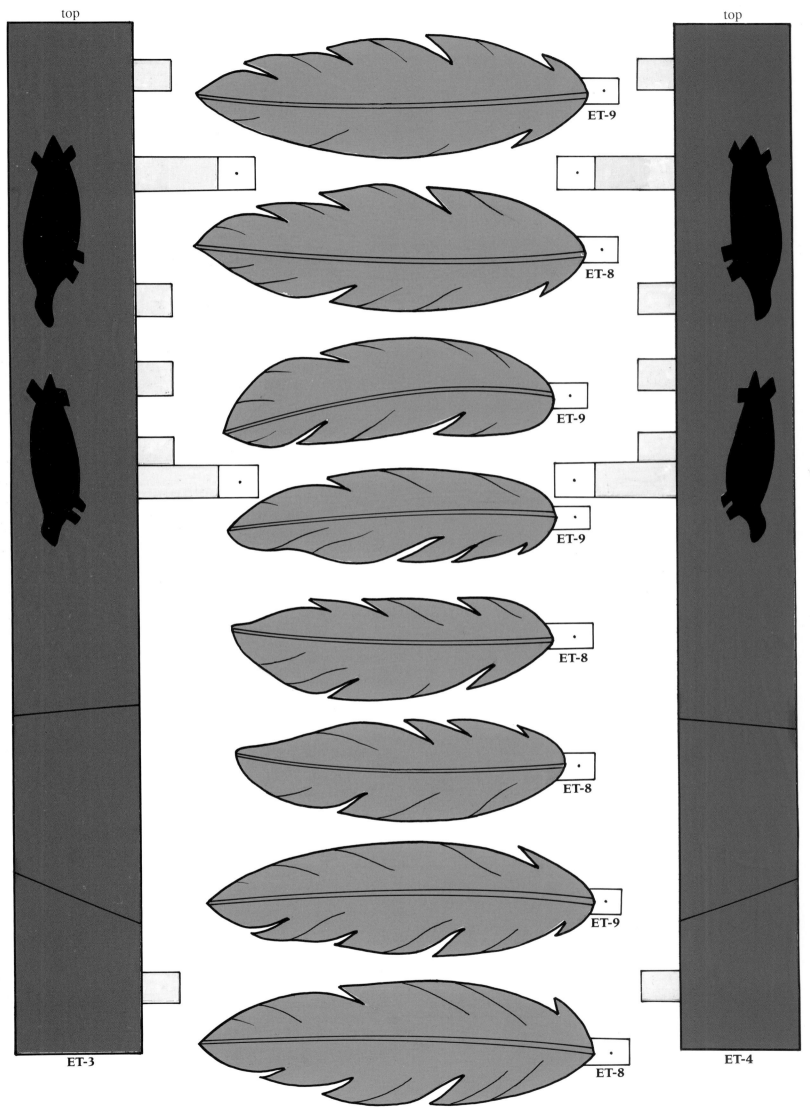

top

top

ET-9

ET-8

ET-9

ET-9

ET-8

ET-8

ET-9

ET-8

ET-3

ET-4

PLATE 4. Eskimo Tunghak Mask

HK-6

HK-2

HK-6

HK-6

Plate 5. Hopi Kachina Mask: Corn Man

HK-4   HK-5

HK-4   HK-5

cut out   cut out

HK-1

PLATE 6. Hopi Kachina Mask: Corn Man

HK-3

HK-7

HK-7

HK-7

PLATE 7. Hopi Kachina Mask: Corn Man

KB-4

KB-5

KB-3

KB-6

KB-2

KB-7

PLATE 8. Kwakiutl Bear Mask

cut out

KB-1

KB-8

KB-9

PLATE 9. Kwakiutl Bear Mask

ES

ES

ES

ES

ES-1

PLATE 10. Eskimo Swan Mask

ES

ES

ES

ES

ES

ES

ES-2

ES

ES

ES

ES

PLATE 11. Eskimo Swan Mask

MR-1

PLATE 12. Makah Raven Mask

top

MR-3

MR-2

PLATE 13. Makah Raven Mask

FF-2

FF-3

FF-4

FF-5

PLATE 14. Iroquois False Face Mask

PLATE 15.
Iroquois False Face Mask

FF-1

cut out

FF-7

cut out
slot for tongue

FF-6

MB-1

MB-2

PLATE 16. Makah Bird Mask

Makah Bird Mask

Makah Bird Mask (Plate 16). Like the Makah Raven Mask, this bird mask has characteristics associated with Makah art: symmetry and bold colors that follow the contours of the mask (which most likely would have been carved from cedar or redwood).

The 2 pieces of this mask are keyed MB. Cut out MB-1 and the black centers of the eyes. Cut out MB-2, which will form the bird's beak. Score along the center black line of MB-2 and along the fold lines for all the tabs; then close the seam at the bottom, gluing the seam tab in place. The beak should have a crease down the center and a curve at the bottom. It should be just the right width to fit into the space provided at the bottom center of MB-1. Glue it in place, letting the tabs follow the contour of MB-1. Attach a string.

Iroquois False Face Mask

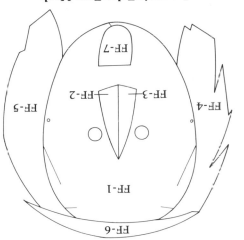

Iroquois False Face Mask (Plates 14 & 15). Among the most spectacular works of art by the Iroquois Indians of the Northeast Woodland area are their wooden False Face masks. Used in curing ceremonies by the tribe's elite medical society, these masks are likenesses of the first Great Doctor of mythical times, whose face was smashed in a contest with the "Creator." The masks always have distorted features, long hair (usually made from horsetails), deep lines in the forehead, a crooked nose and a dark face. The best-known remaining examples date from the nineteenth and early twentieth centuries.

The 7 pieces of this mask are keyed FF. Cut out FF-1 and the black centers of the eyes, the nose opening and the tongue slot. To make the nose, cut out FF-2 and FF-3 and score along the fold lines on all their tabs; then apply glue to the tabs along the curved edge of FF-3, and glue these tabs along the back of the curved edge of FF-2, folding along the scored lines as necessary to allow the tabs to follow the contour of the piece. (The tabs will be folded back quite a bit in this process.) The result will be a curved nose with a crease down the center and two long, straight tabs on either side. Allow the nose to dry; then gently push it from behind FF-1 into the space you have cut for it, and glue the side tabs flat against the back. After the nose has dried, close the five seams on FF-1 and glue the tabs in place.

Now add the three hair pieces (FF-4, FF-5 and FF-6) to the mask. Following the diagram as a guide for positioning, glue FF-4 to the right side of FF-1, FF-5 to the left side, and FF-6 over FF-4, FF-1 and FF-5. Finally, insert the tongue (FF-7) into the tongue slot, and glue the tongue tab in place behind the top of the slot. Attach a string.

Makah Raven Mask

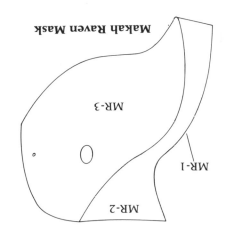

Makah Raven Mask (Plates 12 & 13). The Makah Indians (on the border of British Columbia and the state of Washington) were specialized whale hunters who performed rites for powerful ancestors responsible for a person's wealth and success. A mask like this raven mask may or may not have been a significant piece of ritual equipment. Its design is typical of a wooden Makah mask in its symmetry, surface decoration and colorful painting that follows carved contours.

The 3 pieces of this mask are keyed MR. The mask fits around the sides of your face, with a long protruding beak, and has eyeholes on its sides instead of in the front.

Cut out MR-1 and MR-2 and the black centers of the eyes. Then score along the fold lines of all the tabs on MR-2, and carefully glue MR-2 to MR-1, beginning at the crown of MR-1 with the top end of MR-2. (The top end of MR-2 is indicated on the plate.) Make sure that the top of MR-2 and the crown of MR-1 are lined up before you start gluing; do not make one higher or lower than the other. As you glue, MR-2 should bend to adopt the contour of the beak of MR-1, and end up looking flat and horizontal widthwise, but curved lengthwise. Allow the tabs to dry; then line up the top of MR-2 with the crown of MR-3 and glue the tabs on the other side of MR-2 to MR-3. When all three pieces are attached together, MR-1 and MR-3 will serve as the two flat sides of the mask, and MR-2 will be the mask's curved front.

If all the pieces are lined up together at the top as they should be, MR-2 should extend beyond MR-3 and MR-1 at the bottom of the mask. Bend this extension around the base of the beak and glue the remaining tabs to the insides of MR-1 and MR-3. Attach a string.

This mask may at first be tricky to adjust properly to your face. You should *patiently* experiment with fitting it and adjusting the string to its proper length. Pull it on only until the eyeholes meet your eyes, and allow the beak to stand horizontally by itself. The stiff paper should allow the beak to stand rigidly, and the shape of your face should support the forehead and sides.

Eskimo Swan Mask

Notice that ES-1 has long white areas, each marked with a dot, on the insides of its side curves. Apply glue to these areas, gently push them just behind the sides of ES-2, and press them into place. Finally, cut out all the feathers labeled ES (there are 14) and, using the diagram as a guide, glue them into position.

Attach a string.

Eskimo Swan Mask

Eskimo Swan Mask (Plates 10 & 11). Eskimo masks are well known for their comic or otherwise highly expressive faces. Like other masks from the late nineteenth and early twentieth centuries, this swan mask has a round face carved into a flat background, a tapered oblong shape, feathers balancing erect and an eerie grin.

The 16 pieces of this mask are keyed ES. Cut out ES-1, following its black outline even into the narrow spaces between the sides of the mask and the eyes. Cut out the black eye areas on ES-1. Cut out ES-2 and, applying glue only to the white tab areas marked with a dot at the top left and right, glue ES-2 behind ES-1 so that together they resemble the diagram. (The top center of ES-2, between the two white areas, should *not* be glued to ES-1. The open space is meant to accommodate your nose.)

Kwakiutl Bear Mask

Kwakiutl Bear Mask

Kwakiutl Bear Mask (Plates 8 & 9). The Kwakiutl Indians of the central Pacific Northwest Coast area performed dance dramas about their mythical ancestors, who lived in a time before humans and animals were separate beings. Their wooden ceremonial masks combined a large human or animal face with smaller symbols of humans or animals, and were always crowded with painted designs. Many extant masks similar to this one are dated from about 1850 to about 1900.

The 9 pieces of this mask are keyed KB. Cut out KB-1; then cut out the black centers of the eyes and the space for the nose. Cut out KB-2 (the nose) and score along the fold lines for the three tabs. Push the nose from the back of KB-1 into the space you have cut for it, allowing it to curve until it fits into place; then glue the nose tabs flat up against the back of KB-1, folding as necessary along the scored lines. Allow the nose to dry; then close the four seams in KB-1 and glue the seam tabs in place. Now add the side pieces to KB-1. Using the diagram as a guide for positioning, glue KB-3 behind the top center; KB-4, KB-6 and KB-8 to the right side; and KB-5, KB-7 and KB-9 to the left side. Attach a string.

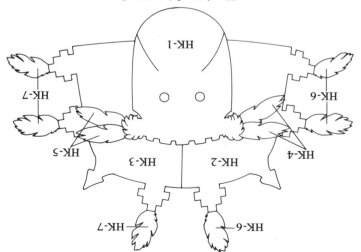

Hopi Kachina Mask

Hopi Kachina Mask: Corn Man

Hopi Kachina Mask: Corn Man (Plates 5–7). To the Hopi Indians of northeastern Arizona, kachinas are spirits that are present with the people for part of the year and help them in various ways. They are impersonated by dancers wearing leather masks in rites that often encourage rainfall and crop growth. Kachina masks were often used over and over again, repainted to represent different kachinas. This mask is a typical late-nineteenth-century Calako Taka (Corn Man) or Calako Mana (Corn Maiden). It probably would have been worn in the traditional Hopi Corn Dance.

The 13 pieces of this mask are keyed HK. HK-1 should be three-dimensional, sloping down on the sides and standing out from the flat headdress. Cut out HK-1 and the eye holes. Close the two seams at the bottom of HK-1 and glue the tabs in place. Glue the top left end of HK-3, by the single long tab, to the corresponding (top right) end of HK-2. When HK-2 and HK-3 are assembled, they should form an arch with an inside gulf that is just the right size for the face (HK-1) to fit into. Place HK-1 into this gulf, to satisfy yourself that it fits there. Then glue it in place, by applying glue to the 17 tabs that point toward each other on HK-2 and HK-3 and pressing them against the inside sides of HK-3 and HK-2 and HK-1.

At the top of HK-1 should be a checkerboard strip with a black puff standing out on each end. Attach the two feathers marked HK-4 to the right puff, and the two feathers marked HK-5 to the left puff, as on the diagram. Attach the three feathers marked HK-6 to the pieces for them on HK-2, and the three feathers marked HK-7 to HK-3. Attach a string.

Eskimo Tungbak Mask

Eskimo Tungbak Mask

ET-1 where shown on the diagram. Attach a string.

seam tabs in place. ET-2 forms the nose. Cut it out and close the seam at the bottom, gluing the tab in place. Allow the seam to dry; then push the nose from behind ET-1 into the space you have cut for it, and glue the tabs flat against the back of ET-1. Attach ET-3 to the right side of ET-1, and ET-4 to the left side. (Make sure that the *top* ends of ET-3 and ET-4 are pointing upward when they are attached; the top ends are specified on the color plates.) The hand pieces, ET-5 and ET-6, also attach to the sides of ET-1 but extend *across the fronts* of ET-3 and ET-4 (see diagram). Glue ET-5 to the right side of ET-1, and ET-6 to the left side. (The thumbs of the hand pieces will point upward if they are glued to the correct sides.)

Because ET-3 and ET-4 have such thin tabs, you may want to glue these pieces to the hand pieces for extra stability. Do this by applying a small amount of glue to the backs of the hand pieces where they pass over ET-3 and ET-4, and carefully pressing them down.

Add feathers to the mask, gluing the four labeled ET-7 to the top of ET-1 as shown on the diagram, the six labeled ET-8 to ET-3 as shown, and the six labeled ET-9 to ET-4 as shown. Finally, cut out the two pieces marked ET-10, close their seams by gluing the tabs in place, let the tabs dry, and glue them to ET-1 where shown on the diagram. Attach a string.